BRUCE ROGERS

A Life in Letters

1870   1957

by Joseph Blumenthal

Foreword by John Dreyfus

AUSTIN · W. THOMAS TAYLOR · 1989

Copyright 1989 by Joseph Blumenthal
Frontispiece courtesy of the Library of the Grolier Club
ISBN 0-935072-16-0

Bruce Rogers: A Life in Letters, 1870–1957

Table of Contents

List of Illustrations	vii
Foreword	ix
Preface & Acknowledgments	xiii
I. The Early Years 1870–1895	1
II. The Riverside Press: Massachusetts 1895–1911	7
III. Free Lance: The Centaur Type 1912–1916	27
IV. The Mall Press: London 1916–1917	38
V. The Cambridge University Press 1917–1919	64
VI. The Affluent Decade in America 1920–1929	82
VII. Homer · Pacioli · Oxford Lectern Bible 1928–1935	110
VIII. Limited Editions Club Books 1933–1954	160
IX. October House: The Late Years 1935–1957	172
Notes	191
Bibliography	198
Index	203

List of Illustrations

Frontispiece. Portrait of Bruce Rogers by Victor Keppler, from *Paragraphs on Printing* (1943).

PLATE 1. Drawings by Bruce Rogers for *Debris*. 1889/1890

PLATE 2. *Homeward Songs by the Way.* 1895

PLATE 3. *Notes: Critical & Biographical.* . . . 1895

PLATE 4. *Sonnets and Madrigals of Michelangelo Buonarroti.* 1900

PLATE 5. *Essays of Michael Lord of Montaigne.* 1904

PLATE 6. *Geofroy Tory.* 1909

PLATE 7. *Geofroy Tory.* 1909

PLATE 8. *The Song of Roland.* 1906

PLATE 9. *Songs & Sonnets of Pierre de Ronsard.* 1903

PLATE 10. *Life of Dante.* 1904

PLATE 11. *The Poems of Maria Lowell.* 1907

PLATE 12. *The Banquet of Plato.* 1908

PLATE 13. *The Parlement of Foules.* 1904

PLATE 14. *The Compleat Angler.* 1909

PLATE 15. *LXXV Sonnets.* 1910

PLATE 16. *Franklin and his Press at Passy.* 1914

PLATE 17. *The Centaur.* 1915

PLATE 18. *Of the Just Shaping of Letters.* 1917

PLATE 19. *Of the Just Shaping of Letters.* 1917

PLATE 20. *The Tempest.* 1921

PLATE 21. *Benjamin Franklin's Proposals for the Education of Youth in Pennsylvania.* 1927

PLATE 22. *The Wedgwood Medallion of Samuel Johnson.* 1926

PLATE 23. *The Journal of Madam Knight.* 1920

PLATE 24. *Priapus and the Pool.* 1922

PLATE 25. *Night and Moonlight.* 1921

PLATE 26. *The Construction of Roman Letters.* 1924

PLATE 27. *The Pierrot of the Minute.* 1923

PLATE 28. *The Pierrot of the Minute.* 1923

PLATE 29. *Ancient Books and Modern Discoveries.* 1927

PLATE 30. *Ancient Books and Modern Discoveries.* 1927

LIST OF ILLUSTRATIONS

PLATE 31. Headpieces from *The Sisters*. 1928

PLATE 32. *Italian Old Style*. 1924

PLATE 33. *Champ Fleury*. 1927

PLATE 34. *Champ Fleury*. 1927

PLATE 35. *The Private Papers of James Boswell*.... 1931

PLATE 36. *The Private Papers of James Boswell*.... 1931

PLATE 37. *The Rime of the Ancient Mariner*. 1930

PLATE 38. *The Odyssey of Homer*. 1932

PLATE 39. *The Odyssey of Homer*. 1932

PLATE 40. *The Odyssey of Homer*. 1932

PLATE 41. *The Odyssey of Homer* (The Hesperides Edition). 1940

PLATE 42. *Fra Luca de Pacioli*. 1933

PLATE 43. *Fra Luca de Pacioli*. 1933

PLATE 44. *Fra Luca de Pacioli*. 1933

PLATE 45. *Aesop's Fables*. 1933

PLATE 46. *Aesop's Fables*. 1933

PLATE 47. *The Symbol and the Saint*, 1924, and a few bookplates

PLATE 48. *Oxford Lectern Bible*. 1935

PLATE 49. *Oxford Lectern Bible*. 1935

PLATE 50. *Utopia*. 1934

PLATE 51. *The Comedies, Histories & Tragedies of William Shakespeare*. 1939

PLATE 52. *The Comedies, Histories & Tragedies of William Shakespeare*. 1939

PLATE 53. *The Complete Poems of Robert Frost*. 1950

PLATE 54. *The Tremolino*. 1942

PLATE 55. "The Atlantic Charter." 1943

PLATE 56. *The Divine Comedy of Dante Alighieri*. 1955

PLATE 57. A selection from the many Rogers printer's marks

Foreword

Odd though it may seem for an Englishman to introduce a biography of an outstanding American typographer, I can give some reasons for taking on the task.

Several of Rogers' greatest books were designed and printed during some of the long periods he enjoyed working in England, where he made a lot of friends and influenced two generations of British book designers. His activities at Cambridge University Press were of special interest to me because I became its typographical adviser, a post first created for Rogers when he joined the Press in 1917. I later knew several of the managers and craftsmen who had worked with him at Cambridge: and I was able to visit the great man at his Connecticut home in 1953, four years before he died.

The author of this biography has been a friend for half my life, or to be more precise, for the last thirty-five years. Like Rogers, he has combined book design with type design; and both men became articulate writers about their craft. They also enjoyed long careers. Rogers died at the age of eighty-seven. Joseph Blumenthal celebrated his ninetieth birthday before finishing this book.

Rogers led an interesting life in agreeable parts of the USA and England. Illustrious printers and publishers on both sides of the Atlantic gave him splendid opportunities to design editions of important or delightful texts. Twice he was able to design a monumental edition of the Bible. He also took on two invitations to design the complete works of Shakespeare. His circle of friends ranged from a few who were rich or famous to a much larger number who were dedicated scholars or fellow-craftsmen, as uncompromising in their concern for quality and detail as he was.

Unless you have become personally involved in book design, you are not likely to be capable of understanding what skills are needed to make an outstanding success in that self-effacing art. For the main purpose of a book is simply to communicate an author's or an artist's ideas to a reader. Intrusive or inappropriate book design can frustrate that purpose as predictably as an ill-chosen picture frame can spoil a painting or drawing. By the same analogy, a well-chosen frame can enhance the effect intended by a painter as much as a suitably designed book can add to the reader's satisfaction. (It will also make reading easier and quicker.)

Blumenthal's long life has brought him a deep understanding of book design and type design. Moreover he has been part of the printing and publishing world in which Rogers moved. Apart from designing an elegant text type named Emerson, and using it with great *élan* in many books printed to his own design at his Spiral Press in New York City, Blumenthal has written several masterly works on the history of design in printing. He is therefore able to assess the importance of Rogers' work within a much broader context than would have been within the compass of most professional printers. Through his long friendship with Rogers, his view has become better balanced than any which might be based solely on the written or printed evidence.

Much of that evidence is to be found among the large number of letters and the comparatively few books and articles in which Rogers expressed himself so fluently and well. Yet there were many aspects of his life about which Rogers was characteristically reticent in what he wrote or published; and there were some periods or projects about which little evidence had survived. With patient ingenuity and acute insight, Blumenthal has managed to piece together a large part of this biography by carefully jointing together extracts from Rogers' own writings. The gaps have been filled in from personal knowledge, or by the biographer's ability to appreciate (sometimes from his own parallel experiences) the essence of the problems experienced by Rogers.

To some readers it may seem that Rogers had a remarkable ability to secure employment or commissions from those in a position to provide ideal opportunities, often contrived by Rogers himself, to show his talents at fullest

FOREWORD

advantage. Few other book designers, except those with printing-houses of their own, have been as lucky as Rogers in the circumstances under which they were able to work. From time to time, Rogers acknowledged that this was true; but he was too much of a perfectionist, and perhaps too often beset by domestic difficulties or complications, to avoid feeling disappointed by his own inadequacies. Tiresome though this must have been for him on many occasions, it has provided an intriguing problem of interpretation to his biographer.

One aspect of Rogers' brand of perfectionism I find wholly endearing, and that is the care he took to stop it from being noticed by his public. The same could be said of many actors, dancers, and musicians, though understandably it can seldom be said of painters, poets, or composers because they being artists (as distinct from *artistes* or artificers) are not conveyors of other people's ideas. The care taken by Rogers to conceal the effort which went into his work served him particularly well in creating a magnificent design for his Oxford Lectern Bible. As he explained, he wanted this to appear as though he was accustomed to "knocking off large folios daily, or at least weekly, as mere routine work."

On a number of occasions, he proved himself to be a real professional in spite of difficult conditions. And that, as Alistair Cooke once said of the way Humphrey Bogart measured his fellow workers, is the real test; because a professional is a man "who can do his best work when he doesn't feel like it." Never in his life was Rogers put to such a severe test as during World War I, when he went to work at Emery Walker's printing-house in London and found himself unexpectedly compelled to act as his own pressman. After the run was finished, he had to take the painful consequences by retouching the sheets with his own hands to cover the defects caused by his own inexperience as a pressman.

He demanded as much of others as he did of himself. When he became dissatisfied with the red ink that was being used in a book for the Grolier Club that was going through Cambridge University Press, the pressman had to stop his machine and wait until Rogers came back from London with another ink that satisfied his meticulous taste.

FOREWORD

Such behaviour was only tolerable because his infinite capacity for taking pains was matched by a much rarer gift—an unerring ability to confer *style* on any book he designed. *Style* was italicized in the report he prepared in 1917 for members of the Syndicate which controlled Cambridge University Press. He told them a distinctive style in bookmaking was then as difficult as it had ever been, if not more so. Nevertheless he argued that the Press ought "to infuse enough of that elusive quality called *style* into its work," so that a glance at a perfectly plain page of type would be enough to identify it as coming from their University Press, without turning to the title-page or imprint. Rogers added that he might go even further "and say that a book ought almost to be identified in the dark, merely by the feel or sound of it."

Did any members of the Press Syndicate think he was pulling their legs, I wonder? Of course that was never his intention. Furthermore, he was acutely aware that to confer style on a book needed unremitting vigilance throughout its making. As he put it, "The success of printing lies in never for one instant relaxing in the inspection of details until the book is actually bound."

Those words show how clearly he understood the role of the responsible artificer in book design. The text which follows gives us a better chance than ever before to understand the character of that great artificer, and also to learn a great deal more about his creative work.

John Dreyfus
London, August 1988

Preface & Acknowledgments

The life of Bruce Rogers (1870-1957) spanned years of enormous changes in society and in the work that engaged his genius. He was born in the American Midwest into a civilization emerging from the prairie; his mature years were spent in scholarly centers in this country and in England when the book was at the heart of culture and enlightenment.

At age twenty-five opportunity drew Rogers to Boston, Massachusetts. In 1896 he was employed by the distinguished publishing house, Houghton, Mifflin and Company, to design trade editions at their own Riverside Press in nearby Cambridge. After four years of involvement in the production of books for wide distribution, manufactured under close budgetary control, Rogers induced his employers to allow him to plan a series of fine limited editions for publication, chosen from the classics of literature, to be designed and produced without restrictions of time and cost. The fifteen years at the Riverside Press, and the remarkable books made there, formed the first important period in Rogers' productive career.

Early in this century, when the Riverside Press Editions were setting the stage for revolutionary changes in book production, Rogers already expressed a deeply felt prophetic wish to live and work in England — an ambivalence that would persist throughout his life. In 1905 and again in 1912, he made short exploratory visits to London, where his Riverside books had already received recognition, and where he formed several enduring friendships. In the ensuing years of free-lance work in the United States, correspondence with English friends led to Rogers' return there in 1917, accompanied this time by his wife and daughter. After two and a half difficult, although not wholly unproductive, wartime years, when hopes for a permanent association had failed, the family returned to New York.

PREFACE

The next nine years in America were extremely productive for Rogers. This was the affluent and expansive decade of the nineteen-twenties when he had his own studio at the Printing House of William Edwin Rudge. At the same time his services were formally retained by the Harvard University Press and the Lanston Monotype Machine Company of Philadelphia. Furthermore, he was deluged with commissions to print books the way he wanted to print them, under very favorable working conditions. Despite the fruitful years in the United States he again made plans that would take him back to Europe.

Although his roots, his family, his closest personal associations, his clientele, and the opportunities for livelihood, were American, he was drawn by temperament to the cultivated and more relaxed ways of British life. A traditionalist at heart, he enjoyed the cosmopolitanism and amenities of London, and explored the English countryside, for which he formed a profound attachment.

In 1928 he was again in Britain, where, with occasional winters in America, he stayed until 1935. On both sides of the Atlantic he found exceptional printing houses that welcomed him and provided the equipment, the craftsmanship, and the understanding he needed to accomplish his work. Although these years in England were relatively few, they were the time of Rogers' fullest maturity. The volumes he produced at the venerable university presses of Oxford and Cambridge and at the Mall Press in London were of paramount importance to his career, and, indeed, to the history of the printed book. After eight years in Europe Rogers returned to his home in Connecticut. In the twenty-two years left to him he produced an extraordinarily large body of work, all printed in the United States.

Together with other dedicated young designers and printers I found it a great privilege to meet Bruce Rogers (known to everyone as "B.R.") at typographic gatherings in New York. I recall, too, the pleasure of dining with him in the 'thirties at his favorite Italian restaurant in London's Soho, and spending a weekend in Oxford with him and John Johnson, Printer to the University. In later years I made frequent calls at his Connecticut home, October House. To the last days of his life B.R. was busy with book com-

PREFACE

missions, had warm friendships among his contemporaries, and enjoyed the attention and affection of a host of young admirers who knew they were in the presence of the master.

The importance of Rogers' new approach to bookmaking was quickly recognized when the limited editions appeared at the Riverside Press. These and the later books designed by Rogers during his long career were acquired during his lifetime by libraries and collectors in this country and overseas at constantly mounting booksellers' and auction prices. B.R. enjoyed his fame despite an innate modesty and a touch of melancholy and self-doubt. Reserved and somewhat remote in manner, he was described by one of his friends as having "a deceptive air of disengagement." Somewhat above medium height, handsome in bearing, distinguished and urbane, he was always well-groomed, usually in tweeds and a bow tie, soft-spoken and never hurried in thought or speech. He had a mischievous sense of humor that could be seen in occasional pieces of printed typographic whimsy. Among his many exhibitions and honors were degrees from three leading American universities and special privileges at Emmanuel College in Cambridge. He received a gold medal from the American Academy of Arts and Letters, and honorary membership in British and American book societies. His printer's mark, the thistle with Father Time wielding his scythe, was cast in bronze for one of the six panels on the doors to the Rare Book Room of the Library of Congress in the nation's capital; another version was carved in wood on a frieze at the Pierpont Morgan Library in New York. B.R. had a skillful hand with pen and ink, and sketched in watercolors; he built exquisite ship models; he loved sailing and the sea; he was a faithful gardener who preferred the country to the city.

Bruce Rogers married Anne Embree Baker in 1900 and soon bought a house in Belmont outside Boston. In due course a daughter, Elizabeth, completed the family circle. The end of employment at the Riverside Press in 1911 marked the beginning of B.R.'s itinerant career. Thereafter an unsettled family life was spent in a variety of temporary quarters in America and England. In 1916 B.R. anticipated schooling in England for his daughter. "Poor child!" he wrote to Emery Walker, "we have moved so frequently of late

PREFACE

that she has never but once had two consecutive years at the same school." Living had become increasingly difficult because of Mrs. Rogers' recurring illness and frequent hospitalizations. Tragically, daughter Elizabeth, whose marriage had failed, died in 1924 at twenty-three years of age, leaving her parents with the responsibility of raising her two-year-old infant son. In 1931 Mrs. Rogers died. Despite all, B.R. coped with family problems and at the same time retained his unique dedication to type and ink and paper.

Bruce Rogers was fortunate in his times. Books were widely read, the library was the center of every literate home, and great book collections were built throughout the United States by men of wealth. Rogers inherited the historic tradition of the noble printed book, and enriched it in moving the art and practice of typography from a handicraft to the processes of the machine. Pertinent here are some closing words of an appreciation that appeared after Rogers' death in *The Periodical*, Oxford University Press (1958), written by Charles Batey, then Printer to the University: "He was fortunate in his patrons too, and the clients who were persuaded to join his genius to opportunity: together they have left to the world many monuments, masterpieces of the printer's craft, which are not likely to be matched again either in number or magnificence."

It is a privilege and great pleasure, on completion of this book, to recall the invaluable help along the way from so many friends and colleagues. The greatest debt is owed to Bruce Rogers himself on whose extensive correspondence and occasional addresses I have drawn heavily. Indeed, almost half the words in the pages that follow come from his fluent and eloquent pen. I am grateful to Rogers' grandson, Bruce Burroughs (a neighbor in Connecticut) for permission to quote from these letters, and for confirmation of family dates.

The manuscript (and its author) has had the great good fortune of full and critical readings by John Dreyfus, Abe Lerner, and Jerry Kelly, each a notable practitioner of the printed page and a scholar of its history. I am also deeply indebted in many areas to Bessie Zaban Jones, Herbert H. Johnson, Harold Corbin, Ronald Mansbridge, and Greer Allen; and as always to the

PREFACE

many librarians who responded so readily to requests for letters and other data, especially to Francis O. Mattson, the New York Public Library; Kenneth A. Lohf, Columbia University; Helen Q. Schroyer of Rogers' own Purdue University; and Gay Walker at Yale's Arts of the Book Room.

For permission to quote from documents, I am grateful to the following institutions: Stanley Marcus–Bruce Rogers Collection, Bridwell Library, Southern Methodist University, Dallas, Texas; the Syndics of Cambridge University Library, Cambridge, England; The Estate of Robert Lee Frost, New Canaan, Connecticut; The Grolier Club, New York, New York; The Harry Ransom Humanities Research Center, University of Texas, Austin, Texas; Special Collections, Colby College, Waterville, Maine; Bruce Rogers Papers, The Newberry Library, Chicago, Illinois; Typographic Manuscript Collection and Random House Papers, Rare Book and Manuscript Library, Columbia University, New York, New York; William Andrews Clark Memorial Library, University of California, Los Angeles, California; Arts of the Book Collection, Yale University Library, New Haven, Connecticut; The Carl H. Pforzheimer Library, The Carl and Lily Pforzheimer Foundation, Inc., New York, New York. I would also like to thank Elaine Smyth for her assistance in pursuing material in these and other locations.

From the first proposal of this work, Tom Taylor, its publisher, has provided enthusiastic and comforting support; and my thanks are also due to Jill Mason at the publisher's office for meticulous care through the volume's production. My wife's essential share in this personal history includes the many visits we had with B.R. on Sunday afternoons as we stopped at October House, returning to New York from weekends at our home in West Cornwall.

Bruce Rogers never wrote his memoirs. I would consider my assignment well done if the present volume has some feeling of the autobiographical—unauthorized to be sure, but convincing withal.

J.B.

Bruce Rogers: A Life in Letters, 1870–1957

1870   1895

The Early Years

Bruce Rogers was born in Linwood, Indiana (now part of the city of Lafayette), on 14 May 1870. His ancestors, of Yorkshire descent, had come overland from Virginia in the hazardous days of the Conestoga wagons, the principal means of transporting household goods before the coming of railroads. His grandfather had been the captain of a river steamboat on the Wabash, and this family memory may have been the source of the grandson's later love of sailing and the open sea.

Albert Bruce Rogers, as he was originally named, was the second son of George Rogers, a baker and confectioner, and his wife Anne (née Gish). A talent for drawing was soon recognized by the boy's father and encouraged. At the same time, the youngster was much drawn to his uncle, a carpenter who lived just across the road from the Rogers' modest frame house. "Bert," as the boy was then known in the family, spent much time in the carpenter shop, where he developed the familiarity with tools that served him well throughout his life.

Of the early years, Bruce Rogers wrote much later:

> Like other children of my age, I played with cubical blocks that had letters printed on each face. I fear I didn't do much with them except to build houses and forts, though I may possibly have learned the alphabet at the same time — which was, of course, the intention of my elders. At any rate I was not entirely illiterate when I first went to school at the age of six, for I was put into the Second Reader class at the end of my first day in a little one-room, brick building, which was still standing

CHAPTER ONE: 1870–1895

(though with no tablet on it) when I last visited my home town of Linwood, in Indiana.

It was not, however, until I had reached my twelfth year, when a cousin of mine devoted to all forms of art gave me John Ruskin's *Elements of Drawing*, that I became aware of letters as something more than mere units in a word. Exercise V. in that book begins: "When you can manage to tint and gradate tenderly with the pencil, get a good large alphabet, and try to tint the letters into shape with the pencil point." Ruskin was not interested primarily in letter forms—only as subjects for practice with the pencil—so I got no further information from him.

But where could I get a good large alphabet, and why should it be good as well as large? Were there, then, *bad* alphabets as well as good, and if so, why? No information on these matters being obtainable in the mid-western town where I then lived, the subject faded from my mind.[1]

Joseph M. Bowles, who would be of crucial influence in the Rogers career, recalled that "sometime between 1883 and 1885 [the young Rogers] had 'issued an edition' of William Cullen Bryant's 'Forest Hymn' in one hand-lettered copy, illustrated with water colors and imitations of etchings on which the plate mark was pressed with a hot iron in the family kitchen."[2]

In a search for the influences that formed a notable career, Bruce Rogers' own recollections are revealing.

My first sight of a really large-paper copy came to me somewhat by accident. McClurg's Book Store in Chicago announced an edition on hand-made paper of Wharton's "Poems of Sappho" at, I think, $2.75. On my ordering a copy (with cash in advance) they wrote that the regular edition was sold out, but that they were sending me one of an edition on large paper, limited to 25 copies, which, on account of a damaged cover, I could have for $8. The book duly arrived, and though I instinctively felt that the proportions of the margins were not all that they should be, the combination of its being a numbered copy, signed by the editor, and the fact that it was already partly paid for, was too much for my resistance, so I somehow got together the remainder of the price and kept the book. It was printed in London and adorned with some of the wood-engraved head-pieces and initials that had descended from Pickering days. Not liking them very much, even then, I painted over the initials with gold and color and added wriggling pen lines which ran up and down the margins in the manner of some bad MS. illuminations I must have seen. I also made stipple copies in water-color of several Greek coins from a Ruskin book I had, and pasted them over the worst of the tail-pieces; and I gilded the name "Sappho" on the title-page and painted, in the lower right-hand margin, a device which I had at that time adopted as a sign of possession. It bore the highfalutin and banal motto in Latin: "Leisure without Literature is Death."

These early attempts at book decoration, though childish and commonplace, will doubtless furnish, to those who like to account for things, an indication of what my later endeavors might be expected to be, but they were hidden from me then, as it was my ambition to become a painter of landscape, or at least, a cabinet-maker or a shipbuilder.[3]

At age sixteen, Albert Bruce Rogers, still known as "Bert," matriculated at Purdue University, only three miles from his home. Because he then expected to become an illustrator, he entered the art class, which consisted entirely of young women except for himself and John T. McCutcheon, who later became a famous cartoonist. In order to gain experience he welcomed the opportunity to join the staffs of several university publications for which he made drawings and lettering.

Referring to the undergraduate years, Frederic Warde, in his invaluable bibliography *Bruce Rogers, Designer of Books* (Harvard University Press, 1925), relates that "even at that time the arrangement of type on paper was of strong interest to him. He tells of bringing home from the library several volumes of the works of the earliest and most interminable American

CHAPTER ONE: 1870–1895

novelist, Charles Brockden Brown, simply because the printing and binding of that particular edition seemed so pleasant to him. He would open and handle the books, turning the crisp leaves; had the text been less turgid, he might even have read it, as a final tribute to typographic merit."[4]

At Purdue the young Rogers' talents were soon recognized. He made drawings and initial letters for the Purdue yearbook, the University catalogues, and the College Quarterly (plate 1). For a few years after graduation, Bruce (the name Bert was being dropped for all time) favored his alma mater with typographic and illustrative contributions.

In 1891, with his college years behind him, Bruce went to Indianapolis and there found a job as an illustrator for the well-reputed newspaper the Indianapolis *News*. This involved assignments to events such as fires and accidents, where it was necessary to make on-the-spot sketches, then hurry back to the newspaper office to prepare the plates for printing to meet the ever-present deadlines. It has been reported that on one assignment Rogers was sent to the morgue to sketch a newly arrived corpse.

Rushing about and working under pressure were not to the young man's liking and he returned to Lafayette for a brief and unrewarding episode in landscape painting. Sketching, however, remained an enjoyable avocation throughout life. In 1892 came a stretch of clerical work in a railroad office in Parsons, Kansas, managed by his brother. In 1893 Bruce was back in Indianapolis as a general draftsman for the Indiana Illustrating Company. Then a chance meeting and the fortuities of time and place set the young artist on a course that would remain constant during a long and productive life.

Joseph M. Bowles, an enterprising young salesman in an Indianapolis art store, bored with selling "wall ornaments" to the ladies of the town, started a magazine, *Modern Art*, in January 1893, when Bruce Rogers was still in Kansas. The emphasis was avant-garde, which then meant works by James McNeill Whistler, Claude Monet, Aubrey Beardsley. Bowles was evidently aware of the lively new Arts and Crafts movement in England. For sale in the shop he imported a few of the smaller titles among the magnificent books then being printed by William Morris at his Kelmscott Press, including *Poems by the Way* (1891), also written by Morris.

THE EARLY YEARS

With Rogers again in Indianapolis, Bowles had occasion to show him the Kelmscott volumes. Although Rogers had already expressed definite interest in the physical book, he was not yet committed. Now the Kelmscott work came as a revelation. "He has said," wrote Warde, "that upon seeing Morris's printing, his whole interest in book-production became rationalised and intensified. He abandoned the prevalent idea that a book could be made beautiful through the work of an illustrator alone, and determined instead to use that curiosity he had always felt as to type and paper, toward a study of the physical form of printed books. Naturally anything which could so thoroughly satisfy his eyes as *Poems by the Way* would have an effect, however transitory, on his efforts."[5]

Bowles secured Rogers' typographic help for the second issue of *Modern Art* in the spring of 1893. Reminiscing much later about these formative years, Rogers told the audience at the opening of his 1938 exhibition at the Grolier Club, "I suppose I must have visited the printing shop in Indianapolis where J. M. Bowles was then having his 'Modern Art' printed . . . and it was he who practically forced me into printing, by giving me commissions for initials and book decorations. . . ."[6] Rogers designed the title page for the second issue, and thereafter until the magazine's close his work appeared in almost every number. A small advertisement in the magazine, autumn 1894, brought him his first professional commissions for lettering and book design.

The first book with the name Bruce Rogers in the colophon was *Homeward Songs by the Way* (plate 2) by A. E. (George Russell), with a few decorations by Rogers, published in 1895 by Thomas B. Mosher in Portland, Maine. (Mosher was the first American to have established and sustained a program, over thirty-two years, of splendid literary output in consistently felicitous typographic form.) Thinking back to his college years, Rogers wrote, on 22 November 1943, to Carl Weber, Curator of Rare Books at Colby College, Waterville, Maine. In this long letter (now in the Colby Library) about his early hero Ruskin, and relating his great admiration for the composition and presswork of the Noah Webster *Dictionary*, first published in 1828, Rogers wrote of Mosher:

CHAPTER ONE: 1870–1895

Now to your query: I first saw some of Mosher's books in our college book-store in Indiana, while I was still an undergrad. As I was doing some lettering and book-designs in my "art" course, I sent some on to Mosher and he gave me an order for lettering the title-page of one of his long slim volumes—I think it was the Rubaiyat. This led to several other small commissions, some after I arrived in Boston.... I met him only once, when he was my guest at tea at the Club of Odd Volumes. As I didn't become a member there till many years later, it must have been 1910 or later that we met. I may have had a letter or two from him after that. Of course in those years I was merely a student and beginner in printing, and I don't think I could have been very interesting to him, personally.... Mosher dictated the form of lettering to be used, to match his other titles of that period. You know what they were like.[7]

A greater opportunity than lettering title pages came when Bowles received a request from William T. Walters of Baltimore, who was a subscriber to *Modern Art*, to produce a book about his art collection. Published in 1895, its full title is *Notes: Critical and Biographical, by R. B. Gruelle, Collection of W. T. Walters* (plate 3). Bowles asked Rogers to help with the design of the book, which, as Mr. Walters requested, was to be similar to the Kelmscott volumes in typographic appearance. Bruce drew a floral design for the title page, which he also hand-lettered. He also drew the headpieces and initial letters. Together, Bowles and Rogers chose Old Style Antique for the type at a time when good type faces were unobtainable. This is one of the few times that Rogers designed in the Kelmscott manner. He later said that he never liked the typography of the 1890s, "except perhaps Charles Ricketts' *Hero and Leander* (1894) and *The Sphinx* (1894)," printed for the Vale Press at the Ballantyne Press in London.

1895 1911

The Riverside Press: Massachusetts

In 1895 Louis Prang, a publisher of "art prints" in Boston, induced Bowles to come to Boston, where the Prang Press assumed publication of his magazine, *Modern Art*, beginning with the winter number of that year. Soon after Bowles' arrival Mr. Prang told him that they needed some typographic help, for which they would pay fifty cents an hour with a ten-dollar per week minimum guarantee. Bowles suggested his friend from Indianapolis, and Bruce Rogers promptly accepted. Nothing could have been more fortunate; the young man concerned with ink and type and paper had come to the uniquely right place at the historically right time.

The Boston to which Rogers came was alive with activity in literature, the arts, and the crafts. Two hundred and fifty years earlier Massachusetts had harbored the first Colonial printers. Now in the 1890s Boston and Cambridge would be the center for an extraordinary confluence of scholars, designers, printers, and publishers devoted to the arts of the book and committed to the history and practice of printing on the highest levels of scholarship and craftsmanship.

Bowles has written that there were no regular hours at Prang's and that nothing was ever in a hurry. Rogers "would work for a few hours, then go to the cashier, get his money and walk in the beautiful Massachusetts country for one or two or three days. He can live on peanuts and pop-corn for as long as necessary; not only can he live the simple life but he actually enjoys it."[1]

Three influential commercial printing plants of considerable size and proven workmanship were already established in Massachusetts. The Riverside Press in Cambridge, which we will soon meet in its decisive relationship

CHAPTER TWO: 1895–1911

with Bruce Rogers, was part of Houghton, Mifflin and Company, publishers of Hawthorne, Emerson, Thoreau, and Longfellow. The University Press in Boston (not a part of Harvard University) was directed by John Wilson, who had come from Glasgow shortly after the Civil War, a scholar who received an honorary degree from Harvard, and who passed the press along to his son. Carl Heintzemann, a young German immigrant originally in the employ of John Wilson, became a key figure in typographic circles. Heintzemann, an accomplished musician, set up a plant with an office designed by architect Bertram Grosvenor Goodhue, who later designed two typefaces. The press became a meeting place for artists and writers, including Henry Lewis Johnson, who became editor of *Printing Art*, an excellent journal true to its name; and Carl Purington Rollins, later the eminent Printer to Yale University, who left Harvard before graduation to serve an apprenticeship with Heintzemann.

In 1887 the Club of Odd Volumes (still active, and holding its monthly meetings at this writing) was founded in Boston, with cultivated interest in the arts of the book, both literary and typographic. The Tavern Club and other groups came together over gustatory pleasures, to talk about books and printing and esthetics, about collecting and exhibitions. A group of artists, architects, and writers put together four large and lively issues of a handsome quarterly magazine *The Knight Errant*, which promised to be "not only an expression of the most advanced thought of our time, but, as well, a model of perfect typography and the printer's art."

Two new publishing ventures were announced by young Harvard undergraduates — Stone & Kimball, and Copeland and Day — who bravely pledged themselves to publish the best in contemporary literature, and to issue their books in elegant typographic dress. In their few years as publishers these young men kept their promises. Their books have aptly been called the delectable 12mos of the nineties.

Of great importance to Bruce Rogers, and indeed to the whole history of fine printing, was the presence in Boston of Daniel Berkeley Updike (1860-1941) and the Merrymount Press, which he established in 1893. Updike was the scion of a cultivated family that had been active in Rhode Island since the eighteenth century. His father, who had been Speaker of the state House of Representatives, died when Daniel was about to graduate from high school. Without funds for a college education the young Updike was forced to look for work. After some temporary employment in the library of the Providence Athenaeum he obtained a job at Houghton, Mifflin and Company in Boston in 1880. After ten years at the publishers' headquarters he was moved to the Riverside Press in Cambridge, where he developed an extraordinary instinct for type and its uses, and became familiar with the potentials of the printed page. Three years later he left and established his own press in order to have complete control over outside commissions that were offered to him. In the craft to which he devoted his life he succeeded with great style; he gave stature and scholarship to his printing house and to the typographic community in which he remained an active participant. Although Updike was ten years older than Rogers, they were the first in an heroic generation of designers and printers who honored the alphabet during a half century of conspicuous achievement in the arts of the book.

Bruce Rogers contributed design and decoration to all issues of Bowles' *Modern Art* from his arrival in Boston until, due in part to Mr. Prang's declining health, the magazine was closed in 1897. In order to supplement his income Rogers had been soliciting free-lance assignments. He designed books for publishers Way & Williams and Stone & Kimball, in Chicago; for Bowen Merrill, Indianapolis; and for T. Y. Crowell in New York.

Rogers' work came to the attention of George H. Mifflin, Houghton's junior partner, who had taken over direction of the Riverside Press during the declining years of its founder, H. O. Houghton. In 1896 Mifflin invited Rogers to come to the Riverside Press to fill the position left vacant by Updike. His duties would be the design of Houghton Mifflin advertising and catalogues, as well as a few dozen trade books each year, and occasional sets and subscription series. Rogers accepted and was thus brought into direct contact with the mechanics and techniques of printing, and was made aware of the infinite detail and vigilance involved in book design and production. At this period his commitment to printing became fixed—he

CHAPTER TWO: 1895–1911

would never change course again. During the years that Rogers was a member of the Riverside organization there were some sixty presses in operation employing some seven hundred workers. A studio was provided for the young designer in a relatively quiet part of the manufacturing complex.

The Riverside Press had been founded in 1852 by Henry O. Houghton. He had a love of literature, pride in the history and importance of printing, and a deep commitment to sound standards of workmanship. From small beginnings he had built a very large and successful plant for the production of books for publishers, including, of course, all the publications of his own Houghton, Mifflin and Company. Houghton was widely praised both for the high standards of printing at the Riverside Press and for its beneficial effect on bookmaking in the United States.

The Houghton Mifflin trade books that Rogers designed during the years 1896 to 1900, and indeed those few done earlier as a free lance, show characteristics that can often be recognized as Bruce Rogers hallmarks. One finds a direct and forthright approach, a subtle lightness in the seemingly easy placement of words on a page — above all a sense of order. In later years of wider scope Rogers' work showed greater audacity and subtlety, but even in these youthful books one may see a certain grace, not easily defined, that was an integral part of both this man and his work throughout a long and productive life. Rogers never forgot that books were meant to be read; his were rarely precious or flamboyant; never *objets d'art* to be preserved behind glass.

At work in the cultural heart of America, close to great libraries and museums, the young Rogers had access to medieval and Renaissance illuminated manuscripts, and to the masterpieces of the printed book from Gutenberg and Aldus to the contemporary European private presses. Soon after joining the Riverside Press the young designer, still in his twenties, felt an irresistible urge to make distinguished books of his own design, free from the crippling limitations of money and time. After several years of persistent persuasion, Rogers was finally able to induce George H. Mifflin to establish a separate department in 1900 for the production of limited editions, with the full resources of the Riverside Press at his disposal. It was called "The

Department of Special Editions," and Rogers was placed in full charge, with adequate financial support to experiment and produce books as he wanted to make them. This was an extraordinarily fortunate meeting of two men of vision and courage in an adventurous association that would produce historic results.

The working quarters were described in an added note to a 1905-1906 catalogue of books published by Houghton, Mifflin and Company: "A special work-room has been provided at Riverside for the production of Riverside Press Editions. One of the old buildings on the river bank has been remodeled and refitted for this purpose. With its walls of brick, large, heavily mullioned windows, and open-timbered roof, this room presents something of the attractiveness of the earlier printing establishments, before the advent of machinery. This attraction, however, is due almost wholly to the substantial and workmanlike character of the fittings, and is not the result of any effort to create an effect. In it some of the methods of the old-time printers are being employed. The only machines are the heavy hand presses upon which occasional volumes of the Riverside Press Editions are printed, for many of these books are printed wholly by hand, and often they are printed directly from the types, and not from electrotype plates."[2]

The first of the Riverside Press Editions to be completed was *Sonnets and Madrigals of Michelangelo* (plate 4). Issued in 1900, it is a small book, 6⅞ x 4 inches (16mo), with a title-page border and decorations by Bruce Rogers. It was set in Caslon italic type and printed damp on a superb handmade paper. The limited edition of three hundred copies was sold out ten days after publication. This is the first book for which Rogers had complete freedom of conception and design, choice of materials, and direct supervision of type composition, presswork, and binding.

During the next twelve years, with sixty limited editions, Rogers initiated a wholly new conception of book design. He broke with the private press tradition of issuing all books with one or two proprietary typefaces in a uniform house style, with limp vellum binding and ties. In this he had some precedence in the work of Daniel Berkeley Updike, but Rogers was much more the inventive and innovative designer. Although always within

CHAPTER TWO: 1895–1911

the dictates of good taste and readability, each of Rogers' Riverside Press books was wholly different in conception, varying in size from 16mo to folio, in a wide range of typefaces, paper, decoration, and binding. Each new title would be a fresh adventure for the designer and a revelation to the collector. It is no surprise that most of the Riverside Editions were sold out before publication or soon thereafter.

It is difficult to describe the pleasure that these books can give. The basic data of type, paper, edition, etc., is provided in bibliographies. Beyond these essentials are the indefinables—Rogers' capacity for charm and gaiety, a sure-handedness in type arrangement, and rare dexterity in the use of initial letters and decoration. Under his design and direction, many of these books became allusive or reminiscent of the period in which they were first published. But to such re-creation, Rogers added his own ingenuity and that most elusive of qualities—personal style. His typographic abilities were soundly based on his close study of the great books of the past. His roots were deep in the grandeur of the books of the fifteenth century in Italy and in the lightness and clarity of the scholarly volumes printed in the sixteenth century in Paris and Lyons. His most illustrious typographic ancestors were Aldus Manutius, Robert Estienne, Geofroy Tory, and Jean de Tournes.

The second book of the Riverside Press Editions, the *Rubáiyát of Omar Khayyám*, also published in 1900, was a favorite title among contemporary private presses. In its light-hearted typographic design, the Rogers volume echoed the enjoyment of life's favors as expressed in the famous poem. This *Rubáiyát* is of special interest because it is Rogers' first use of the Brimmer type, a vigorous, transitional face that he found in a corner of the Riverside composing room. Many years earlier it had caught the eye of H. O. Houghton, who had ordered it from England. It was later recognized by Stanley Morison, the English historian of the printed page, as the Bell typeface, designed in the eighteenth century in England. Rogers drew some special swash characters to be added to the font, which he then used in one or more Riverside Press books each year. Although the *Rubáiyát* was the first of the Riverside Press Editions to be undertaken, the Michelangelo *Sonnets* came out in advance of it, as there was only enough type to set four pages at a time, elec-

THE RIVERSIDE PRESS: MASSACHUSETTS

troplate, distribute, and then set the next four, which took about a year.

By the end of 1903, nineteen Riverside Press Editions had been completed, each with its own typographic individuality. Included were the first two volumes of the monumental folio edition, *The Essays of Montaigne* (plate 5), page 14½ x 9⅝ inches. The third volume was issued in 1904, for a grand total of approximately fifteen hundred pages. Portrait frontispieces in the Renaissance manner were engraved in wood by M. Lamont Brown for this edition; initial letters and decorations were redrawn by Rogers from Geofroy Tory books printed in Paris early in the sixteenth century. Of special significance was a new type designed by Rogers for the Montaigne volumes. Much later he wrote of the origins of the Montaigne type, as it was called, in the booklet, *The Centaur Types*:

> At an exhibition of books at the Boston Public Library I saw for the first time a copy of Nicolas Jenson's *Eusebius* of 1470, and I was at once impressed by the loveliness of its pages, indifferently printed though they were. This early judgment was confirmed for me many years later (though by then it needed no confirmation) when Berkeley Updike wrote of them: "to look at the work of Jenson is to think but of its beauty, and almost to forget that it was made with hands."[3]

Rogers found a collector who owned a *Eusebius* and, at the Harvard College Library, found a *Suetonius* also printed by Jenson. With photographic enlargements made of type pages from both books he "began the search for what I fondly thought would be the ideally perfect type; not knowing then that it was something like the quest of the Holy Grail." He continues, in *The Centaur Types*:

> After several years of work with Houghton, Mifflin & Company, when the specially printed Riverside Press Editions had achieved a measure of success, I prevailed upon George H. Mifflin, then head of the firm and an enthusiast for good bookmaking, to let me have a new type made for a folio edition of Montaigne's *Essays* then under consideration.

CHAPTER TWO: 1895–1911

I had in the meantime bought Ongania's *Early Venetian Printing* . . . [from which] I adapted several decorations for Riverside Press books, at the same time making acquaintance with other early Venetian types; but Jenson's was still my ideal. So, with Mr. Mifflin's kind authorization, I blithely set to work to make drawings from enlargements from my Jenson photographs. These designs, through the agency of Mr. J. W. Phinney, head of the Boston branch of the American Type Founders Company, were put into the hands of John Cumming of Worcester for the cutting of the punches. Cumming was the best punch cutter of his day. He was a retired athlete and oarsman, with great clumsy-looking hands; but the way he could handle a minute graving tool was a marvel. He was also a marvellous potato masher, as I discovered when I once lunched at his home. I suppose he enjoyed the relaxation of wielding a larger and freer implement than the graver.

The first proofs of the type were faintly disappointing to me, even in the excitement of seeing my drawings transmuted to metal. For Cumming worked almost free-hand, with only occasional measurements, and had not preserved all the niceties of either Jenson's letter or my adaptation of it. But Mr. Mifflin was delighted with the new type, and after several of the least successful letters were recut I decided it would have to do—for the time, at least—until I could have another try for my ideal type.[4]

Early in 1902, the young Carl Purington Rollins must have seen *A Report of the Last Sea-Fight of the Revenge*, a Riverside Press Edition that had been printed in the trial font of the Montaigne type. He wrote to Rogers about the type. Rogers replied on 5 December 1902 in a letter that revealed much of Rogers' attitude toward type and book design, which never changed. (The letter is now in the Arts of the Book Room of the Yale University Library.)

Dear Sir—
I regret to say that your letter of Nov. 24th was mislaid and although I searched several times for it, it did not reappear till this morning. My apparent negligence in replying to it was due to the fact that I had not

your name and address. I now hasten to answer your queries and hope it is not too late for your purpose.

1st. The design of the type may properly be called my own, though it is modelled closely as to size and proportions upon Nicolas Jenson's 15th century Roman face. Still enough individuality has gone into the handling of the details of its construction to produce an original face — as originality goes nowadays — and I am free to say that [frankly] speaking, I am not a believer in "originality" as generally understood — that is, the sort of originality that discards all preceding models as far as possible and boldly strikes out with the announced intention of producing something "new" — The results may be "new" but they are almost invariably bad, at the same time — and I prefer to be accused of copying rather than to produce eccentricities. There is large field for the play of genuine originality and personality even in the endeavor to reproduce standard models in any art. I may say here that in many respects I consider the "Montaigne" type distinctly inferior to Jenson's, while better fitted in some respects for modern work.

2nd. At the present date the "Montaigne" type proper has not yet appeared in any publication but the 1st volume of Montaigne's "Essays" from which it takes its name, will be issued before Christmas. — This will answer your 4th query also.

3rd. There are some minor differences between the type to be used in the "Montaigne" and that of the "Revenge" — the latter being really a trial stage of the finally accepted type. Several letters were recut after the "Revenge" was printed notably the lower case o which was made rounder and the lower case g which was lightened — The g has since been still further modified and will require one more recutting before meeting my entire approval. In addition to these modifications the whole fount was given a wider set, 1/3000 of an inch being added to the body of each letter to open up the page a little more. The effect is hardly discernable even when attention is called to it but the improvement is there.

Trusting that these replies will answer your queries satisfactorily. I

CHAPTER TWO: 1895–1911

shall still be glad to give you any further information desired if I can, but I must ask to be excused from putting it in writing as I have not the time to give to it in that way. I shall be very glad to see you at the Press at any time, but will ask you to let me know beforehand, as my hours here are uncertain.

Concerning the reproduction of the "Montaigne" type. I am adverse to having it reproduced by zinc etching, particularly if it involves reduction—but if you will tell me the size and shape of plate desired I shall be pleased to have a block of it set and send an electro for your use to be returned to us afterwards.

The Montaigne type was not a wholly satisfactory accomplishment and was recognized as such by Rogers. Nevertheless he used it with consummate skill in four more Riverside books: Boccaccio's *Life of Dante* (1904), *Augustus St. Gaudens* (1907), *The Banquet of Plato* (1908), and *The Constitution of the United States of America* (1911). He also used it for two large broadsides: *The Declaration of Independence* (1906) and the *Emancipation Proclamation* (1907).

The *Geofroy Tory* (plates 6/7), a Riverside Press Edition of 1909, one of Rogers' great books, is of added interest for its type, which became known as Riverside Caslon. Rogers was unable to find an existing type that would reflect the atmosphere of the books of sixteenth-century France, when Geofroy Tory, artist and printer, made his memorable books. To resolve the problem, Rogers used a foundry Caslon as a base and combined 12-point capitals with 14-point lower-case characters. With a graver he remodelled every letter in the font, then slightly rubbed down the type in order to increase its depth of color, and reduced the fit of the type to bring the characters closer together. After a great amount of trial proofing, electrotype matrices were made, which were then used to cast sorts (individual type characters) on a Monotype machine for the book's hand composition.

The illustrations for the new edition were taken from original Tory books. Photographic prints were made which Rogers retouched or redrew in order to compensate for the less than perfect impression on textured papers of the early editions. During the exacting work, he suffered such intense headaches that he had to forego all other activities until the new photo-engraved lineplates were made and ready for press.

In addition to the Montaigne type, the Riverside Caslon as remodelled, and the Brimmer for which Rogers made swash characters, a number of other typefaces appeared in the Riverside Press Editions. Three books were given a medieval look, employing black-letter (gothic-style) types: *The History of Oliver and Arthur* (1903) in Priory Text; Chaucer's *Parlement of Foules* (1904) in *lettre bâtarde*; and *The Song of Roland* (1906), a tall folio, also in *lettre bâtarde*, and with *civilité* for marginal notes. The *lettre bâtarde* and *civilité* were especially imported from France. *The Song of Roland* (plate 8), printed in red, blue, brown, and black, one of the most popular of the Rogers books, was notable for drawings made by Rogers from the stained glass windows of the cathedral of Chartres, printed from line blocks and hand colored. Caslon type was a Rogers favorite during the Riverside years, as was Brimmer, but he also used Scotch Roman, Oxford, Didot, and Original Old Style italic.

In recording typefaces it is well to remember that type is only one of the essential elements of bookmaking. A fine volume involves many choices of materials and design; all must be fully realized and interrelated. In *Paragraphs on Printing* (page 22), Rogers said, "You may take the most beautiful type in your stock, and if it be carelessly set, if it be too large or too small for the page, or the page badly placed on the paper, then no beauty of type or paper will compensate for any one of these violations of proportion."[5]

George H. Mifflin was so proud of the tall folio volume *The Song of Roland* that he sent a copy to President Theodore Roosevelt in the White House. The President, himself an author, acknowledged receipt of the book with thanks, adding, "Incidentally, I am proud as an American that such a bit of work should be done in America." Then on 23 January 1907, he wrote to the publishers again, at their offices in Boston:

Gentlemen:

Would it be agreeable to you if I stopt at 4 Park Street on the morning of the 23d of February to look at some of your special editions like that Beautiful "Song of Roland" which you sent me? I am not an

CHAPTER TWO: 1895–1911

expert on these matters, but comparing that "Song of Roland" with other modern printing (notably with a very handsome edition of a great German book I have) it seemed to me far ahead, and almost like some of the very beautiful printing of books at the end of the Fifteenth Century. The other day I saw a Livy, tooled in Florence in 1476, which was so beautiful, altho so very expensive, that it really needed heroic self-denial for me not to purchase it.

Mifflin replied by return mail:

Dear Mr. President,
    It will be altogether delightful to have you call at 4 Park Street on the morning of Feby 23, and we shall have the greatest interest in showing you all our Special Editions, and presenting to you our Mr. Bruce Rogers their designer. The writer further hopes to have the pleasure of meeting you at the Porcellian rooms the same evening.[6]

President Roosevelt arrived as planned and looked at Riverside Press books. It was a great day for a publishing house, for Bruce Rogers, and for American bookmaking.

At the opening of the exhibition of his books at the Grolier Club in 1938, when his greatest work had been accomplished (although nineteen years of life and many fine books lay ahead), Rogers told his audience that, of the more than four hundred books on display, he owned "only about seventy-five . . . and I could reduce that number to perhaps thirty, and still have all those that I consider entirely successful."[7] Anyone familiar with the Rogers opus would deplore such self-evaluation, or perhaps devaluation—a diffidence that persisted through a lifetime. Nevertheless those books are of special interest because they are the designer's expressed favorites. Their titles may be found on page 119 of *Paragraphs on Printing* (1943), "Elicited from Bruce Rogers in Talks with James Hendrickson on the Functions of the Book Designer." This book is a remarkable summation with rare insights into Rogers' attitudes and methods. It will be referred to frequently in the present volume.

THE RIVERSIDE PRESS: MASSACHUSETTS

Nine of those thirty severely selected books are from the Rogers years at the Riverside Press. They are the product of his youth—ardent, ebullient, lyrical works, the best of which can stand shoulder to shoulder with his more mature masterpieces. The nine titles are: Ronsard's *Songs and Sonnets* (1903) (plate 9), Boccaccio's *Life of Dante* (1904) (plate 10), Chaucer's *Parlement of Foules* (1904) (plate 13), *The Song of Roland* (1906) (plate 8), *Poems of Maria Lowell* (1907) (plate 11), *The Banquet of Plato* (1908) (plate 12), Walton's *The Compleat Angler* (1909) (plate 14), *LXXV Sonnets* of Wordsworth (1910) (plate 15), and *Ecclesiastes* (1911).

The beauty, ingenuity, and variety of the Riverside Press Editions changed the course of typographic history. To employ a designer on staff or free-lance, to design a book from the manuscript, was unheard of before the young Updike broke ground at the Riverside Press. With the path somewhat prepared, Rogers made book design an acknowledged and respected profession. He was, in fact, the first artist-typographer. After the Rogers years it has become standard practice among publishers and cultural institutions to employ professional typographers to design their books.

As early as 1903, when a dozen of the Riverside Press Editions had been printed and acclaimed, Rogers already had the vision of the great book and the knowledge that he would ultimately have to find printers who would provide him with adequate and congenial working arrangements. Meantime it is of interest for us to see that certain lifetime attitudes had already been formed, and to have some realization of the handicaps he was able to surmount in achieving brilliant examples of pure craftsmanship. He had received a long and very favorable review in the *Inland Printer*, a trade journal. After thanking the writer, Thomas Wood Stevens, Rogers continued, in a letter of 4 March 1904:

> Almost needless is it to say that I am greatly pleased with the reserved quality of the praise that you give certain volumes and the contrast of this quality with the rather exuberant tone of some recent notices of them is most refreshing. When it comes to saying that a piece of work is the "most perfect ever produced" it casts a shade on my confidence in

CHAPTER TWO: 1895–1911

the ability of the writer to judge intelligently. Such wholesale praise soon becomes nauseous—but is unfortunately characteristic of much of our modern exaggeration in almost everything.

The latter quality is one I strive most assiduously to avoid in my work, even at the expense of its resulting in rather commonplace books. I confess that the temptation often comes to break away from the limits I have set myself and to introduce more striking effects of typography or decoration, but after keeping the sketches of such work before me for a while I usually abandon them for something simpler and less pronounced—less original if you please. I can readily see that your sympathies are with the more unique treatment of bookmaking and up to a certain point I am with you. I have great admiration for the Kelmscott books and a little less for the Vale Press and Doves Press editions—but without having much desire to attempt to follow in their footsteps even if I thought myself capable of it. My criticism of them is that the "Art" element stands out too strongly in them all—they are objects of art first—books to be read secondly—and somehow I would prefer to have my work primarily bookish—the art concealed or subordinated to the literary quality. I can not perhaps make my meaning quite plain but you will guess what it is. To this end I am not so particular whether the ornament I use is new and original or copies from older work—it is not of enough vital importance to my scheme to bother over. If I could without difficulty get present-day designs that equaled the old in my opinion, I should use them in preference to borrowing from older work—but I have really not had time enough to discover any—with the exception of the border to the "Raleigh" which was designed by a friend of mine here in Boston and which seems to me only indifferent good—though I believe the attempt to retain the character of Elizabethan ornament is accountable for its shortcomings.

I take issue with you on only one small statement in your article and that is perhaps only a matter of taste. Men probably *have* learned a great deal about the art of design since Tory's time—too much, perhaps—but I sincerely believe that no initials or ornaments have been designed that surpass in beauty of line and proportion and style the work that he produced. I do not say that it could not be done by several living men, but it is rare that a man of the first rank as a decorator nowadays will condescend to do carefully and conscientiously so small a thing as an initial. They are too busily engaged upon larger schemes of mural painting or architecture. I had some difficulty in persuading Blashfield to do the drawings for Spenser's Songs, as his time was so occupied on a large mural decoration. If I do not bore you utterly, it may interest you to see the sketch I sent him to indicate the effect I desired on the page. A similar scheme was sent to Pyle for the "Revenge."

Had I anticipated the character of your last paragraph I could possibly have prevented the regret you express at its beginning. It would need a personal visit to the Press probably, the pleasure of which I hope you will some day give me, to explain to you the somewhat peculiar position I occupy here, but I can perhaps give you an idea of it. The firm is one of the ultra-conservative kind and with the exception of Mr. Mifflin, the senior partner, not in the least bookish. He has well grounded ideas of good books along one or two well beaten tracks, and it is only by his approval that I am allowed to have full swing in these special editions. Usually the details of their design are never questioned—and it is only in the manufacture of them that I meet, not opposition but apathy. The two or three workmen I have (not always the same ones) are interested enough usually, but they are not under my direct control, and the foremen generally consider the whole scheme foolish and a mere fad.

I have been at the Press over seven years—always with the idea of making fine books—but unable to induce them to let me try until two years ago. Up to that time I had part only in designing the advertising matter, title-pages, etc., etc., apparently good practice, but really, I believe, very injurious training for the kind of work I want to do—as it is almost impossible under such conditions for a man to shake off the tradition that attaches him to the manufacturer of the ordinary book — which by the way is still all under my supervision within certain limits.

As to equipment, with the exception of my two special types it is of a character that could be surpassed by almost any second class job office in the country, and while there has been some improvement lately, it is too difficult to induce them to buy proper material to make it worth my while to fight for. Withal the personal associations are pleasant and although I at regular intervals declare that I will quit and look somewhere else for an opportunity to carry on my work, I usually settle down again to the routine of it, varied only occasionally by the pleasure such articles as yours give me in it. You will see that while I do not have the mechanical difficulties of bookmaking to contend with personally — (though it requires my closest supervision to have the composition and printing as well done as it is) I should gladly welcome them in a small private establishment instead of the more wearing ones that I meet here almost daily. So I can not agree with you in thinking that we "lack nothing that the task requires." We lack the chief thing almost — enthusiasm.[8]

In 1905 Rogers made an exploratory trip to Europe. In England he called on, among others, Alfred W. Pollard, Keeper of Printed Books at the British Museum; and Emery Walker, printer and photographic engraver, who had been a mentor and associate of William Morris at the Kelmscott Press, and a partner with T. J. Cobden-Sanderson at the Doves Press. Rogers also visited the Netherlands, where the interest in fine printing had been continuous since the fifteenth century, when the native Laurens Coster was believed, by certain Dutch patriots, to have been the inventor of printing from movable type.

From a letter written five years before leaving the Riverside Press, we can see that Rogers already had the compelling, and prescient, desire to live and work in England. He could not then have known that he would spend much of his working life in England; that he would there spend some of his happiest years; and that at presses in London, Oxford, and Cambridge he would produce his greatest books. On 24 October 1907 he wrote to Pollard:

> If you can recall me to your memory at all, it is doubtless as a person who troubled you somewhat, two years ago, by an apparently useless call upon you at the Museum.
>
> So far as I can remember, my only excuse was to ask some information regarding books decorated by Tory, in anticipation of a projected translation of Bernard's "Life." You were good enough to express some interest in the undertaking and I believe I promised to send you some specimen pages. So many things have delayed the book that I have only recently got so far as to have specimen pages pulled—two or three of which are enclosed herewith. The type is a modification of Caslon, which I have myself recut in the hope of getting something of the effect of the French Renaissance letters without making it too difficult to read. The decorations throughout, will be reproductions of Tory's own designs. (You will discover that the pages on the sheets I send are not consecutive. The folios are fictitious.)
>
> As you specially commended some pages of a little Chaucer volume I had with me, I got together some time ago, a complete set of the sheets to send you, but have held them back for a year or more hoping to have the Tory pages to enclose with them. I regret that some sheets are imperfect but they were all that remained.
>
> I send also one of the recent lists of Riverside Press books that you may see what a variety of undertakings I am called upon to encounter—too frequently with very indifferent results.
>
> That you may not mistake my motives in writing to you, I would like to say that I am in no wise concerned with the sale of these books nor with their advertising—so pray do not suspect me of trying to "interest" you in them—at least from the commercial point of view. My only excuse is an enthusiasm for well-printed books and for the work of Geofroy Tory—both of which you, through your writings, have had a large part in fostering.

CHAPTER TWO: 1895–1911

> My ambition is still to come to England to live and work, wherein I am encouraged by at least two of our mutual acquaintances, Professor Eliot Norton and Mr. Liddell — Mr. Liddell, by the way, has established a hand-press at his house and is preparing to print his Shakespeare himself.
>
> I hope therefore to sometime have the pleasure of seeing you and of study among the treasures of the Museum.[9]

The Riverside Press Editions for which Rogers had complete freedom in design and control of production included some of his finest books. But it must be remembered that during the sixteen years of his association at the Riverside Press, as an employee he was also required to design, re-design, or dress up, hundreds of Houghton Mifflin trade books, catalogues, and advertising items. These trade duties were accomplished at the same time that Rogers was absorbed in the design and production of the Riverside Press Editions. Hence it is not surprising that he looked to a future when he could devote himself wholly and without distraction to his own chosen work. On 30 July 1910 he wrote to S. H. de Roos, the Dutch artist and type designer, who had written a few years earlier asking for specimens of Riverside Press Editions:

> We, in America, are always in such a rush to be *doing* something, that we take little time to enjoy life or really *be* something more than machines. However, I have always looked forward to living, for a term of years at least, either in England or on the Continent — possibly allying myself for part of the year at least, with some already established business. Not of course as a daily worker but as a designer or artist director of such part of their work as I might be competent to undertake.
>
> My present agreement with the Riverside Press expires next year.... They pay me very well, even for this country — (6000 dollars per annum) but they give me no leisure except two weeks vacation yearly. And now leisure for my own pursuits has come to mean more than money to me, and unless I can arrange for a yearly term of perhaps three months to enable me to visit Europe occasionally (with a cor-

responding reduction in salary) I shall probably withdraw from the connection.[10]

A close professional relationship which lasted a lifetime had begun between Rogers and Henry Lewis Bullen (1857-1938), the director of the excellent typographic library and museum at the American Type Founders Company in New Jersey. The Library (later acquired by Columbia University) was established in 1908 by Bullen under the enlightened presidency of Robert W. Nelson. It consisted of some forty-six thousand items of historical and contemporary importance concerned with the art and techniques of printing.

On 7 October 1910, Rogers wrote to Bullen and told him of his expected departure from the Riverside Press and about his uncertain thoughts about the future. The relationship with the Press had about run its course, and the break would come with mutual consent:

> I have occasionally spoken to you of the probability of my leaving the Riverside Press and it is now an established intention on both sides. I shall probably finish my present agreement with them which lasts till April 1, 1911, though if something offers before that time I am at liberty to quit them at any time on short notice. I shall put through all the books in hand (except the Dante which will be abandoned) and we part company with mutual good-will. In fact I shall probably do many more books with the types and ornaments which I have been instrumental in getting together but the department of fine printing will be discontinued.
>
> The plain fact is that it doesn't pay—at least not well enough to please the newer and younger element in the firm, and in the general retrenchment now going on, my head, as that of the highest salaried man in the concern was naturally one of the first to fall. I am really greatly pleased, though I haven't an idea yet as to what I shall do.
>
> I think however, it will be designing, entirely upon my own account, of whatever may turn up in the way of commissions—from an initial letter to a complete set of books or cover designs. However time will

CHAPTER TWO: 1895–1911

doubtless make clearer the best course to pursue. My inclination is of course, for a small printing establishment, but that means business and business means capital and a partner—and I don't just know where to look for either.

In any event I shall try to have a little more personal freedom and one of the first uses I shall make of it will be to familiarize myself with your collection, which looks so tempting on the occasions I have had glimpses of it.[11]

1912 1916

Free Lance: The Centaur Type

Finally, in 1911, Rogers concluded his formative years at the Riverside Press and freed himself from the constraints of the weekly salary and the necessity of accepting direction from an employer. For the balance of his life (excepting only two years at the Cambridge University Press on a part-time advisory basis) he would devote himself completely to the nuances, the vagaries, and the infinite detail of the printed book. He would steadfastly refuse any entanglement involved in plant ownership and in problems of personnel.

In 1912 he sailed for England, hoping there to find significant work that would also provide the wherewithal for the necessities of life. During the crossing he wrote an interesting account for the London *Times* Printing Number on "Progress of Modern Printing in the United States," unsigned in accordance with the custom of the *Times* at that period. Included was a rather critical section on his own work at the Riverside Press:

> In twelve years some sixty titles have been placed in this series, and the volumes composing it present almost as many different typographical studies. There has been little attempt at originality of style. Old *motifs* have been followed with varying degrees of fidelity and success. The workmanship has been unwaveringly conscientious and in most cases excellent. A few books have been printed on handpresses, and some are decorated with woodcuts executed in the open-line manner that harmonizes so well with vigorous typography. . . .
>
> In so ambitious an effort frequent failures are to be expected, and our expectations are not entirely unfulfilled. Some of the volumes are

CHAPTER THREE: 1912–1916

unpleasing in proportion, and the taste in type and paper is not always impeccable. Mr. Rogers evinces a fondness for the use of italic or cursive type, especially for the printing of poetry, doubtless on account of its greater poetic character and suavity of line.[1]

During the summer spent in England in 1912, Rogers was unable to make satisfactory working arrangements, and returned to the United States to face several years as a free-lance designer. He had earlier expressed the whimsical hope that he might one day become a "tramp printer" with a home in the country at a converted water mill, with a limited amount of type, a small portable press, and a sketch pad. That escape from reality remained a dream that recurred whenever Rogers became fed up with the frustrations and the labyrinthian details of book production.

During three unsettled years—1912 to 1915—Rogers maintained himself with a variety of printed work which, with his growing reputation, brought him into contact with museums, book clubs, other cultural institutions, and book collectors. He found temporary living quarters wherever his work took him—but most often in New York, a city for which he had little affection. Books and ephemera were still printed for him and at his direction by the Riverside Press. He also produced work at the Munder Press in Baltimore; at the Bartlett-Orr Press in New York; and, of especial significance, at both Carl Purington Rollins' Montague Press in Massachusetts, and the Metropolitan Museum Press in New York.

In 1912 *Les Points de France* was printed at the Riverside Press for the Metropolitan Museum of Art, but the present writer finds nothing of the Rogers magic in this paperback volume. Also produced at Riverside in 1914 were *Mr. Ryan's Collection*, privately printed; *A Political Romance* by Laurence Sterne, a reprint of the first edition of 1759 for the Club of Odd Volumes in Boston; and *Franklin and His Press at Passy* (plate 16) by Luther S. Livingston, commissioned by the Grolier Club of New York. The Franklin is an octavo volume, set in Fry, Brimmer, and Oxford types, an example of allusive typography, in which Rogers suggested Colonial American printing. The Oxford type was probably designed by James Ronaldson. It was first shown in a Binny & Ronaldson specimen book in 1812, called Roman No. 1. In a letter of 30 March 1930 from London to Laurence Siegfried, Rogers wrote that Will Bradley was the real discoverer of the type later called Oxford, but that Updike later developed its use.

Rogers was occasionally accused of being imitative when he gave his books some feeling for the period in which the book was written and first published. But his original and subtle manipulation of type always raised his books beyond the imitative. He wrote about this subject in *Paragraphs on Printing*:

> Making an "allusive" format for a book — that is, casting it in the style of the period of the original text — is in a small way something like planning the stage setting for a play. An up-to-date style for an ancient text would compare with staging *Hamlet* in modern dress. However novel and effective in its own way, you feel it to be strange, and this sense of strangeness is an annoying distraction; you are forced to think of the setting and the designer rather than of the text.[2]

With his usual modesty, and apparently unaware of his own contribution to the history of book design, Rogers commented further on the subject of allusive typography when speaking to his audience at the Grolier Club in New York, at the preview of his exhibition in 1938:

> Even a casual look round the room will show that apparently no basic principle has actuated the production of all these books, no new organic theory has been demonstrated. They are as miscellaneous as they look to be; and therefore, as a collection, not nearly so impressive as a set of Kelmscott or Ashendene or Doves Press books. Yet there *has* been a sort of principle on which I have worked, however mistaken it may have been. It is to have, conceivably, pleased the *author* of the work that I had in hand, by the form which I gave it. This has indeed actually happened, when the book was by a writer still living, as several letters in my possession will testify. But as it has been my fortune to have been most frequently called upon to print authors of the past, rather than those of the present time, it seems logical to have cast their words in

CHAPTER THREE: 1912–1916

the forms that were familiar to them in their own day, instead of trying to impose upon them any of my own typographic interpretations or peculiarities. My contribution has been mainly to take advantage of modern improvements, to print their books better if possible than they were done in their own times.

This conception of my functions as a printer naturally resulted in what has come to be called "period" or "allusive" typography. I do not mean to imply that it was my invention; it has been practised at times by many earlier printers and publishers, amongst whom Pickering comes most readily to my memory. He occasionally had the Whittinghams reprint early works in a style that simulated their original editions without being attempts at facsimile.

But the practice of period printing by no means precludes sympathy with modern, even ultra-modern, styles. It merely happens that I have never been called upon to print, say, Gertrude Stein, or James Joyce, or Ezra Pound—though E. P., when we last parted at Rapallo, did invite me to come back and help him with a new printing of his "Cantos," and I have always regretted that circumstances prevented my doing so. No, it isn't the modernity of modernistic books and types that I dislike; it is the visual ugliness of most of them. And when we come to analyze them we find them, after all, not so modern as their ostensible creators would like us to believe.[3]

It should be noted that allusive typography was no longer a factor in the later years when Rogers put into type the timeless words of Homer, Shakespeare, and the Bible.

During the years in New York Rogers cemented a lifetime friendship of personal and professional importance with Henry Watson Kent, then Secretary of the Metropolitan Museum of Art, later President of the Grolier Club and of the American Institute of Graphic Arts. In *The Centaur Types* (1949) Rogers wrote about their first meeting many years before. It was when Rogers was living on Pinckney Street in Boston "that Henry Watson Kent and John Cotton Dana came to call on me, and then and there I made the acquaintance of two of the most accomplished and scholarly men in America whose secondary interest, at least, was printing. Till meeting them I had not definitely decided to become a printer or a book designer, having remnants of an ambition to be an illustrator or a painter. But their enthusiasm and encouragement decided me to remain in what I had thought to be but a temporary occupation."[4]

John Cotton Dana, the cultivated librarian of the Newark (New Jersey) Public Library, recognized the significance of the work Rogers had done and in 1916 gave him his first comprehensive exhibition. In collaboration with Dana, the Carteret Book Club, a group of New Jersey book collectors, issued a printed catalogue of the exhibition. In addition to "A List of Books and Other Pieces of Printing Designed by Mr. Rogers," it contained an extended essay by Alfred W. Pollard, "Modern Fine Printing in England and Mr. Bruce Rogers," which was also the title of the publication. Pollard was one of the first of the scholarly historians concerned with printing to appreciate the seminal worth of the Riverside Press Editions: "I believe that no other printer, since printing began, could point to so varied an output of so high a standard of craftsmanship within so short a time. Certainly no other books I have ever seen embody more successfully the lightness of touch, gaiety and colour which have their place among the ideals of fine printing no less than splendour and dignity."[5]

Henry Watson Kent, who had a keen appreciation for fine printing, and who was dissatisfied with the pedestrian printing that had been done for the Metropolitan Museum of Art, bought type and presses, hired a compositor and a pressman, and established the Museum Press on the institution's basement floor. With a natural gift for typography, Kent designed new, attractive exhibition labels, charming invitations, splendid posters, and other ephemera. In 1938, a quarter century of printing at the Museum Press was celebrated by an extensive exhibition at the Pierpont Morgan Library in New York, "In appreciation," stated the catalogue, "of the work initiated and furthered by Mr Kent, in raising the standard of institutional printing to that of one of the Fine Arts." For books and catalogues and other assignments beyond the capacities of the Museum Press, Kent called in

CHAPTER THREE: 1912–1916

several of the prominent designers and printers during these years, including of course, his friend Bruce Rogers, whose forthcoming new type which enjoyed Kent's financial support, became an important Museum acquisition. Kent also asked Rogers for part-time help in the management of the Press. An enchanting small pamphlet, *Amycus et Célestin*, of sixteen pages, 8⅛ x 5¼ inches, designed by Rogers, was printed in the Centaur type at the Museum Press in 1916. It contained two delightful woodcuts by Timothy Cole after designs by Bryson Burroughs.

Never satisfied with his Montaigne type, Rogers had always intended to try again. Between 1912 and 1914, in his second attempt, he succeeded magnificently. The new type, ultimately called Centaur, is a design of historic importance. For a starting base and guide, Rogers again turned to the type of the *De Evangelica Praeparatione* of Eusebius, printed by Nicolas Jenson in Venice in 1470, itself a development from the marvelous letter forms written by the scribes of the Italian Renaissance in their glorious manuscripts.

Rogers made fugitive prints (pale impressions) enlarged from the Jenson photographs and then wrote over the lower-case letters with a broad pen as rapidly, he said, as he could drive the pen. The capitals required more careful drawing, as was probably done by Jenson himself. Rogers has written that "after writing a page which contained practically all the letters of the alphabet the best of them were selected and their obvious imperfections touched up with a brush and white."[6]

Instead of the ancient practice of cutting punches by hand from which matrices were then struck, the Centaur matrices were made on a pantograph machine by Robert Wiebking in Chicago from the Rogers drawings. "The result," wrote Rogers, "was a much closer approximation to the original Jenson than the Montaigne type had been. It was not, however, a facsimile, for I had purposely altered some of the details of a few letters, and Wiebking had made slight alterations, for practical reasons, in others, but they were nearly always improvements over my designs.... With only a few recuttings the matrices were completed in their present form and the first type was cast from them by the American Type Founders Company.... The only size made was 14-point, though later on Mr. Kent, Director of the Metropolitan Museum Press, had capitals cut in one smaller and several larger sizes for labels in the display cases at the museum."[7] The 14-point Centaur for hand composition was commissioned by Kent for the Metropolitan Museum. Its use was restricted to work done at the Museum Press and to printing by Bruce Rogers as co-owner. Some fifteen years later the Centaur type was made available to the trade for machine composition by the English Monotype Company.

The Centaur type is an original design of rare cultivation and grace. Because of its classic elegance and its aristocratic Renaissance ancestry, the type calls for special handling. Indeed it has had no success in advertising or commercial printing. On the other hand, among devotees of fine printing it has been accepted as one of the great type designs, and once the cutting was completed for the Monotype machine, it was welcomed by sensitive designers and printers for many of their best books and ephemera. (The type you are now reading is the 14-point Monotype version.)

The original 14-point casting for hand composition made its first appearance in a book, *The Centaur* (plate 17), translated by George B. Ives from the French of Maurice de Guérin. (The first use in this volume gave the type its name.) The book's colophon reads: "One hundred thirty-five copies printed by Bruce Rogers at the Montague Press in November, 1915. One hundred copies for sale." The book is a tall quarto of sixteen pages of a handmade paper, 12⅛ x 8 inches, with a headpiece and an initial letter drawn by Rogers in the Geofroy Tory manner. In its one size of type throughout, *The Centaur* is a book of typographic eloquence—of forthright, dramatic simplicity.

In the autumn of 1914 Rogers and his wife found agreeable rooms in Montague, Massachusetts, and stayed through the winter in a boarding house conducted by an ex-Unitarian minister and his wife. Rogers was made very welcome and given a desk at the Dyke Mill, a converted structure in which Carl Purington Rollins had set up type and presses and which he had named the Montague Press. Rogers found the country setting extremely congenial

CHAPTER THREE: 1912–1916

and, with complete freedom to work, returned frequently over the years. He and Rollins had first met when they were both in Boston at the start of their respective careers. Their relationship at the Dyke Mill strengthened a warm and productive lifelong friendship. Rogers expressed his feelings in a footnote on pages 3 and 4 of *Paragraphs on Printing*:

> In this book no attempt has been made merely to chronicle famous names, and those mentioned serve only to illustrate some point in the text. But I cannot refrain from occasional memories of the men whom I have known best; and of these Carl Rollins easily comes first as the master craftsman. Besides furniture and all sorts of gadgets in wood and iron he has built two pleasant houses; and he rebuilt his famous Dyke Mill almost annually (I should say) over a long period of years. When his energies were transferred to Yale his propensities for hand-work entered the larger field without diminution. Not only the work from his private press, but all the printing of the Yale University Press still bears that desirable, indefinable quality of having come out of the work-shop rather than off the drawing board.[8]

In addition to *The Centaur*, for which Mrs. Rogers hand set the type, Rogers produced two privately printed volumes at the Montague Press during 1915: a memorial volume, *Luther S. Livingston, 1864-1914*, by G. P. Winship, was set in Caslon type, two hundred copies printed; and *An Account of Descriptive Catalogues of Strawberry Hill and of Strawberry Hill Sale Catalogues*, with a bibliography by Percival Merritt, edition of seventy-five copies, in Riverside Caslon type.

The hand-set Centaur type was also used later in Dürer's *Of the Just Shaping of Letters* in 1917, Tory's *Champ Fleury* in 1927 (both books commissioned by the Grolier Club), and two or three lesser books and pamphlets, including a brochure, *Spare Your Good* (1919), privately printed at the Cambridge University Press in England.

Fortunately for the typographic communities on both sides of the Atlantic Ocean, the Centaur type in a full range of sizes was made available for machine composition. Rogers wrote about that in *The Centaur Types*:

FREE LANCE: THE CENTAUR TYPE

New problems arose when the Monotype Company in Philadelphia asked me to let them cut the design for their machines, in all the usual sizes of a series. For various reasons, but chiefly because I was going back to England for a year or two, it was decided to have it made by the Monotype Company of London. There we spent a year or more revising it to fit their composing-machine requirements and making several sets of patterns for the diversity of sizes from six- to seventy-two point. To match their other series of book faces an Italic was desirable; but not feeling prepared or competent to design such a letter I prevailed upon Frederic Warde to revise his beautiful Arrighi italic to accompany the Roman founts.

The first specimens of the Monotype version, so far as it was completed (1929) were displayed in a pamphlet called, "The Trained Printer and the Amateur," written at my request by Alfred W. Pollard, then Keeper of Printed Books at the British Museum.[9]

The Monotype version of the Centaur first appeared in book form in 1932 in *The Odyssey*, surely one of Rogers' greatest books and, in the judgment of the present writer, one of the most beautiful printed books of all time. The Monotype Centaur type was also used for the *Pacioli* in 1933, and for the Oxford Lectern Bible published in 1935. These three titles, books of special importance, will be described in detail in later pages.

Before leaving discussion of the origins of the Centaur type it will be of interest to have Rogers' own evaluation, made in *The Centaur Types*:

> I have often been asked what I myself think of Centaur, and although one usually has a bias in favor of his own productions the whole matter is now so far in the past that I believe I can view it without prejudice. My opinion, then, is that, whatever its intrinsic merits may be, it is too definitely an Italian Renaissance letter (which I have tried to suggest by the classic column in my initial drawing). It is a little too elegant and thin for our modern papers and methods of printing, and is seen at its best when printed on dampened hand-made or other antique papers, and with more impression than you can ordinarily get a press-

35

CHAPTER THREE: 1912–1916

man to put on it. He, and most of us, want printing as well as many of our other outlines in life to be as sharp and hard and definite as possible. (I rather think that, in printing, Bodoni inaugurated this fashion, and was thus as "modern" as his types.)

The three qualities named, sharp, hard, and definite, are no doubt admirable ones in their place; but Centaur does not take to them readily and naturally, and profits most when somewhat carelessly printed on paper that wouldn't be passed as perfect in any modern paper mill. It looks surprisingly well on news stock, but we can't make books of that. It is what might be called a "cool" type unless humored in the composition and press-work.[10]

And, finally, some comment follows, extracted from a review of the Centaur type by Stanley Morison, famous British paleographer and historian of the printed book, in Number VII of *The Fleuron* (London, 1930):

A comparison of the two types [Jenson's and Centaur] reveals that if, as Mr Rogers says, he drew over the enlarged photographs of the Eusebius type he also drew away from them — with the happiest results. It would be cheeky, perhaps, to say that the farther Mr Rogers draws away from Jenson, the nearer he draws to our ideal face. . . . That Mr Rogers has assimilated rather than redrawn his original is, therefore, matter for congratulation. There are differences in detail and in mass which are conspicuous. Instead of the very ugly double serifs of the original, which were so carefully retained in the Doves fount, we are given an entirely new and very beautiful M. . . .

The most notable difference, however, between the original Jenson and the Centaur founts is in the distribution of weight. When Mr Rogers began to make enlargements of the original he was "at once struck by the pen-like character of the lower-case," a character, indeed, which has been strengthened rather than weakened in his own drawings. The calligraphic basis of the design which evades the eye in the smaller sizes is beautifully seen in the 72 point. . . .

In the book sizes of the type, *i.e.* 18 point and below, the face disposes itself on the page with a unique grace, carrying the sense of the text with an easy and modest individuality.[11]

On 18 October 1915, Alfred W. Pollard of the British Museum presented a paper, which was read for him, to members of the British Bibliographical Society about the work of Bruce Rogers. A small exhibition of Riverside Press Editions was on view. For the work of an American printer to be discussed at considerable length by this organization was a most unusual event. In the course of the essay Pollard included the statement, "Even the little which is shown here this afternoon will, I hope, suffice to convince you that in Mr. Rogers we are dealing with the work of a printer of unusual importance, in connection with whom there is no exaggeration in using the word genius."[12]

1916   1917

The Mall Press: London

Over the years Rogers resolutely pursued the hope of working and living in England. Since his first trip to London in 1905 he had kept in touch with Alfred W. Pollard and Emery Walker, probably the most influential men concerned with fine printing and the British private press movement. Some time before Rogers finally left the Riverside Press, Walker was already aware of Rogers' firm expectations. In a letter of 18 November 1910, he wrote to Rogers that, "You might possibly find some scope for your activities in connexion with my business.... I am nearly 60 years of age so should be glad in the course of a few years to take things a bit easier."[1]

Emery Walker (later Sir Emery) delivered a famous lecture on the printed book on the evening of 15 November 1888 at the inaugural exhibition of the newly formed Arts and Crafts Exhibition Society in London. In the course of his lecture Walker projected enlargements by lantern slides of pages from early Italian humanist scribes and printers. In the enthusiastic audience sat William Morris, a friend and neighbor of the speaker. As the two friends walked home after the lecture, Morris, inspired by the enlargements he had seen, turned to Walker and proposed that forthwith they should make a new font of type. Then and there the Kelmscott Press was born. Morris invited Walker to become his partner. Walker declined but remained at Morris' side as his wise and trusted counselor through the great years of Kelmscott books, until Morris' death in 1896.

The year 1900 began an ill-fated partnership with T. J. Cobden-Sanderson at the Doves Press, where Walker supervised printing operations, and pro-

duction of the Doves Press type for which the Jenson type was the model.*
Walker was also instrumental in the production of the Subiaco type for the
Ashendene Press. Subsequently Walker aided Count Harry Kessler† in Germany in the production of a new type (also based on the Jenson type) and
in book production, until the arrival of Hitler, when Kessler had to flee
his country.

During Rogers' visit to London in the summer of 1912, he and Walker
doubtless discussed an eventual English relationship. Over the next years
when Rogers was at work in New York and Massachusetts, the future in
London was surely an important subject in the letters exchanged. On 19
February 1915, Walker wrote a long and warm letter in which he responded
with pleasure to Rogers' proposal that the time had come for a mutual
working arrangement. A few excerpts from Walker's letter follow:

> I duly received three days ago the parcel of printed sheets from the
> Montague Press you kindly sent, and the next day your long and most
> interesting letter.
>
> I am very glad to hear that you have got to work again. I congratulate
> you upon your Centaur type. It is certainly one of the best romans in
> existence. The lower case in the *Champ Fleury* pages is quite as good as
> the capitals. I think the large size of the latter are quite admirable. . . .
>
> It would be delightful if we could work together on a job of the
> kind you suggest. We often do catalogues of works of art and have just
> completed two—one of English Earthenware and the other of late
> Venetian pictures, both for the Burlington Fine Arts Club, a Club
> which exists chiefly for the purpose of getting up exhibitions of works
> of art of all kinds. Of course we could send a photographer and if it
> was in any way possible I should like nothing better than to pay a visit
> to America in such circumstances. I feel pretty sure that together we

---

*T. J. Cobden-Sanderson (1840–1922), a lawyer turned printer and bookbinder,
established the Doves Press with Walker's help.
†Harry, Graf von Kessler (1868–1937), was proprietor of the Cranach Press in
Weimar, Germany.

CHAPTER FOUR: 1916–1917

might make a much handsomer catalogue than the series that were done at enormous expense for Pierpont Morgan, which have nothing in the least distinguished, from a typographical point of view, to recommend them.

I hope your wish to come to England this summer may be realized. You would like our village at Yattendon, which is in a fairly remote part of the country, though it is only about sixty miles from London by rail and rather less as the crow flies. It is at the top of the Berkshire Downs and is really very pleasant as there are only three new houses and neither of them very ugly, whereas the rest of the village is quite charming. Our house was built in 1702 and is a fair specimen of the ordinary building of a manor house at the time of Queen Anne. . . .

There are scores of other things I should like to talk to you about but I must leave them over to-day. For one thing I haven't mentioned the War, which makes one forget almost everything else. One reads the same sort of reports every day and we seem to be no nearer the end. Yesterday the Germans promised to begin their new "frightfulness," but I see two of the Zeppelins, which are used in the North Sea as scouts, are said to have been wrecked, so possibly we may have a respite. Anyhow, the seafaring people do not seem to have been much alarmed and insurance rates haven't gone up. Almost everyone one knows has relatives fighting or preparing to fight. The unanimity of the country is wonderful, and as far as one can tell from people one meets there is a kind of grim determination to go on to the bitter end.[2]

A year and a half after receiving this letter, Rogers was ready to make his commitment to go to London and join Emery Walker in some form of partnership. In a very long and revealing letter about himself, his plans and his hopes, Rogers expressed his pleasure at what lay ahead. These long letters are the quintessence of Bruce Rogers the man, and Bruce Rogers the most eminent producer of the printed book. To edit, condense, or abstract such letters would diminish their value and diminish our knowledge of the man who wrote them.

THE MALL PRESS: LONDON

In view of the wide acclaim already given on both sides of the Atlantic to the Riverside Press Editions, it is difficult to understand Rogers' deep-rooted humility as seen in the letter to Walker of 9 July 1916:

> Your letter has touched me deeply—the generosity of the proposal in itself and your confidence in me and my aims to which it bears witness are beyond me to requite in words—even if I could find fitting ones to try to express my pleasure in the prospect you open up before me.
>
> For five or six years, now, I have struggled against a growing sense of despondency and discouragement—lightened frequently, it is true, by some prospect of a bit of work in which I could take pleasure, and still more often by sympathetic letters from dear friends, such as you and Pollard—and of late, particularly by Pollard's unstinted praise of my past attempts at bookmaking.
>
> Nevertheless I have felt that I was accomplishing nothing worthy of the encouraging start I had made at Riverside, now (it seems) so many years ago—and the prospect of an outlet for the many ideas that still bubble up within me seemed almost definitely closed. Almost as a final resort I took up the study of binding (or rather tooling) this winter, as an art which can be practiced with small equipment and in either town or country. Printing, in comparison, requires an outfit of implements and workmen which I hadn't either the capital or the ability to establish and keep going. Such an undertaking over here, even on a small scale, would mean an entry into the competitive field, to a certain extent—and with price-cutting, labor troubles and the difficulties of unskillful help, was not to be thought of, without a trained business partner—and such a man hadn't as yet turned up—the returns from a distinctly printing business being, apparently, lower than from almost every other branch of industry—and no one anxious to embark in it.
>
> I didn't mean to go into details—but you will see something of the state of mind I was in when your letter arrived with its proffered oppor-

CHAPTER FOUR: 1916–1917

tunity of all I most desire—satisfying work in congenial company, and, furthermore, life in England, even in an England so deeply engaged in such a glorious though heart-breaking struggle. The news, now for the past few days over here, is at last vastly encouraging, and we, who are with you heart and soul, begin to hope it is the beginning of the end. As Pollard says, it is better to go on than to stop before complete victory is won—but the cost is a great one—Pollard's own losses are *unspeakable**—but his courage has been wonderful.

I have taken several days to turn your proposition over in my mind, but I think my decision was made as I read your letter.

Beyond two or three small commissions on which I am working, there is nothing to tie me to this side of the Atlantic (barring, of course, a natural regret at having to part with a few dear friends). I have never formed any interest in the Montague Press. We lived there winter before last, only while my friend Rollins, who owns the old mill, printed two or three little things for me. We came to New York about Dec. 1st and have lived in two rooms in a suburb, where Elizabeth attended a very good public school. Elizabeth is now 15 and taller than her mother (I enclose two little recent photos of her, and also one of myself—with a dear friend of mine—an Oxford man—in the foreground.)

As I have already said, I took up finishing—working every morning for three months with Edith Diehl, pupil of Douglas Cockerell's and one of our best binders here. I have already commissions for some six or eight bindings (one on *The Centaur* for Pierpont Morgan's library) but they can be done at my leisure and as well in London as here. Then my friend H. W. Kent, secretary and acting head of the Metropolitan Museum, asked me to help direct the printing office at the Museum—which is his especial hobby there—and that took one or two afternoons of every week. Of printing I have had during the winter only two or three small commissions—but now I have in hand a little book for the Carteret Book Club of Newark N.J. containing Pollard's paper on my

*Pollard's two sons had been killed in France.

THE MALL PRESS: LONDON

own work and a list of all the books etc. which the Club exhibited at the Newark Library recently — (notice enclosed). The same exhibit is wanted at the Cleveland Art Museum and possibly the Indianapolis Art Museum also, during the summer, and Kent wants to put it up at the Metropolitan Museum next Autumn. I have also had a proposal to show it at the Library of Congress, Washington — so I seem to be turning showman rather than printer. However, it all means a growing reputation over here, which we may turn to ultimate advantage — though it has taken much of my time this spring.

In addition to the little book, the Carteret Book Club have proposed a more important publication consisting of several woodcuts of Newark* to be made by a friend of mine here — printed in colours — with many vignettes in the text — the plan and printing of the book according to my designs. This will take some 18 months to prepare — but can be done as well over there.

I have just submitted a scheme for a new book to the Grolier Club, which was favourably received by the Publication Committee and only awaits the approval of the Council to be put into course of execution. The *Champ Fleury* of which I sent you trial pages, I think, having proved too expensive for publication by them just at this time, it occurred to me that I could take Dürer's treatise on the making of letters out of his *Geometry*, and put it into exactly similar form — it making only 48 pp. as against 275 of *Champ Fleury*. My friend [R. T. Nichol] in the little photograph will translate it from the Latin edition, and it will make a trial-horse for the *Champ Fleury* — which the Club will eventually print — so Kent says.

The printing of the Dürer will have to be done here, as one of the Club members is a printer† (and a very good one) and they feel he ought to do it, but the Centaur type will be used, and my plans followed accurately.

*This book was later entrusted to Updike in Boston, entitled *Newark: A Series of Engravings on Wood* by Rudolph Ruzicka.
†Rogers no doubt referred to Walter Gilliss, but Rogers printed the Dürer himself in London.

CHAPTER FOUR: 1916–1917

Then there are two elaborate catalogues in course of preparation here — of the collections of two of our millionaires — which will be fully illustrated and will attempt to rival Morgan's publications (which, typographically, oughtn't to be difficult). Kent — who is at the bottom of most of the good things done over here, just as you are behind all the best printing in England — says there oughtn't to be any difficulty about our getting them both to make, as one man is one of the Metropolitan trustees and the other is an intimate friend of his. I read most of your letter to Kent and he advised me not to stop to write but to take the next ship over, and said if we made satisfactory arrangements we should make him American agent. He joked, of course, but some such arrangement might not be at all impracticable and, as I said, everyone comes to him, as he is a power in the museum and library world over here.

In addition to all this, I am far from believing that the interest in special publications such as the Kelmscott and Doves Press books is exhausted over here, and an occasional book of that nature would more than pay for itself at least. My experience with the little *Centaur*, which was not advertised or reviewed in any way — proved that, satisfactorily — though I made so few that it was expensive, and gave away half the edition, largely to people who would otherwise have been purchasers, I still more than made expenses of printing and binding. Did I tell you that Mrs Rogers set the type? Her first attempt — but she was fascinated by it. I am sending you two additional copies to give to whoever you think might care for it. I've sent copies to Pollard, Hornby* and Dent.†

While I am on the subject, let me say that I shall be very glad to send a copy to your friend Mr. Rowe, and if he wants to pay for it, let him, and apply the sum to my dues in the Arts & Crafts society — to which I shall consider it a great honour to belong, if they see fit to elect me. As to the exhibition, it was of great interest to hear of the Academy's offer. "The world do move!" as the old nigger preacher said. Con-

---

*C. H. St. John Hornby (1876–1946), proprietor of the Ashendene Press, London.
†J. M. Dent (1849–1926), British bookseller and publisher.

THE MALL PRESS: LONDON

cerning my own part in the exhibition, would it (in view of my possible coming over, and association with you) be of any advantage to you and to me—(it is perhaps premature to say *US* though the temptation is great)—to show a pretty complete lot of my books—and other pieces of printing. In Newark they filled 16 showcases each about 2 x 5 feet and in addition there were 7 or 8 broadsides and about 100 circulars, title-pages, trial pages—cards, etc. etc. mounted on grey cartridge paper and fastened on screens. Altogether they fairly filled a room about 30 x 50 feet—on three sides. It would, of course, be impossible, I suppose, to obtain that much space, and many of the things shown here might not be desirable—some wouldn't pass the Jury—but I can send over (almost) the whole lot—two cases will contain it—if you see any advantage in making a display imposing for its extent if not always for its quality. My feeling is that as a (possible) new member it might be an advantage to present all the credentials I can muster, at the first concours. What is the date of the exhibition as Constables might still have some of my books?

I have so much to say to you that may have a possible bearing on the great issue mentioned in your own letter, that this is, I fear, a scrappy and wandering epistle. I'll try, however, to get everything said somehow and then come back to the main proposition.

In mentioning the several projects I have under way, I neglected to write of the most important and interesting of all—which is this: the Grolier Club (Kent, of course) some little time ago asked Pollard to write them something, to be put into my hands to print. He (P) proposed a combination of a series of papers on the various parts of a book —their treatment historically and aesthetically—the whole to make from 40,000 to 60,000 words.* Pollard was afraid his price was too high and that they wanted something right off—but Kent says they considered it very favourably and that the book will almost certainly go through—at the maximum. Kent's idea is to illustrate the various points made in the text, not by facsimiles of old work—but by setting

*This project was later abandoned.

CHAPTER FOUR: 1916–1917

new pages in various types and with various decorations done in accordance with the practices described in the text. This would make it most desirable for me to print the whole book in direct touch with Pollard, and the Club consents to this. I have written Pollard that I should probably come over to do it this autumn—and asked if he didn't think we could get Hornby to print it at Letchworth under my direction; or even, perhaps, induce you to take a hand and get together two or three workmen to produce it. I haven't yet had time to hear Pollard's own views—but you see the chances were already strongly in favour of my making at least a temporary stay in England sometime not far in the future—and perhaps this is the very thing to try a combination of forces upon.

I am not losing sight of the fact that you may have very different views of my possible usefulness to your business—nor of the fact that that business is not altogether printing or bookmaking as I have practised it.

Printing is now, of course, an old game to me, though mastery in it seems almost as far off as ever. But I must warn you that I have no training in business, whatever, and that, even in printing, I have relied upon others for all estimates of cost, handling of men and accounts, and general executive management—devoting my own efforts to the solution of the artistic and technical problems. The few workmen whom I trained to do the sort of work I required all seemed, however, to take pleasure in working for and with me and greatly regretted going back to the routine work of the Press when I left. When I took the book on *Franklin's Press at Passy* back to Riverside to print there, my old pressman actually had tears of pleasure in his eyes when he found we were to collaborate on a piece of press-work again. So it is fair to say that I can get along well with men of the stamp of your employees, and they usually like me.

You will understand that I have no practical experience either, of the photogravure and other reproductive processes, except the photo-

THE MALL PRESS: LONDON

engraved zinc plates—by which nearly all my recent books have been illustrated or decorated.

Your letter leaves me a little in doubt as to just what sort of position I shall be expected to fill. If it is one concerned with typography or general arrangement of printed matter and illustrations I think I may say that I feel competent to do that already. If it concerns the management of the business or the technicalities of various reproductive processes, then I can only say that I am ready to learn.

In the latter case I feel constrained only to stipulate that I shall have at least a portion of my time to practice printing—book-printing—for, after all, that is my proper *métier* and I still have dreams of doing something finer in a fully developed style of my own than has yet been accomplished. I do not, for an instant, think that I can ever surpass Morris or Sanderson or Hornby on their own grounds—but my own ideal book is still far from being a realization and I must keep working toward it, however slowly and painfully. With you for a counsellor and inspiration, the progress may still be a slow one but it would be the reverse of painful—it would be a never-ending pleasure.

Taking up the business end of the matter, I have, as I think you know, a small income from more-or-less wise investments—the result of savings while my salary was a high one. This income suffices fairly well for my family, to whom I have turned it over. My own immediate wants are not extravagant, and I have felt the shortage of cash in the last four years chiefly because I wanted money to put into types, papers and occasional books for study. I should hardly feel justified at present in withdrawing any of this capital from its present use as it would have to be done at some sacrifice—but I would suggest that I come over in the Autumn to learn more definitely just what your proposed arrangement is; that I try it for a stated period on some salary that would at least enable me to live over there; and that then, if you thought me fitted to take up the partnership you propose, we could make the arrangements to that end. Eventually then, if we found it worked, I

CHAPTER FOUR: 1916–1917

should of course be glad to put in capital of my own if necessary.

Does this sound too hesitating, too cautious, as though I did not fully appreciate your open-handedness and open-heartedness? I don't mean it so in the least, dear Emery Walker. It is only that the prospect in certain lights in which I view it, seems too good to be true, almost. It is so entirely different from all my previous experiences that I can't help feeling that it is, on your part, another fine example of British courage—to make such an offer to a man you haven't seen for four years—(or five)—and I want to do all I can to safeguard you from what an American business man would perhaps consider your own rashness.

At any rate I have tried to throw as much light as possible on my own attitude toward the possibilities of the proposal and I shall eagerly await your verdict.

My wife is fully as enthusiastic as am I, at the prospect of once more being in England. My daughter is a little aghast at leaving her newly made friends here—but I suppose the problem of school for her there is not a difficult one, and she makes friends readily. Poor child! we have moved so frequently of late that she has never but once had two consecutive years at the same school—but she is rather ahead of girls her own age here—probably a little behind them in England. At any rate it will be a good thing for her to get out of this rapid, modern, superficial, kind of life that seems inevitable over here. She is a very companionable child and has, I think, a good mind.

You will pardon, I am sure, a smile at your reference to your 65 years, when I tell you that my father is 84 and last Autumn took his two granddaughters on a month's trip to California and exposition—travelling nearly all the time, managing the whole expedition himself, and fairly tiring out the girls. He lives, still, in our old home in Indiana, and works daily in a real-estate office there. We expect him to visit us in August. His mother lived to 93. Elizabeth, when she was quite a small child, told some one that her grandfather had all his faculties except his hair. So, on the whole, I insist on thinking 65 the prime of life, especially when I recall how you showed me the Adelphi

PLATE I.

Drawings by Bruce Rogers for the Purdue University senior class publication, *Debris*, 1889/1890

HOMEWARD SONGS
BY THE WAY

A.E.

PLATE 2. (1895)

PLATE 4. (1900)

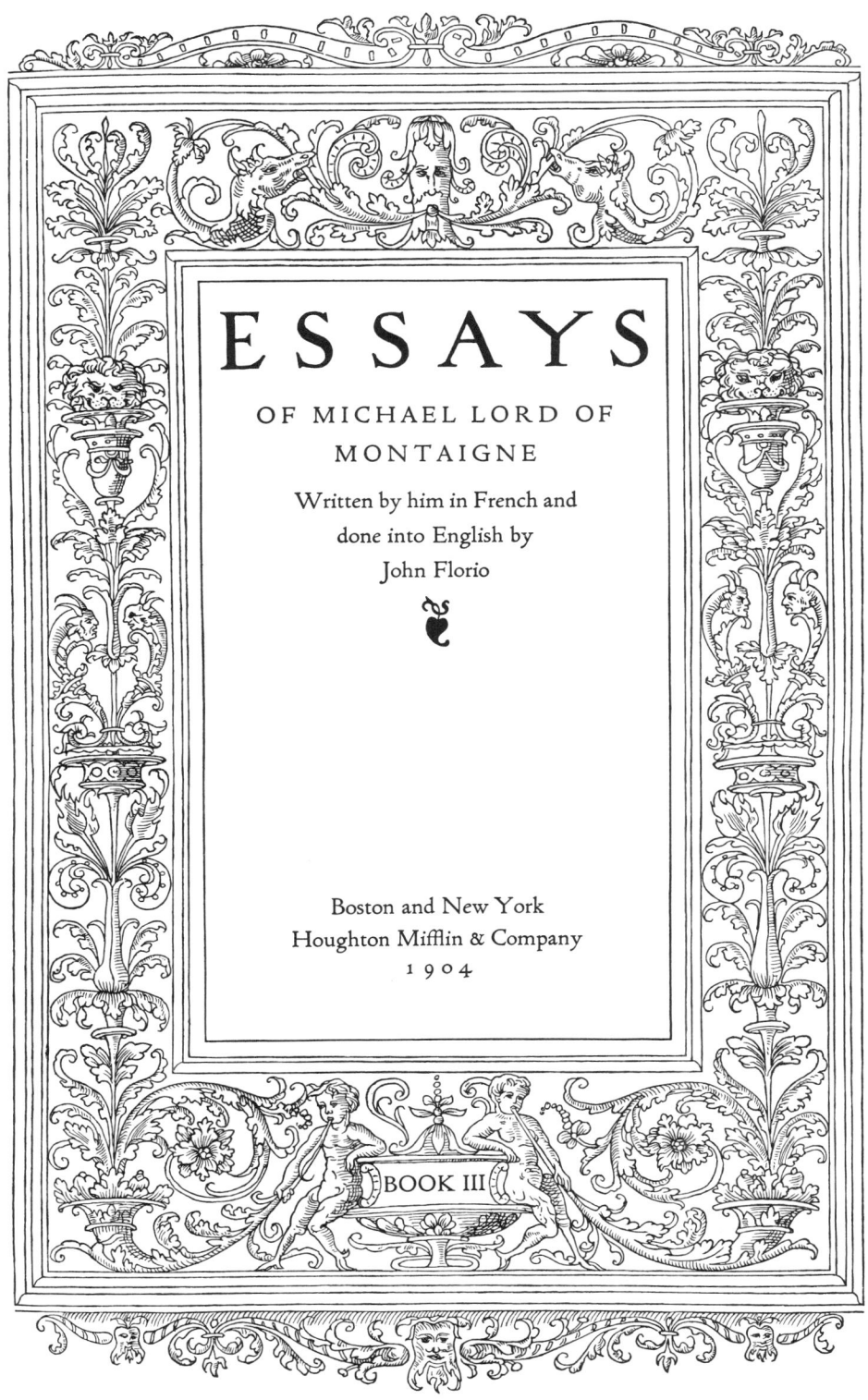

PLATE 5. (1904) Reduced

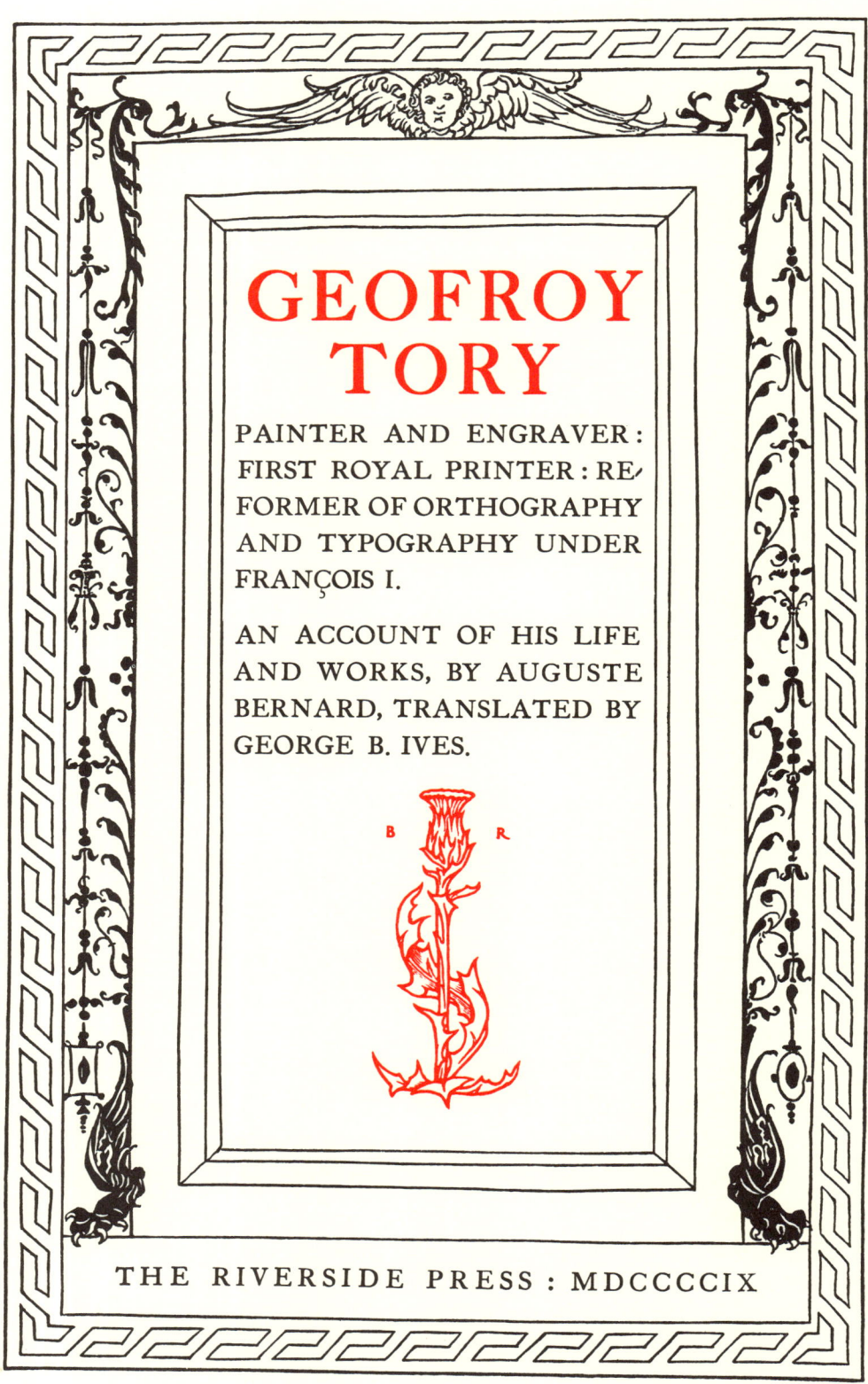

PRINTERS' PREFACE.

BERNARD'S *monograph on Tory was first published in* 1857, *when M. Bernard was already a recognized authority on the history of typography. In* 1865, *after an interval devoted largely to a search for further information concerning Tory, and for probable examples of his work as an artist, a second edition of the book appeared, enlarged by more than one-half, arranged more systematically, and embellished with several additional engravings of designs which are, in the author's opinion, attributable to Tory. The Iconography, which forms the third part of this revised edition, did not appear as such in the first edition, although a small part of the material it contains may be found scattered through that edition. It now occupies more space than the Biography and Bibliography combined. The new arrangement necessitated more or less repetition where, as in many instances, the same book is referred to by M. Bernard in more than one section of his work; and this repetition sometimes reveals discrepancies between the different descriptions. Where such discrepancies have been discovered by him the translator has endeavoured to correct them, generally, in the absence of an opportunity to inspect the volume in question, assuming that the description in the bibliographical section is more likely to be trustworthy; in a number of cases, however, inspection of title-pages themselves, or of reproductions thereof, has enabled him to correct numerous minor errors in transcription.*

The Song of Roland

I

The Treachery of Ganelon

Charles the King, our great Emperor, has been for seven long years in Spain; he has conquered all the high land down to the sea; not a castle holds out against him, not a wall or city is left unshattered, save Saragossa, which stands high on a mountain. King Marsile holds it, who loves not God, but serves Mahound, and worships Apollyon; ill hap must in sooth befall him. ⁋King Marsile abides

Marsile takes counsel against Charles

faith of the Christians, and to become his man in all honour & loyalty. If he would have hostages, send them to him, or ten or twenty, to make good the compact. We will send him the sons of our wives; yea, though it be to death, I will send mine own. Better it were that they lose their lives than that we be spoiled of lands and lordship, and be brought to beg our bread. ⁋By this my right hand,' saith Blancandrin, 'and by the beard that the wind blows about my breast, ye shall see the Frankish host straightway scatter abroad, and the Franks return again to their and his counts, saying: 'Dear, lords, what evil overwhelms us; Charles the Emperor of fair France has come into this land to confound us. I have no host to do battle against him, nor any folk to discomfort his. Counsel me, lords, as wise men and save me from death and shame.' But not a man has any word in answer, save Blancandrin of the castle of Val-Fonde. ⁋Blancandrin was among the wisest of the paynims, a good knight of much prowess, discreet and valiant in the service of his lord. He saith to the King: 'Be not out of all comfort. Send to Charles the proud, the terrible, proffer of faithful service and goodly friendship; give him bears and lions and dogs, seven hundred camels and a thousand falcons past the moulting time, four hundred mules laden with gold and silver, that he may send before him fifty full wains; and therewith shall he richly reward his followers. Long has he waged war in this land, it is meet he return again to Aix in France. And do thou pledge thy word to follow him at the feast of Saint Michael, to receive the

will have no word nor tidings. The King is proud and cruel of heart, he will let smite off the heads of our hostages, but better it is that they lose their lives than that we be spoiled of bright Spain, the fair, or suffer so great dole and sorrow.' And the paynims cry: 'Let it be as he saith.' ⁋So King Marsilie hath ended his counsel, he then called Clarin de Balaguer, Estramarin, and Endropin, his fellow, and Priamon, and Barsan the Bearded, Machiner, and Maheu his uncle, Joimer, and Barbien from oversea, and Blancandrin; ten of the fiercest he hath called, to make known his will unto them. 'Lords, barons,' he saith, 'go ye to Charlemagne, who is at the siege of the city of Cordova, bearing olive branches in your hands in token of peace and submission. If by your wit ye can make me a covenant with Charles, I will give you great store of gold and silver, and lands and fiefs as much as ye may desire.' 'Nay,' say the paynims, 'of these things we have and to spare.' ⁋King Marsilie hath ended his council, & he saith to his men: 'Go ye forth, lords, & bear in your hands

And sends to him toy Ambassadors

PLATE 8. *The Song of Roland* (1906). Considerably reduced

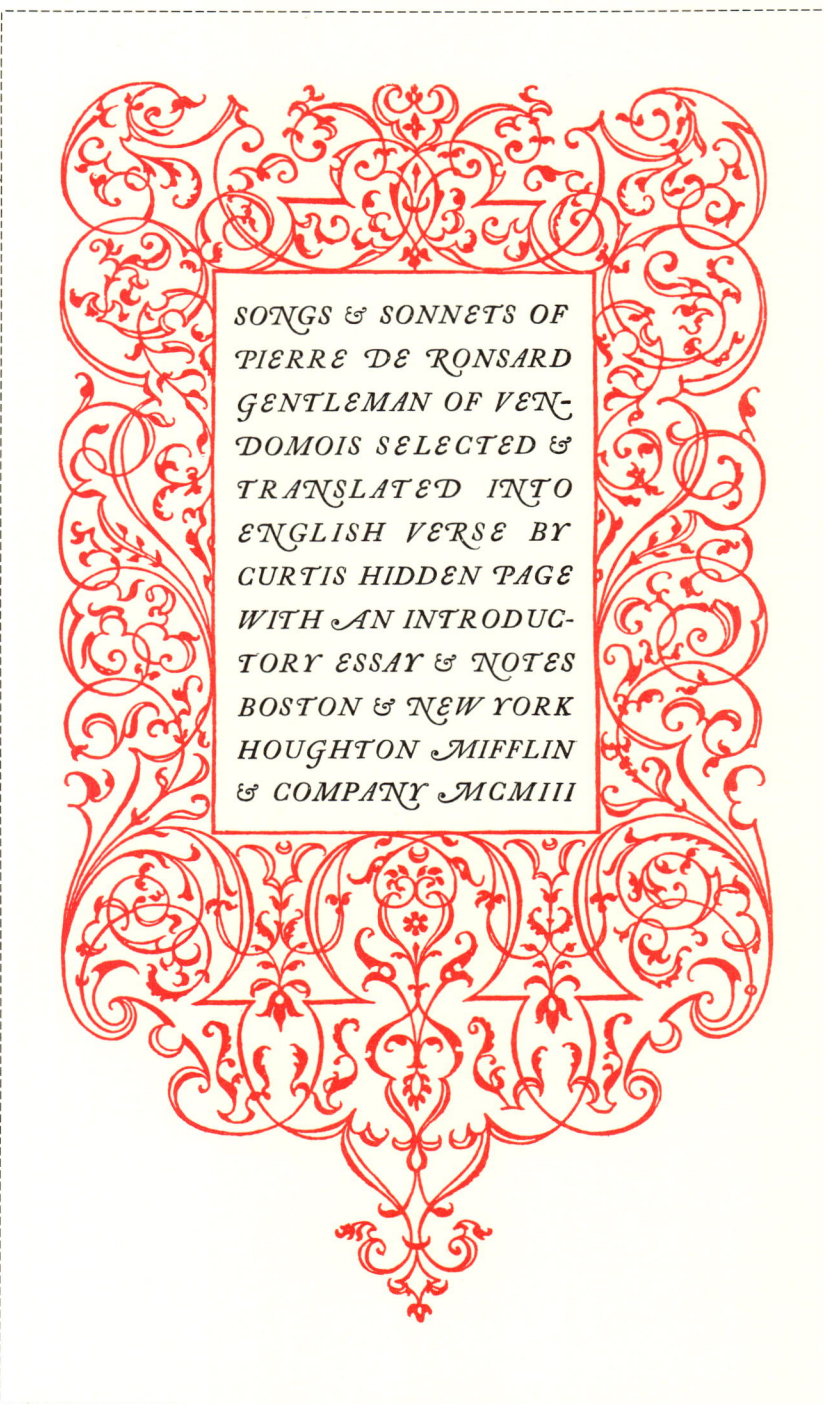

PLATE 9. (1903)

LIFE OF DANTE

WRITTEN BY GIOVANNI BOCCACCIO AND
NOW TRANSLATED FROM THE ITALIAN BY
PHILIP HENRY WICKSTEED

THE RIVERSIDE PRESS
MDCCCCIV

THE POEMS OF
MARIA LOWELL

CAMBRIDGE
THE RIVERSIDE PRESS
1907

THE BANQUET OF PLATO TRANSLATED FROM THE GREEK BY PERCY BYSSHE SHELLEY

youth than an amiable lover, or to a lover than an amiable object of his love. For neither birth, nor wealth, nor honours, can awaken in the minds of men the principles which should guide those who from their youth aspire to an honourable and excellent life, as Love awakens them. I speak of the fear of shame, which deters them from that which is disgraceful; and the love of glory, which incites to honourable deeds. For it is not possible that a state or private person should accomplish, without these incitements, anything beautiful or great. I assert, then, that should one who loves be discovered in any dishonourable action, or tamely enduring insult through cowardice, he would feel more anguish and shame if observed by the object of his passion than if he were observed by his

11

And that for/gevyn is hir weked dede;
Than shal they come in/to that blysful place,
To whiche to comyn God synden us grace!'
The day gan failen, and the derke nyght,
That revith bestis from here besynesse,
Berafte me myn bok for lak of lyght,
And to my bed I gan me for to dresse,
Fulfyld of thought and busy hevynesse;
For bothe I hadde thynge that I nolde.
And ek I ne hadde thynge that I wolde.

But fynally, myn spirit at the laste,
For/wery of myn labour al the day,
Toke reste, that made me to slepe faste;
And in myn slepe I mette, as that I lay,
How Affrican ryght in the same a/ray
That Scipion hym say by/fore that tyde
Was come and stod right at myn bedis syde.

The wery huntere, slepynge in his bed,
To wode a/gen his mynde goth a/non;
The juge dremyth how hise pleis been sped;
The cartere dremyth how his carte is gon;
The riche of gold; the knyght fyght with his fon;
The syke met he drynkyth of the tunne;
The lovere met he hath his lady wonne.

I can nat seyn if that the cause were
For I hadde red of Affrican by/foren,
That made me to mete that he stod theere,
But thus seyde he: 'Thow hast the so wel born
In lokynge of myn olde bok to torn,

PLATE 13. *The Parlement of Foules* (1904)

THE COMPLEAT ANGLER
Or, The Contemplative Man's Recreation

BEING
A DISCOURSE OF FISH AND FISHING
NOT UNWORTHY THE PERUSAL OF
MOST ANGLERS

The Riverside Press Edition
1909

TO THE

Reader of this Discourse

BUT ESPECIALLY TO
THE HONEST
ANGLER

I Think fit to tell thee these following truths; that I did not undertake to write, or to publish this Discourse of Fish and Fishing, to please my self, and that I wish it may not displease others; for I have confest there are many defects in it. And yet, I cannot doubt, but that by it, some readers may receive so much profit or pleasure, as if they be not very busie men, may make it not un-

LXXV SONNETS

William Wordsworth

The Riverside Press

FRANKLIN

And his Press at Passy

AN ACCOUNT OF
THE BOOKS, PAMPHLETS, AND LEAFLETS PRINTED
THERE, INCLUDING THE LONG-LOST
'BAGATELLES'

BY

LUTHER S. LIVINGSTON

NEW YORK
THE GROLIER CLUB
1914

THE CENTAUR. WRITTEN BY MAURICE DE GUÉRIN AND NOW TRANSLATED FROM THE FRENCH BY GEORGE B. IVES.

I was born in a cavern of these mountains. Like the river in yonder valley, whose first drops flow from some cliff that weeps in a deep grotto, the first moments of my life sped amidst the shadows of a secluded retreat, nor vexed its silence. As our mothers draw near their term, they retire to the caverns, and in the innermost recesses of the wildest of them all, where the darkness is most dense, they bring forth, uncomplaining, offspring as silent as themselves. Their strength giving milk enables us to endure without weakness or dubious struggles the first difficulties of life; yet we leave our caverns later than you your cradles. The reason is that there is a tradition amongst us that the early days of life must be secluded and guarded, as days engrossed by the gods.

My growth ran almost its entire course in the darkness where I was born. The innermost depths of my home were so far within the bowels of the mountain, that I should not have known in which direction the opening lay, had it not been that the winds at times blew in and caused a sudden coolness and confusion. Sometimes, too, my mother returned, bringing with her the perfume of the valleys, or dripping wet from the streams to which she resorted. Now, these her home-comings, although they told me naught of the valleys or the streams, yet, being attended by emanations therefrom, disturbed my thoughts, and I wandered about, all agitated, amidst my darkness. 'What,' I would say to myself, 'are these places to which my mother goes and what power reigns there which summons her so frequently? To what influences is one there exposed,

OF THE JUST SHAPING OF LETTERS
FROM THE APPLIED GEOMETRY
OF ALBRECHT DÜRER
BOOK III.

NOW, since architects, painters & others at times are wont to set an inscription on lofty walls, it will make for the merit of the work that they form the letters correctly. Accordingly I am minded here to treat briefly of this. And first I will give rules for a Latin Alphabet, and then for one of our common Text: since it is of these two sorts of letters we customarily make use in such work; and first, for the Roman letters: Draw for each a square of uniform size, in which the letter is to be contained. But when you draw in it the heavier limb of the letter, make this of the width of a tenth part of the square, and the lighter a third as wide as the heavier: and follow this rule for all letters of the Alphabet.

First, make an A after this fashion: Indicate the angles of the square by the letters a. b. c. d. (and so do for all the rest of the letters): then divide the square by two lines bisecting one another at right angles—the vertical e. f. the horizontal g. h.: then, in the lower line, take two points, i. and k., distant respectively one-tenth of the space c. d. from the points c. and d.: then, from the point i. draw upwards to the top of the square the lighter limb; & thence downwards the heavier limb, so that the outer edges of both may touch, respectively, the points i. and k.: then let a triangle be left between the limbs, and a point e. be fixed at top in the middle of the letter, and next join both limbs beneath the horizontal line, and let this limb be a third as broad as the heavier limb.

Now let the arc of a circle, applied to the top of the outside edge of the heavier limb, project beyond the square. Then cut off the top of

PLATE 18. *Of the Just Shaping of Letters.* Reduced

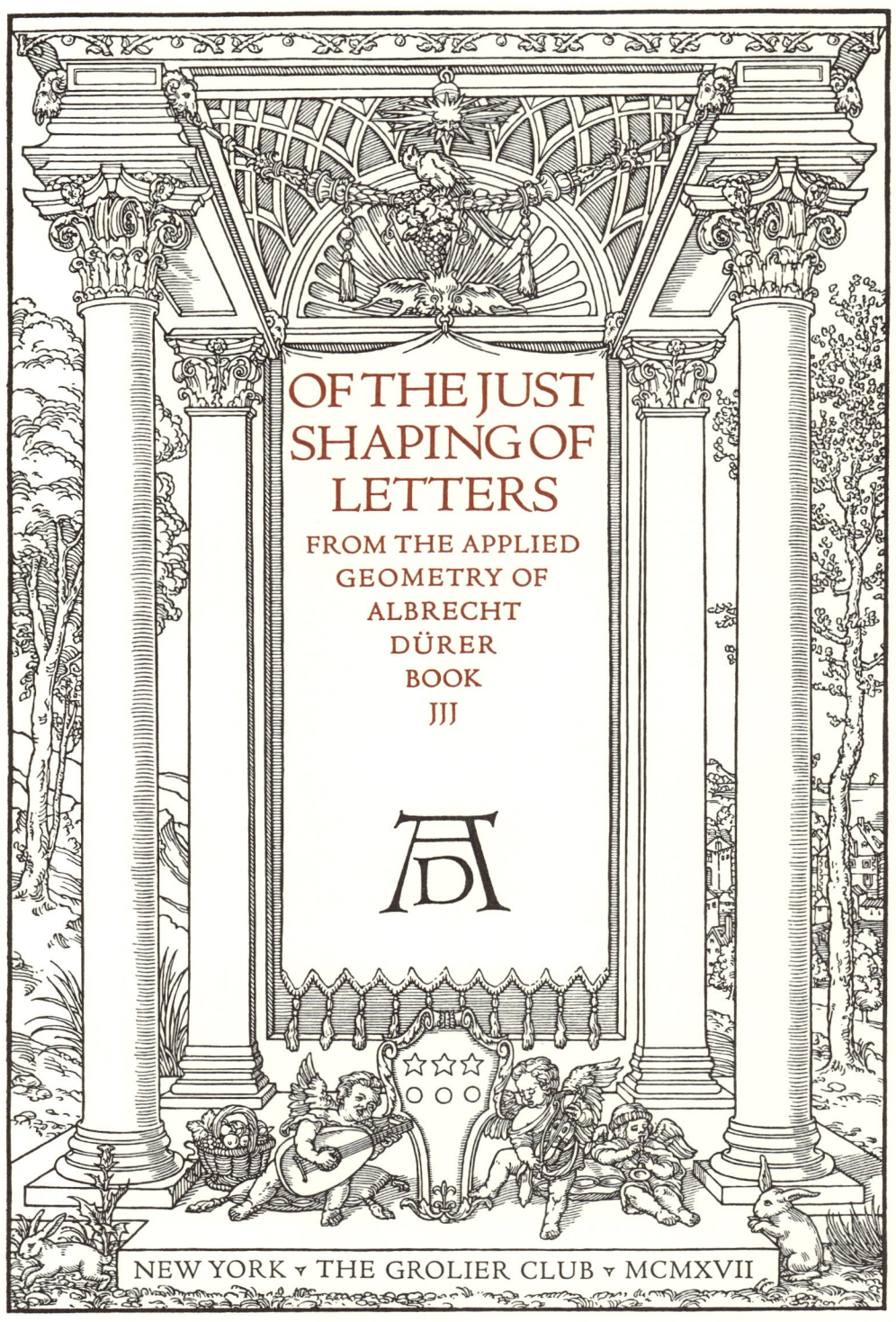

PLATE 19. (1917) Reduced

THE TEMPEST

CAMBRIDGE
AT THE UNIVERSITY PRESS
1921

BENJAMIN FRANKLIN's PROPOSALS FOR THE EDUCATION OF YOUTH IN PENNSYLVANIA

1749

ANN ARBOR

The William L. Clements Library

1927

THE
WEDGWOOD MEDALLION
OF
SAMUEL JOHNSON

THIS likeness of Samuel Johnson was made at some time during the last year and a half of his life, for inclusion in Josiah Wedgwood's famous and popular series of 'Illustrious Moderns.' It is an oval cameo in black and white (or pale blue and white) jasperware, measuring four inches by three inches, the original mould of which is preserved in the Wedgwood Museum at Etruria, Stafford. From the time of its first manufacture in 1784, it has been familiar to all collectors of Wedgwoodware, as one of the finest of the portraits of eminent men cast in this and similar forms; but it has been strangely overlooked by such critics and literary historians as make use of illustrative documents, and, in particular, by that odd race of enthusiasts who call themselves *Johnsonians* and

[1]

THE
JOURNAL
OF
Madam *KNIGHT*.

Monday, Octb'r. y^e second,
1704.

ABOUT three o'clock afternoon, I begun my Journey from Boston to New-Haven; being about two Hundred Mile. My Kinsman, Capt. Robert Luist, waited on me as farr as Dedham, where I was to meet y^e Western post.

PRIAPUS AND THE POOL

BY CONRAD AIKEN

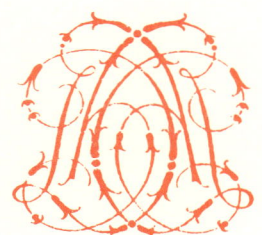

DUNSTER HOUSE : CAMBRIDGE

1922

NIGHT
and
MOONLIGHT

✧ ✧
✦

HENRY D. THOREAU

NEW YORK
HUBERT RUTHERFORD BROWN
1921

PLATE 25. (1921)

THE CONSTRUCTION OF ROMAN LETTERS BY ALBRECHT DÜRER

Dunster House : Cambridge

1924

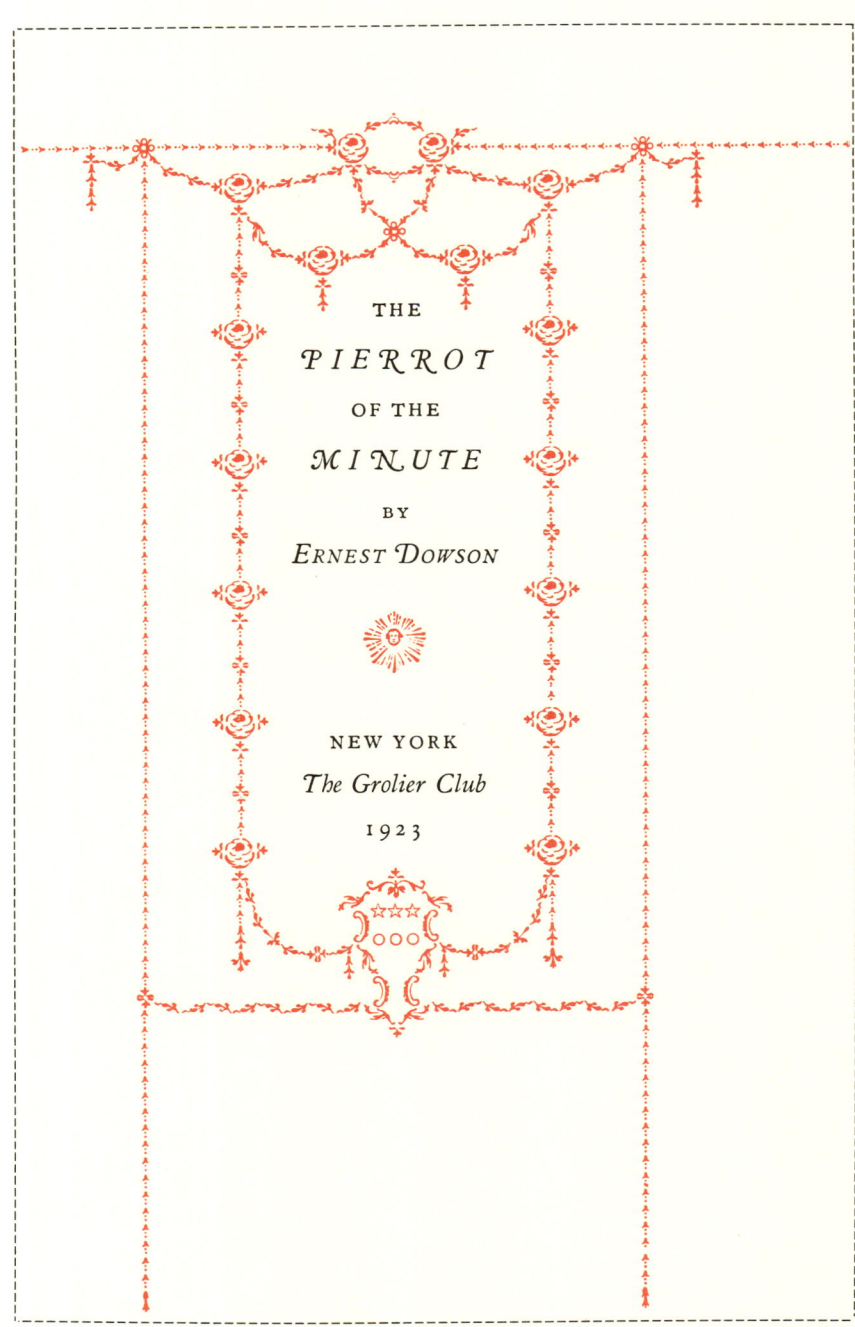

PLATE 27. (1923)

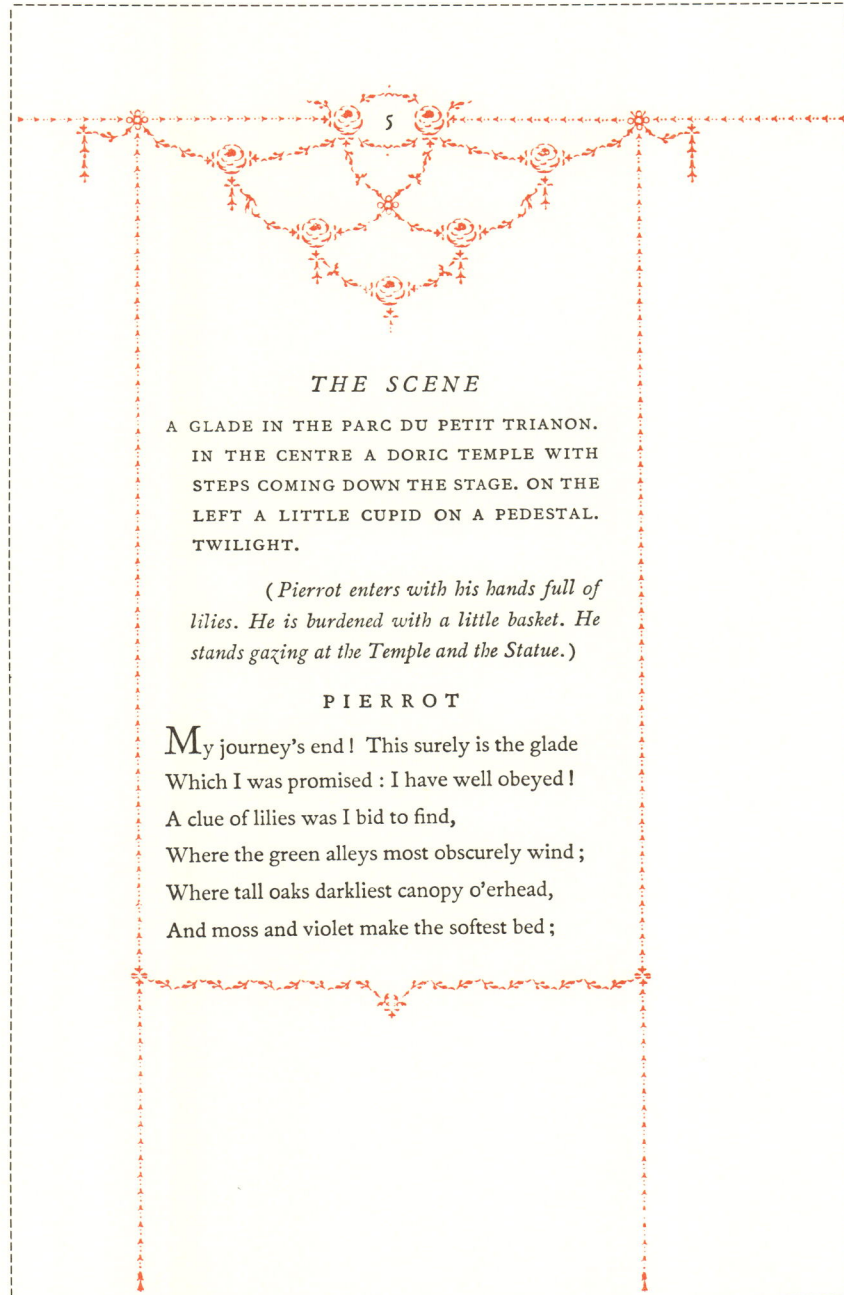

5

THE SCENE

A GLADE IN THE PARC DU PETIT TRIANON. IN THE CENTRE A DORIC TEMPLE WITH STEPS COMING DOWN THE STAGE. ON THE LEFT A LITTLE CUPID ON A PEDESTAL. TWILIGHT.

(Pierrot enters with his hands full of lilies. He is burdened with a little basket. He stands gazing at the Temple and the Statue.)

PIERROT

My journey's end! This surely is the glade
Which I was promised: I have well obeyed!
A clue of lilies was I bid to find,
Where the green alleys most obscurely wind;
Where tall oaks darkliest canopy o'erhead,
And moss and violet make the softest bed;

PLATE 28. *The Pierrot of the Minute*

ANCIENT BOOKS AND MODERN DISCOVERIES

By Frederic G. Kenyon

The Caxton Club: Chicago

1927

CHAPTER I.
The Antiquity of Writing

THE purpose of this essay is to give some picture, according to our present knowledge, of the various methods by which man has endeavored to commit his words,—the repositories of his experience or his thoughts—to permanent record by some form of writing. The perpetuation of the spoken word in enduring form is one of the most potent elements of civilisation; and the manner in which it has taken place in different times and in different countries has fundamentally affected the course of the intellectual development of nations. The inquiry is not, therefore, a mere matter of antiquarian interest. The literary history of a country is only intelligible if the manner in which its literature was preserved is understood; and some literary problems of the highest importance, such as the origin of the books of our Bible, or, in secular literature, of the Homeric poems, which are the fountain head of Greek, and therefore of all modern, literature, need for their interpretation some acquaintance with this material question.

The present summary does not pretend to be exhaustive, in the sense of covering all countries and all periods. My

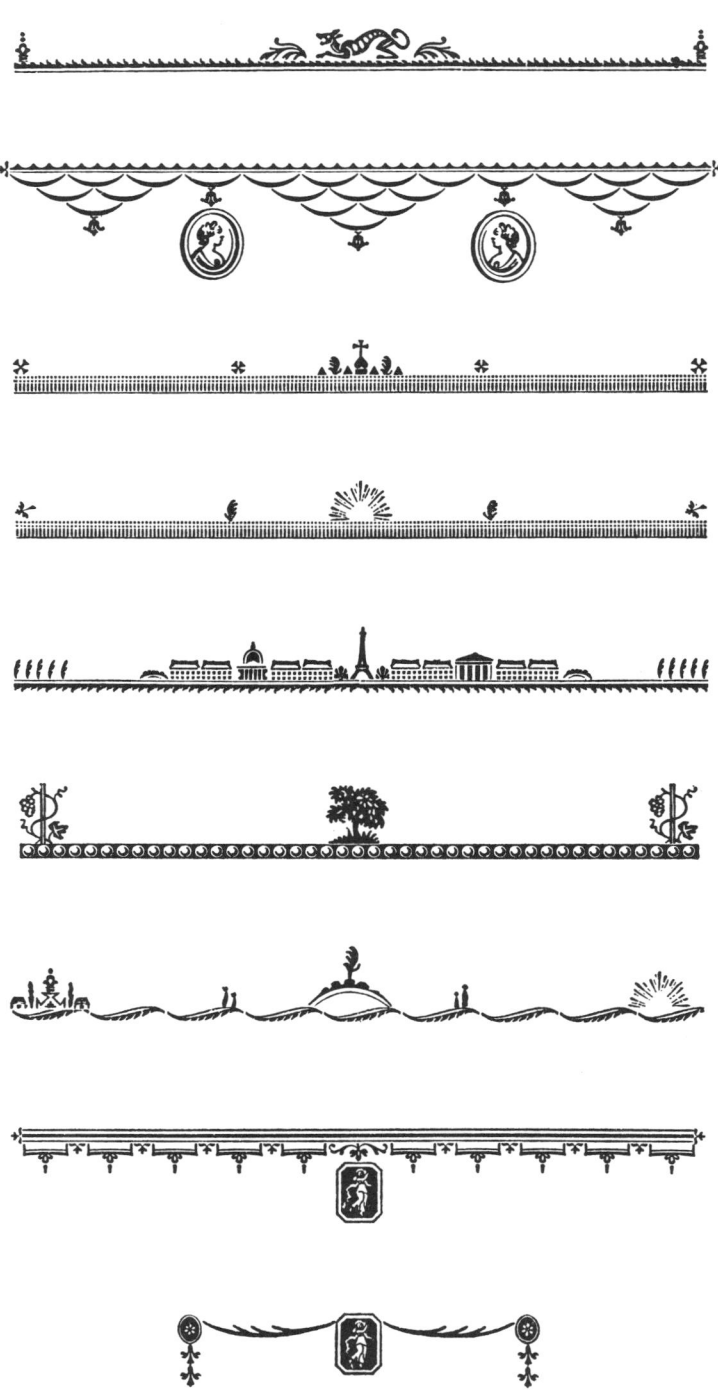

PLATE 31. Headpieces from *The Sisters* (1928)

THE MALL PRESS: LONDON

terrace at 1 or 2 in the morning, the evening we met Gordon Craig*
and Count Kessler. I wonder where they both are. I'd like to send Craig
a *Centaur* tho' I'm afraid he wouldn't care for it. By-the-bye the paper
is a Batchelor make—one I had him make several years ago. It was a
bit too thin and transparent and I had to keep the press-work light and
rather grey—but I wanted to show the type clearly.

My family have gone to the shore or they would join me in affectionate regards to Mrs Walker and Miss Dorothy. As for me—you
have given me a great deal to think about and be thankful for. Between
you and Pollard, life seems once more to be worth living and working for.[3]

Rogers' next letter to Walker, from Montague, Massachusetts, was written on 11 September 1916. Quoted in full, it again tells us much about the man and his work:

Your note containing Prof. Chase's address reached me a few days
ago, and I knew by it that you had written, before it, a letter which had
never reached me. I was on the point of writing to apprise you of its
non-arrival, when I had notice of a registered letter for me in New
York—and on sending over for it, you can imagine my relief and
pleasure to find that it was yours. We have been up here in the hills for
about 3 weeks and will stay only a few days longer—so my address will
remain 131 East 31st St., N.Y.—as before.

I appreciate and was greatly interested in the outline sketch of your
business and of your connection with it, and am further greatly obliged
to you for your frank statement of its present conditions and future
prospects, which with you, I am convinced are capable of developing
soundly after war; and I will say at once, without further preliminary,
that I am proud and pleased to accept your offer of a position with you
—tentatively if you so think best, until we see whether I am capable
of the work that you have for me to do. The salary you mention is quite

---

*Edward Gordon Craig (1872–1966), stage designer, made wood engravings for the Cranach Press editions of *Hamlet*.

CHAPTER FOUR: 1916–1917

satisfactory and ample, I think, for my needs, unless I should find living expenses very much increased over what they formerly were. In fact, under the conditions, I think you are more than generous in fixing it so high as you do, and if I find I can do with less, I hope we may readjust it—or else, better, put it into special equipment if the work develops a necessity for it. I'm always buying odd lots of papers and types as they turn up and I've always found it good investment, as they come into use sooner or later. But that might not be good policy over there, where you are so near the sources of supply.

I hardly see how I can come over before the latter part of October—though I'd like, of course, to see the Arts & Crafts Exhibition—as it would at once familiarise me with what is now being done there. But I *must* do one more little book that is just about ready to print, at the Metropolitan Museum, and our various belongings are so scattered that it will take some little time to get them together under one roof and ready to leave. But I will write you again just as soon as I get back to New York, and go over the ground with the various people with whom I've been doing various things there. My engagement with the Museum does not expire until Jan. 1—but I can easily arrange that. One book that I'm binding will have to be finished here—but the larger and more elaborate one I can arrange to bring over with me.

Mrs. Rogers is delighted with the prospect of again going to England, and particularly with again seeing your wife and daughter, to both of whom she was greatly attracted. We have not yet definitely decided whether she and Elizabeth had better come over with me at once, or remain here during the winter—principally on account of E's school, to which she became greatly attached last winter. I rather think, however, that they will come with me, particularly if my negotiations with Professor Chase [to live in his London flat] turn out satisfactorily. I have already written to him but have not yet had time for a reply. Our household effects have been stored for four years past, in a shed attached to our little house near Boston (and the house rented) so that they will only need some little overlooking and arranging to leave as they are. When we settle definitely over there I shall sell the house and move them over. Some of my books I shall want with me, and will endeavour to send in a small case. As soon as I get to New York I will despatch the more portable ones by mail, as you suggest, and I hope they may arrive in time for the exhibition. Hornby has at least two of my books—*Banquet of Plato* and *Compleat Angler*—and, I think, also Boccaccio's *Life of Dante*.

By-the-bye, I'm afraid I didn't make my meaning clear as to the two extra copies of the *Centaur*. I meant to say that I had *already* sent copies to Pollard and Hornby and J. M. Dent, direct. These two were to be used as you pleased—perhaps Merton would like one. I have several remaining, I think.

It's very pleasant to think of Merton as a lover of printing too—I hadn't that idea of him before; judging from what you had written that he was more keenly interested in the financial side of the business—so the new light you throw upon him is welcome. I just remember him as a quiet and pleasant young man—having met him for only a few minutes, outside your door.

If I come over next month, I shall probably have to bring with me the book on which I am engaged for the Grolier Club—the translation of Dürer's treatise on the alphabet—from his *Geometry*. I enclose with this a very rough proof which will give you some idea of the page—of which I figure there will be about 48 pp.

I have only about 140 lb. of Centaur type in which the book is to be printed—but if I find that I can get the type sent to England safely, perhaps I had better have more cast up and shipped. Or had I better bring over the matrices? They would probably have to be re-fitted for casting over there. Can you estimate from the pages sent, and by consulting one of the original editions of the work (the translation is made from the Basel edition of 1535, as no Nuremberg edition was available here—the plates are, I believe, slightly different in the two editions, and the earlier Nuremberg edition would be preferable to use) the cost of manufacture of 200 copies?—to be bound in narrow vellum

CHAPTER FOUR: 1916–1917

back and paper sides—(I'm allowed 85 cents per copy for binding over here).

I have made tracings of some of the cuts from which I proposed making zinc-etchings—photo-engravings—and re-touching them by hand for printing on dampened hand-made paper. I don't think handpress work is essential to this particular book—but it might be just as economical over there. The paper ought to be a good grade of handmade—not necessarily Batchelor's best make, though.

A word from you on this whole proposition would be welcome and if you think we might do it together before or after I actually took up my position with you, I'd like nothing better—but it ought to be put in hand before long and if I could hear from you regarding it before I leave, I would know better how to arrange matters here.

I have agreed to do the book for the Club for not more than $1500.00—$100 of which goes to the translator, a friend of mine—(an Oxford man) here. I can't remember the various items but I believe the total cost of manufacture came to about $900, leaving me $600 commission—at the maximum. If it cost more than I estimated, I was to pay the difference out of my commission.

If we printed it over there we should have to add the import duty (15% I believe it is now) but paper and ink would be cheaper there, and perhaps the labour. At any rate I want to carry it through, whether I am left any profit or not—as this is a "trial horse" for the much larger undertaking of the *Champ Fleury* which the Club will put through some day—of which I believe I sent you specimen pages last year. (I'm sending the dummy volume for the A[rts] & C[rafts] exhibition—if they will admit unfinished products.) I am under great obligations to you for proposing me for membership in the Society—but I'm under so many others, to you, also, that it seems hopeless to try to enumerate them, and I'm only hoping for opportunities to requite you for all your kindness.

I've rambled along, in this letter, about material things and plans and have said little to the point, I fear. But the pleasure of the anticipation of soon seeing you all, and really living and working near you, makes it difficult to write very connectedly about things that we shall soon be talking about face to face.

I hope I have not disappointed you in the approximate date I fixed for sailing—but I will do all I can to put it earlier on the calendar than I mentioned, and will write in time to give you fair warning when to expect me.

Mrs. Rogers joins me in warm regards to Mrs. Walker and Miss Dorothy, and with renewed (but quite inadequate) thanks to your most kindly self, I am,

Affectionately yours,
Bruce Rogers[4]

Although Rogers had expressed his intention to leave for England late in October, he and his wife and daughter finally sailed on a Dutch ship in December 1916, and spent Christmas on board. On a neutral vessel, they arrived without incident from submarines, and docked on New Year's Day of 1917 in an England at war. Rogers carried with him the commission to design and print a book for the Grolier Club. Albrecht Dürer's treatise on letter forms, *Of the Just Shaping of Letters*, would be his first work on English soil—the first of the volumes that he would make in the country that had long nourished his fondest expectations.

Of the Just Shaping of Letters was ultimately printed by Rogers in England and bound there, despite the desperately difficult war-time conditions described in letters (below) which Rogers wrote to his friend Henry Watson Kent. The high hopes that Rogers and Walker had had of printing and publishing books in the manner of the Kelmscott and Doves presses evaporated to their great regret as they faced the realities and the difficulties involved in the proposed partnership. Actually, the Dürer book was the only edition ever completed at the Mall Press, the name given to the joint undertaking. Nevertheless, Rogers and Walker remained close friends and associates throughout their respective careers. Rogers stayed in England until 1919, thanks to a forthcoming appointment to the Cambridge University Press and other activities.

CHAPTER FOUR: 1916–1917

In his first letter to Kent since departure from New York, Rogers told about the ocean crossing, and about the circumstances which forced him to do the actual work himself of printing the Dürer book on a small German job press under the most bizarre and trying conditions. The letter, begun in January and completed on 27 February 1917, was written from Digby Mansions, No. 1, Lower Mall, Hammersmith:

> Well—we're here because we're here because, etc.—but I hardly know why. When I consider the matter calmly, it seems a slightly mad undertaking to transplant one's family and to ship some 700 or 800 lb. of Centaur type to London in the midst of a great war; all to produce one book which will hardly pay anyone concerned. For the partnership with Walker and continuing the traditions of the Kelmscott and Doves presses doesn't seem much of a prospect at present. Both those presses were financed out of private means and were not what you might call financial successes, even though they may not have actually lost money. So I predict the Mall Press will not last much beyond its first commissions—"And what will poor Robin do then?" with no barn to fly to.
>
> This is the first opportunity I've had to write, as settling in has been a considerable undertaking. The voyage was without incident and the only excitement was a somewhat nervous tension as we approached the submarine zone. We had a little rough weather for a few days but it didn't interfere with the Christmas festivities on board. There were so few passengers in the 2nd cabin that there was only single service in the dining-room. They were mostly Dutch or Belgians returning home—and a few English.
>
> As we entered the Channel the name of our ship blazed in 8-ft. letters on each side and a spot-light played on the Dutch flag at the masthead. We moored in Falmouth harbor just as the New Year came in—but there was no celebration. Most of the passengers were to have another ten days on board, as the boat had to go back out around Ireland and across the North Sea by way of the Orkneys. I didn't envy them their trip.

THE MALL PRESS: LONDON

So few landed at Falmouth that we had little delay at the Customs and we left about 1 P.M. in a train that wandered all over south-west England—taking on and putting off carriages all the way (as the railway service was very much condensed) and so, instead of reaching Paddington about 7 P.M., it wasn't until 11:30 that we arrived to find Walker and his daughter still waiting for us.

We had had nothing to eat but some sandwiches which somebody in Falmouth advised us to buy (there was no restaurant car on the train) so we first had supper in the station and then Dorothy Walker, Anne and Elizabeth stayed in the hotel all night while Walker and I and the baggage (I should say "luggage" now) took a cab for Hammersmith. The Walkers had built fires in two of the grates earlier in the day, but they had burned out long ago without having any appreciable effect on the chill dampness of the rooms.

After getting the luggage in and as I was wide awake, having slept in the train, I accompanied Walker to his house, about ¾ of a mile up the Mall, in the snow and slush. We had so much to talk about—what had happened since we had last met, and the plans for the Grolier Club book (he told me at once that the Centaur type boxes had arrived a week or so before)—that when we reached his house he said he would go back to see me home, though it was then 2 o'clock. And then when we reached our flat I went back again with him to 7 Hammersmith Terrace, returning alone. London was very eerie, blacked out, with all the gas and electric lights shrouded except for a very small ray of light on the pavements immediately beneath them. And the tugs in the river showed only navigating lights. But you'd know it was London by the smell—a distinctive odor of coal-smoke, soot, fog and damp. I love it.

I crawled in between cold sheets at last about 3 A.M. So passed New Year's Day.

Anne and Dorothy and Elizabeth arrived the next morning about 9 with the remainder of the luggage and we finally got the apartment comfortably heated (or rather warmed) by noon. It is a pleasant suite of rooms on the second floor (first in England) including a long living

CHAPTER FOUR: 1916–1917

room with three french windows opening out on to a narrow balcony overlooking the river. It is right at Hammersmith Bridge and had recently been occupied by James Norman Hall, the writer, who had gone off to the war. He'd left a lot of his books and magazines so we are well furnished in that line.

Our first job was to get ration books—and then rations. There seems to be plenty of food, though we are limited as to choice sometimes. The worst of it is the waiting in queues—but even that is interesting—listening to the people's talk. They are of course mostly women. Coal was the worst problem, but we got our janitor to fetch it in for us and so escaped the long lines of home-made soap-box wagons and prams that besieged the coal-sellers' yards.

But enough of our domestic difficulties, and to the printing ones.

Sussex House, which houses part of Walker's establishment, is up the Mall about half way to his residence from ours. It sets back from the pavement with a neglected garden in front behind high iron palings. Some of his workrooms are across the narrow Mall in a house next to the Doves Bindery. The Doves pub is a little farther along, then Cobden-Sanderson's house and then Kelmscott House.

C. S. and Walker, as you know, are having difficulties over the dumping of the Doves type into the river from Hammersmith Bridge. According to their original agreement the type was to revert to Walker when the press closed, and he has been considering a suit against C. S. over its destruction—mats and all. At any rate they are not on speaking terms, and one morning Walker came to me in great amusement with a note from C. S. which read: "Mr. Cobden-Sanderson presents his compliments to Mr. Emery Walker and suggests that it would be an improvement if he were to clear up the waste-paper in his front garden."

C. S. for a week or two had been trying various colors, pink, blue, ochre, on the narrow front of his bindery across the Mall—so I suggested to W. that he reply: "Mr. Emery Walker presents his compliments to Mr. Cobden-Sanderson and begs to inform him that he does not approve the color of Mr. C-S's house this morning."

THE MALL PRESS: LONDON

Feb. 27 — Had to break off here and now it is almost a month later. I should have sent off this much at once, but you'll know by my cablegram that we got here safely.

To resume: Our "composing room" is set up in an abandoned green-house in the back garden of Sussex House — the equipment being a stand and four type-cases that Walker got from Jacobi of the Chiswick Press and a small coal stove that takes off a little of the chill. There is plenty of light as the roof is all glass. Our "comp" is an old chap whom I think Jacobi also furnished — said to be a good typesetter in his day — but his day seems about over. We have no proof press and proofs are taken by tapping lightly on a board laid over the paper.

The press is about 1½ miles from the Mall, up in Shepherd's Bush. Walker's collotype presses are located in one of two houses belonging to Walker's manager and chief workman (a very fine man, also named Kent) who lives next door. You realize, of course, that the force is a skeleton one with only the essential men kept out of the army and a few small boys and girls for helpers. And of course there's no one left with enough time to even attempt to keep up appearances. So the house and the press-room, in a glass-roofed building put up over the back garden, are a litter of all sorts of unrelated stacks and bundles of papers, covered with dust and grime. It's just about the most depressing set-up for a press that you could imagine.

We shall print only two pages to a form and these pages are locked in a chase in Hammersmith. I carry them out through the back garden and up a lane to Hammersmith Road, where I wait for a tram that takes me to the foot of Coningham Road and I then carry it the rest of the way to the printing works. It gets pretty heavy at the last.

The press itself is a little, much repaired, German jobber that will just take the two page forms. It is placed in the most ingeniously devised place for inaccessibility that you could think of.

You go through the deserted house, out to the scullery in the back garden, in through a room crowded with discarded machinery, and there is the press, set between a brick wall and the glassed partition that

CHAPTER FOUR: 1916–1917

shuts it off from the main press-room, from which comes all the light it gets. You can't get around the press to change the set of the ink fountain, without going out in the passageway and into another room, also filled with machines. Then back again the same way to the front of the press to test your adjustment of the ink.

Of course *I* didn't have this to do on the first two sheets of the book, but then our last pressman was called up and the only thing to do was to volunteer for the job myself. I'd never run a press of any kind, but with a little instruction from Kent I found it simple enough—except for the running to-and-fro through the mechanical jungle, from the front to the back of the press.

There is of course no heat anywhere and I have to dampen the Kelmscott hand-made in the converted kitchen. Both my hands and feet have developed chilblains.

St. John Hornby came out to see me one day at the printing works, and he, who has a luxurious press-room with every convenience, was horrified at the whole set-up. I've got round to thinking of it as a joke, but much of the work still carried on in England is done under similar handicaps in these critical days of the war. It's dogged as does it.

We found some so-called vellum at Band's works at Brentford, now making only drum-heads, though one would think there isn't much use for drums in *this* war. It is really goat skin that had been made for Count Kessler's Cranach Press in Weimar. But Band thought he would probably never hear from Kessler again, so consented to sell it to us. There is just enough for three copies of the Dürer if I don't spoil more than one sheet to a form. Let's hope I don't, but it is a risky gamble. So far I haven't spoiled *any*, but some of the solid black letters will have to be touched up with a brush and ink. By the way, Walker has decided to call this venture The Mall Press—but I don't see how it can go on after the Grolier book is finished, unless the war is over by that time.

We were of course too late to see any more Zeppelin raids, but we did see the famous day-light raid. When the sirens went off practically everybody rushed out into the streets to see what it meant. The firing was tremendous over the city but it seemed a long way off. We finally did see five German planes very high, almost invisible in the bright sunlight. But no bombs were dropped in our section and the whole thing lasted only a few minutes. There have been two or three night alarms but no bombs in our neighborhood. When a raid is on the search-lights make a wonderful show. There is one near the other end of Hammersmith Bridge and there are always one or two captive observation balloons (sausages) there in day-time.

Whenever we go into London for dinner, which isn't often, as the Soho restaurants have only very sketchy menus now, we always come back on top of a bus that takes the long way round to Hammersmith, careening along through almost pitch darkness with only an occasional patch of light under a gas lamp. It might be London in the 17th Century, except there are no link-boys.

I really must stop here and get this off to you. I hope you're well— we all are (except the chilblains).[5]

Type composition, printing, and binding the forty-eight pages of Dürer's *Of the Just Shaping of Letters* completely absorbed Rogers' time and energy for nine months of almost intolerable frustration and delay. After he had been only two months at work, Rogers wrote to Ruth Shepard Granniss, Librarian of the Grolier Club, explaining why it had become clear that the promise of delivery could not be kept. Characteristically, he offered to accept cancellation of the commission if the Club so desired. His offer was not accepted and the book ultimately became one of the Club's finest publications. An excerpt from a letter of 4 March 1917 to Miss Granniss follows:

I received your letter of inquiry about the "Dürer" several days ago —but I've waited until I could go over the question with Mr Walker, in the hope that I could give you a satisfactory answer. But with the best endeavours, I'm afraid I can't. At the rate we are going, the book will not be ready till June—and there seems, at present, to be no way of speeding it up. We have only enough type to set about 10 pages at a

CHAPTER FOUR: 1916–1917

time — then print and distribute and print again. The unforeseen delay comes in the press-work. Mr. Walker has only one press capable of printing it, and this is so engaged on printing maps for the Government, that it is available at present only about two days a week. And on these two days, we can print only about 4 to 6 pages. Things may improve later or they may get worse (which is more probable). But at the present rate you see it will take about 2½ months to print the 60 pp. [finally only 48 pages] which the book will probably run to. There are only a handful of men left in Mr. Walker's establishment, many having been called up long ago and some going now — while several are making maps at the Admiralty. New regulations prohibit him from hiring others even if he could get them. His superintendent and I ran the press for printing what pages are already done and I find I have most of the details to do myself on this book. So altogether I think it impossible to promise it for any definite time, but as I said, will do my best to have it in June if that is not too late....

We've all had influenza and have been pretty miserable generally. However, if I could only get ahead with my work I shouldn't mind so much the physical annoyances. But the slowness and the delay get on my nerves.[6]

With the Dürer volume finally completed and ready for shipment, Rogers wrote two days before Christmas in 1917 to his friend Kent in New York. Rogers' story of the infinite labor which he found essential in the edition before it could leave his hands is a typical revelation of the standards, regardless of time or money, which Rogers would always demand of himself. These unseen details are at the heart of craftsmanship. Further paragraphs are evidence of Rogers' incapacities for, or inattention to, the matters that are usually called good business sense:

> I wired in response to your cable but there seemed to be no use in replying to your note and your later letter until I had something definite to write about the Dürer. I can now finish the story.
>
> When I finally got the actual printing finished in August I thought

THE MALL PRESS: LONDON

the worst was over, but as it has turned out, it had only begun. I'll not go over the whole disagreeable tale in detail, but suffice it to record that my lack of skill as a press man resulted in most of the large letters coming out grey and broken—so for more than a month, with the help of two young women in Walker's establishment we patched them up with brush and pen.

As there are 164 of these in each copy and quite half of them were defective in each, these, multiplied by 200, would give 16400 individual letters—which I don't think is an exaggeration of the number we "blacked up."

In the meantime we had arranged, on Walker's recommendation, to have the binding done at Longman's "Ship Bindery" and I had searched for and found at a marblers, sufficient marbled paper to cover the sides (of the same make as on the "Franklin's Press at Passy").

I engaged the lot—but owing to the delay in actually turning the books over to the binder, the marbler thought I had given up my claim on the paper, and *sold* it to someone else.

Then there was a long search to find any more white paper suitable for marbling—another delay of 3 or four weeks in getting it marbled and of course a still further delay in getting the covers made.

In the meantime I had to come to Cambridge to take up my job here, and could only go to London on Fridays to look after matters—and by correspondence, which is most unsatisfactory when working with new people. They did pretty well—mechanically—but they succeeded in spoiling about 70 covers in making them, by not matching up the marbled paper properly for the sides. As no more paper was to be had the only thing I could do was to put the spoiled ones into plain brown paper (khaki) and call them "war bindings." On the whole I like them quite as well as the marbled ones and if I had had any preconception of the difficulties in getting marbled paper and getting it on right, I would have put them all into plain paper at once.

I have personally examined the 200 copies and although a few of them are not quite what I should have liked as to binding I think I had

CHAPTER FOUR: 1916–1917

better let them go as they are, as there seems little chance of getting anything better done here, or in any reasonable time.

You have, I'm sure, little conception of the difficult conditions for getting some passably good work done now in London—at any price. The material simply isn't to be had and most of the skillful men have gone. The remainder work long hours and the binderies as well as other establishments, have more than they can possibly do and are all declining work continually—It was only by Walker's influence that I got this bindery to take the job at all.

I regret the continued delays and the long postponement of the shipment—but I have done my utmost to get the commission finished and with at least enough merit so that it would not be a disgrace to the Club as a publication. . . .

Walker & the binders are arranging the shipment, consular invoices, etc. and I will cable you when the cases actually start—(you will get it before you do this, as they *ought* to be off the latter part of this week). . . .

For your private information only—not for the Publication Committee—I'd like to say that I'm out of pocket on this book just about the amount of the commission—or $1500—And when my first payment from the Univ. Press came, we were down to less than £4. As to Walker, I think, and hope, that he will come out even at least on it, as I shouldn't like to feel that I had got him into a financial loss, as well as all the bother I've given him.

When I found that I couldn't go into his business (I can't go into particulars, but it is in a very bad way financially, and I can't afford to work only for glory as Walker and Merton do—having independent incomes) I couldn't, of course, go on taking a salary; so after two months it came to a stop and we have been living on what we brought over with us. So in 9 months my actual receipts have been only £55, and if this Cambridge job hadn't come along I don't know what we should have done. It was a close squeeze. I don't in the least regret the year's experience, and the present one in connection with the Press here promises to be less strenuous at least—but what I'm giving you all these details for is to hear me out in saying that I must consider the Dürer as the last book I shall attempt to print on commission. It can't be done the way I want to do such books without paying too heavily out of my own pocket for the privilege—I have lost considerably on all the books I have attempted to do on my own account, and have at last been compelled to break into the small principal that I saved while at Riverside. The war has reduced the income from the balance of it to about half. We shall be able to live on my salary here, as long as it lasts, but I don't believe my engagement here will prove to be either a permanent one or a long one, as I am engaged principally, I think, to coach the Manager of the Press—(a very good business man but with no experience as a book-maker).[7]

The books were finally shipped to the Grolier Club early in 1918. They were offered to the membership in November at $12.00 per copy. The edition of *Of the Just Shaping of Letters* by Albrecht Dürer (plates 18/19), translated by R. T. Nichol, consisted of 215 copies on a British handmade paper and three copies on vellum. It is a slender folio of forty-eight pages, 12¼ x 8½ inches; the decorative title page was printed in black and red. The type was hand set at the Mall Press in the 14-point Centaur that had been shipped from the United States. The text included the admonition from Dürer: "Now, since architects, painters and others, at times are wont to set an inscription on lofty walls, it will make for the merit of the work that they form the letters correctly." Rogers reproduced all the Dürer drawings of the letters of the alphabet, each 1¾ inches high, printed in a fine, rich, velvet-black ink, and then laboriously retouched the weak spots as described in the foregoing letter. It is one of Rogers' great books, done with noble and dramatic simplicity. The present writer finds the book to have a maturity—perhaps an elusive magic—less evident in the more youthful work. And Rogers included *Of the Just Shaping of Letters* as one of the thirty books that he considered "successful."

1917   1919

The Cambridge University Press

During the months that Rogers was at work in London, John Clay, the University Printer at the Cambridge University Press, died. Clay was succeeded by J. B. Peace, a member of the Board of Syndics of the Press, a member of Emmanuel College, and a lecturer in engineering. Peace was not a printer by training, and was unfamiliar with the intricacies of book production. The quality of the Cambridge books then being printed, using worn type and antiquated equipment, had deteriorated to a marked degree.

Sydney Cockerell, who had been William Morris' secretary and partner when the great Kelmscott books were being printed, and who had been associated with Emery Walker, was Director of the Fitzwilliam Museum in Cambridge at the time that changes were to be made at the University Press. He deplored the lack of workmanship, the poorly designed and badly printed books that were being published over the Cambridge imprint. Cockerell, who was already familiar with Rogers' work, and who was aware that Rogers was in London, made it his mission to bring Rogers' gifts to the University Press. Fortunately for Cockerell's maneuvers a Printing Committee had already been appointed to deal with criticism of the Press output. (The Committee was also charged with later consideration of the four-hundredth anniversary in 1921 of Cambridge printing.) A. T. Bartholomew, Under-Librarian of the University Library (with whom Rogers later formed an especially warm friendship), had been invited to join the Committee, and soon became an ally in Cockerell's effort to convince the Syndics of the need for a radical change. In short, after many meetings, the Syndics authorized

Peace to discuss with Bruce Rogers the possibility of his coming to the Press either full or part time.

During the spring of 1917, when Rogers was still deeply involved with the Dürer book, Peace invited him to come to Cambridge. After several visits Peace found it possible formally to offer Rogers a year's engagement, with four days per week at the Press, at an annual salary of £750, to begin in September at the start of the new academic year. The exact nature of Rogers' responsibilities was never spelled out in writing, but it was perfectly clear that as "typographic consultant," he was employed to improve Cambridge printing. Since it was no longer possible for Rogers to continue at the Mall Press, and since his financial resources were largely depleted, he welcomed the offer to join the Cambridge University Press for a limited period.

During the summer, in anticipation of the new relationship, there had been some discussion with Peace concerning the advisability of a new typeface that Rogers might design for exclusive Cambridge use. New, proprietary types, then considered hallmarks of their respective presses, had been made for Kelmscott, Doves, Ashendene, and Eragny books in England, and Rogers and Updike had followed similar paths in the United States. Rogers concurred about a new type, provided he could retain the right to use it for his own work, as had been arranged with the Metropolitan Museum of Art in New York for the Centaur type. Although the Syndics agreed, the project was never undertaken, owing perhaps to the difficulties of life and work in a country at war.

With the presswork of the Dürer finally completed (although the binding and its problems remained), the Rogers family moved to Cambridge on 29 September. Mrs. Rogers was still convalescent from a recent operation, and daughter Elizabeth would attend the Perse School in Cambridge.

In a long letter written on 9 November to John Cotton Dana, B.R. included a paragraph describing his office "in the *old* Syndics Room and library of the Press, with three large windows looking out on the court-yard and across to the Gothic tower and windows of the original Pitt Press building (the 'Freshman's Church') still covered with green and yellow and red vines.

CHAPTER FIVE: 1917–1919

The room itself is a fine old one about 20 x 30 lined with books (the older publications of the Press, which I greatly prefer as companions to the later ones). In one section are all the Bibles, Prayer Books and Hymnals ever printed, I should say, including King James's original Bible, Baskervilles, etc. etc. A long council table runs down the middle, there are real Chippendale chairs, a nice old rug, and last, *and* least—an open coal fire. Someone said, when I told them that I had an open fire and walls lined with books, that as winter drew on I'd be glad to have it reversed—one book and the walls lined with open fires; which I suspect is true."[1]

Rogers spent much of the autumn on a long report to the Syndics which he was to deliver the day after Christmas. An unhappy first month was followed by better living conditions. Two letters that follow show that Rogers had begun to enjoy life in Cambridge and the people he met there. He wrote to Kent on 23 November and again on 29 December 1917:

> After a month of starvation in a miserable boarding-house on Trumpington Street we are now completely settled in lodgings on Park Place facing Parker's Piece, a big broad playing-field out beyond the University Arms Hotel. We have a living room on the ground floor and two bedrooms on the second floor. The intermediate floor is occupied by a very pleasant elderly man who is slightly crippled by paralysis —though he goes every day to business. He is a partner in one of the large furnishing stores in Cambridge (his name is Paine). On one block there are Paine, Sadd, Greefe and Death! And there is also an establishment in another section which announces: "Merry: Undertaker"! English family names are sometimes curious things. There is a butcher near Victoria Station in London who has altered his cognomen to "De Ath."
>
> We follow the usual custom in Cambridge lodgings: we buy the provisions and the landlady cooks and serves them and takes care of the rooms. For the grate in our living-dining room our ration of coal is one hod per diem. But the landlady uses about half of that to "air" the rooms with both windows wide open, an hour before we come down

at eight. Must somehow stop that, but don't quite know how.

Our landlady is a second Mrs. Malaprop—very genteel. On inquiring why the grass didn't grow better under a tree in the back garden she said it was because the roots of the tree "took all the suction from the grass." And when her dog Flossie, a thoroughbred "from a famous aviary," presented her with a litter of pups she said Flossie had "matriculated"! But everything is spotless and she is a good cook.

At the first boarding house we met a pleasant young couple from Harrogate. He is a Captain in the R.O.T.C. which is quartered in various colleges. He is a fine musician and has composed some excellent light music. (He occasionally asks me in to the Chapel of Pembroke to hear him practice and improvise.)

They left the boarding-house, about the time we did, for lodgings not far from ours. As an officer he has a much greater meat allowance than they can possibly use, so they frequently contribute some of the surplus to us—a most welcome addition to our rations. The shops have generally been better supplied than they were in Hammersmith, so we don't find foraging very onerous.

The present University Printer is a fine sort—J. B. Peace—and we shall get on well together, I'm sure. In addition to managing the Press he also runs the city gas works and is Bursar of Emmanuel College—yet he always seems to have time to talk with me. I am to draw up a series of recommendations about their stocks of type (tons of it) saying what to discard as old metal—which the War Office wants badly—and what fonts to keep or add to, whenever it is possible again.

Through Peace's influence I have been made a member of Emmanuel Parlour, which means that I can dine at the high table in hall with the five or six elderly dons still left, on giving notice in the morning to the steward. I don't abuse the privilege as I know the difficulties of getting supplies. Most of the Fellows are on war work and all the students are gone into the services except a few physically disabled ones. But two of the long tables in Hall are filled with Siamese undergraduates. They can have beer, but the wine-cellars are closed for the duration.

CHAPTER FIVE: 1917–1919

Occasionally Master Giles has as a guest someone high up in the War Office or a Fellow home on leave. And then in the sanctity of the Parlour, over the sherry and port, we hear inside news of the operations from authentic sources — more than the public ever hears. We had an Admiral a few evenings ago.

Dec. 29

We celebrated Christmas at the High Table by having a special treat. The American wife of the Librarian had grown two little pumpkins in her garden and under her direction her cook had made a couple of little pies. I'm afraid the old johnnies didn't care much for it, and I wasn't surprised. They spooned it up out of the crust.

Everybody has been most kind to us and we are invited to many teas. Lady Darwin, who is an American, asked us to a tea on her lawn when we first came. On my first visit to Cambridge, long ago, I paddled up the river in a canoe and saw people at tea on the lawn which slopes to the river back of her house, never dreaming that some day I would be one of the guests there.

Sydney Cockerell — through whose good offices I was invited to come to Cambridge — has several times invited us to his house for luncheon, and there we always meet celebrities of some kind.

Mrs. Cockerell is beautiful, but she has been an invalid for many years — goes about in a wheel-chair. Cockerell's Fitzwilliam Museum is a treasure-house of beautiful things, and some not so beautiful that he has to keep on exhibition because they are from the bequest of the donor. Cockerell has exquisite taste and has directed the formation of the Chester Beatty collection of MSS. and I think also that of Henry Yates-Thompson. The nucleus of Y-T's collection consists of 100 of the most beautiful MSS. and printed books obtainable; when one is found that is better than one he already has, he discards an old one.

He lives in a mansion in Portman Square and has a beautiful country place on a hill near Aylesbury where Walker and I spent a week-end several years ago. My chief recollection of it is the peach-house — all glass and covered with trained trees bearing peaches larger than tea-cups.

I want to get this off to you, so no more at present — [2]

The "Report on the Typography of the Cambridge University Press" was delivered to J. B. Peace at the end of December after Rogers had had three months to familiarize himself with conditions at the Press. In a covering letter of 27 December 1917, Rogers wrote:

> I hand you, herewith, the report and recommendations that I have been so long in preparing.
>
> I have never before attempted such an undertaking, and I fear that you will find it very badly put together, and full of what may seem inconsistent and unconsidered statements. It contains, however, my general conclusions on the various matters dealt with, and I can at any time go more fully into details with you on any point you may care to take up. With a little difficulty I can probably produce concrete examples to bear out any statements that I make, which may seem to you to require further corroboration.
>
> I have gone into the matter of type more fully than into other factors of bookmaking, because in a way, it is a more permanent part of a Press's equipment.
>
> Papers and inks come and go, but a new outfit of type is not to be bought without careful consideration of its future as well as its present value.
>
> My suggestions as to new types might be enlarged or changed after better opportunities of studying other type-founders books — the assortments of them at the Press is very limited and out-of-date, without being *enough* out-of-date.
>
> You will rightly conclude that my chief remedy for the present conditions is to buy new materials.
>
> I can perhaps put it more strongly to you, personally, than I would have done in the report — but I can not believe that any other printing-house of equal standing can have gone on for so many years with such

CHAPTER FIVE: 1917–1919

an inferior equipment of types—they are, in my opinion, bad beyond belief, and the ornaments little better.

I don't know if the Syndics of the Press can be made to see this, as it is largely a matter for ocular demonstration, and if he hasn't an "eye for printing" it is difficult to convince him—

An afternoon at almost any book-shop amongst the newer books from a number of publishers—and chiefly, perhaps, the smaller publishers of war poems and papers—ought to open his eyes to the fact that most excellent work is being done in various quarters, not withstanding war conditions.

I hope I have not been too strong in any of my statements, and that I shall [not] give offense to somebody concerned, in the conclusions I have drawn. All work, and especially in one of the arts, is wholly an impersonal matter to me, and should be discussed on its merits alone, regardless of whoever may be concerned in or responsible for it—and it is in this conviction that I have written.[3]

The Report as submitted was a sober and rather pedagogical document of some eight thousand words. It reviewed the unsatisfactory conditions of printing at the Press, discussed its existing type and equipment, offered recommendations for replacements, and proposed improvements in workmanship. The opening paragraph of the introduction stated, "A distinctive style in book-making is now quite as difficult of attainment as it has ever been, if not more so. When printers were their own type-founders, ink-makers, and sometimes paper-makers, the products of various presses were easily distinguished and were, in a sense that we have now nearly lost, a much closer reflection of the printers' individual tastes and capabilities."[4]

The main thrust of the report consisted of ten individual sections. They covered "Old Face Types," "Modern Face Types," "Display and Poster Founts," "Ornaments and Initials," "Monotype Faces," "A Private Type," "Papers," "Inks," "Binding," and "Future Policy." Inasmuch as Rogers touched on the basic steps involved in the printing process—selection of type, the uses of paper, the essentials of presswork and binding—the report also became a kind of credo of a typographic practitioner.

Rogers' period of association with the Cambridge University Press was also a time of transition in the production of printing. In the final section of his "Report," with an eloquent plea for the sanctity of the printed word, Rogers touched on the need for change to machine composition of type, and for the advisability of a new department at the Press. In the section called "Future Policy" he wrote:

> In the foregoing suggestions and recommendations I have been concerned almost wholly with the physical and aesthetic qualities of the products of the Press, and with means for their improvement. I have ventured few opinions on its policy, feeling that questions of that kind are not strictly within my province. But even in my brief connection with the Press, the desirability (almost the necessity) of formulating and pursuing fixed policies along several new lines has become apparent to me; and I venture, somewhat diffidently, to call attention to two or three of them here, as an appendix to the main body of recommendations.
>
> The first is the question of hand- versus machine-composition. Until recently I have always been an advocate of hand-set type; but recent developments in the machines themselves now permit the possibility of doing quite as good work as by the older and slower method. For the very finest printing and for certain varieties of books, hand-composition is perhaps as yet unavoidable, but it has been proved, I think, on the whole more expensive and much slower than composing-machines, and in the coming days of keener competition and higher prices all round, I believe hand-work should be brought to an irreducible minimum, while machine-work should be correspondingly developed.
>
> In no other similar craft, which at all permits the use of machines,

CHAPTER FIVE: 1917–1919

does hand-work still play so large a part to-day as it does in printing, and it will be increasingly impracticable to obtain adequate prices for hand-work in a market dominated by a machine product. Even in printing, it is only the composing-room that has lagged in development and (in America at least) it has long been an accepted fact that composing-rooms "don't pay." The press-rooms make the profits, but press-rooms have been modernized and have long ago discarded the hand-press, of which hand-composition may now be considered the contemporary.

There will, of course, always be a limited field for hand-work in display composition and in connection with and supplementary to machine-composition, but otherwise I believe it is in a fair way to becoming obsolete. I believe, therefore, that at the Press the problem of changing over from the old type bodies to the more modern point system should be further resolved into changing over as much as possible of the old type into additional facilities for Monotype composition.

Finally, as my own connection with the Press (in fact my residence in England) is only a temporary one, I shall perhaps not be suspected of any ulterior personal aim in recommending that my present function should be made a permanent department of the Press, and an incumbent found for it who shall have practically complete supervision (of course under the Manager's control) of all details of design and make-up of the books and other printing. At present these details are not (or, at least, in the past they have not been) sufficiently correlated; either within the making of a single book, or between various books of similar nature, or (still more important) with the best historic precedents. They have apparently hitherto been left largely to proof-readers, clickers, and machine-room superintendents, who, however excellent in their own special departments, can hardly be expected to have a comprehensive grasp of the problem of book-making as a whole, or as broad an acquaintance with, and appreciation of, the best typography of both present and earlier days as to enable them to turn out a finished product as good as the best of any period.

This responsibility for details (frequently conflicting details) should be concentrated in one man, and it does not seem impossible to find a competent man for the place among the younger school of printers now growing up in England. It is perhaps superfluous to say that he should not be too much of an idealist to conform to necessary and practical limitations, but it is equally important that he should be idealist enough to maintain, in a stronghold of science and scholarship like Cambridge, that art is as fundamental as any other source of civilization; and that printing, however it may serve to further the ends of literature and the sciences, is no less a servitor of art — a servitor of too great a lineage and too much dignity to be restricted wholly to mechanical employment.[5]

Despite the continuing gravity of the war in 1917, the Syndics accepted the Rogers report. His broad proposals were adopted as conditions allowed, and in post-war years the plant was completely modernized. During the twenty-one months that Rogers spent in Cambridge he put his precepts into practice, and emphasized the need for constant vigilance in every phase of design and production.

Twenty-four books and brochures, printed at the Cambridge University Press, which received special care from Rogers, were shown at the 1938 exhibition at the Grolier Club. *Address at the Unveiling of the Roll of Honour of the Cambridge Tipperary Club* (1918), a brochure 10 x 6¾ inches, and *Spare Your Good* (1919), a thin booklet 9 x 6¼ inches, with stiff board covers, were hand set in Centaur type. A charming octavo brochure, *On Friendship* (1918), sixteenth-century verses set in Caslon italic type and privately printed for A. T. Bartholomew and Bruce Rogers, included arabesque designs made from units of type ornament. Such decoration would engage Rogers increasingly in the future in preference to embellishment drawn to order and reproduced. *A Collection of Books about Cats* (1918), an octavo with notes by Percy L. Babington, set in Georgian Old Style type, must have been pleasing to Rogers since he put his printer's device on the title page.

CHAPTER FIVE: 1917–1919

Two trade books, *Euclid in Greek* and Shakespeare's *The Tempest* (plate 20), should be noted inasmuch as Rogers included them among the thirty books he considered "successful." Although both volumes are attractive, they are not among his great books, and it is difficult to understand why he should have chosen them when other volumes done under more favorable circumstances are of much greater significance. *Euclid in Greek* (1920) by Sir Thomas L. Heath, page 7¼ x 4¾ inches, was set in Monotype Old Style and Greek types, clothbound. *The Tempest* (1921), the pilot volume of the "New Cambridge Shakespeare," page 7 x 4½ inches, was set in Monotype Old Style type, clothbound. The editors, Arthur Quiller-Couch and John Dover Wilson, planned to issue each play in a separate volume at the rate of six plays per year, but the series was not completed until 1966. Although Rogers later expressed himself as not wholly satisfied with the design of The Cambridge Shakespeare, he hoped to use the Cambridge text for a more luxurious format which the Grolier Club might issue in a limited edition. However, the Club never accepted Rogers' proposal.

One of the happiest relationships that Rogers formed in England was with Francis Meynell, scion of a distinguished British literary and publishing family, who had established his own Pelican Press in 1916. In his autobiography, *My Lives* (Random House, New York, 1971), Meynell wrote of his own beginnings: "Bruce Rogers, the great American typographer, was my hero. What he had done for book design in the United States I now tried to do in the design of 'jobbing' printing—catalogues, posters, press advertisements, political manifestos."[6] Meynell went on to establish the Nonesuch Press in 1923, where his stated purpose was "to choose and make books according to a triple ideal: significance of subject, beauty of format and moderation of price."[7] These highly desirable objectives were achieved in a brilliant succession of more than a hundred published books of great typographic diversity, from 1923 to 1935.

In the summer of 1917 Meynell wrote to Rogers, then in London, sent samples of work printed at the Pelican Press, and invited Mr. and Mrs. Rogers to dinner. He explained that they lived simply and promised some piano playing by Mrs. Meynell. Rogers accepted in his letter (below) of 11 August 1917. Meynell later printed this and other correspondence in his autobiography, as he recalled their friendship and work together when Rogers was in England.

> Dear Mr Meynell, I'm much relieved to find that you live in a slum, and don't dress—for I haven't had a dinner jacket for ten or twelve years. For the past five, we have lived from hand to mouth and knocked about from one lodging to another—dining mostly at cheap restaurants or making a stew over a gas-burner—so please tell Mrs Meynell we shall be frightfully disappointed if she gives us a regulation English dinner, and goes to a lot of trouble—don't let her, please.
>
> I may add that we usually impress our own guests into service for the wash-up afterwards—but we of course don't insist upon this if there is a piano![8]

In his book Meynell wrote that the dinner was a delightful occasion. "I found his personality a complete confirmation of his work as a typographer. His line of talk was as firmly gentle as his drawing of a border or typeface. He was a propagandist but he was kind; he admired a great tradition and showed how one could adapt it to modern use; he treated the young aspirant as a fellow-worker."[9]

With Rogers in Cambridge the friendship ripened personally and professionally. On one occasion Meynell took his American friend to a cricket match. "It was a lovely summer day," Meynell wrote, "and I decided that there was one thing in the world at which I could be his instructor."[10] Meynell sent much of his printing for Rogers' criticism, which was freely given—and praise, too, for "your magnificent specimen-sheet."

During the autumn of 1918 Meynell asked Rogers to accept a commission to design a poster type for the exclusive use of the Pelican Press. After a few preliminary exchanges, Rogers wrote on 5 December 1918:

> In regard to the type-design, your offer is a tempting one, just at present when income taxes are about due, though of course the problem of a lower-case is more vexing than of caps alone. I enclose some

sketches of both, but I am not at all confident that they are what you want. I fear I am not much good at this kind of letter as I'm not wholly in sympathy with the idea of making type look like drawn lettering, even in a mild degree.

Especially in lower-case when a single letter is repeated so frequently, the eye soon tires, I believe, of any marked eccentricity in its form. I have therefore made the lower-case even more regular than the caps — with the result that you will probably not like any of it. But you mustn't hesitate to say so, as I should hate to feel that the result did not meet your entire approval. It's really *your* type, you know — I'm just the draughtsman. So you will tell me frankly if you don't altogether like the sketches, and give someone else a trial. It would be comparatively easy to get more attractive letterforms in this genre if it were not for the limitation in width. A narrow, and at the same time a heavy, letter is almost certain to be a somewhat gross one.[11]

Rogers worked on the poster type during the winter, and was able to send Meynell some examples with his letter of 5 February 1919:

I've been working at your poster type design the last few days and I've got it pretty well "roughed in." But I have so many misgivings about the design that I'm sending it on to you in its present state to find out whether it is going to be what you want.

I fear it hasn't enough of the unusual in its make-up to satisfy your requirements and I don't want you to take it unless it does. I haven't been able to turn up any satisfactory (heavy) model for the caps (the lower-case doesn't exist I suppose) except the one Goudy used — and I mustn't lay myself open to the charge of copying Goudy — even if I liked his type — which I don't. It looks well enough as he has shown it — just a line or two. But it would have become most tiresome and disagreeable in any quantity, I'm sure, and especially if enlarged.

I don't really like any of Goudy's types — except the Forum caps for very limited use. So I have fallen back on my own devices and started such a letter as I think I might like to use myself — but as I said in the beginning, I'm not at all sure it is what *you* want. You mustn't, however, take each letter as its final form, for they will doubtless all have to be modified more or less after they are all in ink (especially the A) but I can't do that at the present state of the drawing.[12]

Meynell was much pleased by the finished drawings of the complete alphabet of roman capitals, lower case, punctuation, and figures, which he arranged to have cut in wood. The wood type was successfully used to print a considerable number of posters, but unfortunately the design had not been transferred to metal, and the wood inevitably showed signs of wear. After Meynell had left the Pelican Press for other duties he found that the worn wood letters had been destroyed. In any event, the original drawings are in the possession of the Victoria and Albert Museum in London. Rogers was never altogether happy with the results, believing that some of the freedom had been lost in the cutting.

The armistice was signed and four years of war had finally come to an end on 11 November 1918. The winter of 1918-1919 was especially difficult for Rogers, who suffered from the Cambridge climate. He had become restless and discouraged because he had not had the opportunity to produce the kind of work that would "satisfy his soul." His ambivalent nature, which frequently made him unhappy with his immediate surroundings, caused him to look forward to his return to the United States. Once there he would look back with nostalgia to the Cambridge experience. A month before leaving, he had written a letter to Kent (on 27 May) expressing his unhappiness and adding thoughts about a printing and publishing business to be established on his return, but which never became a reality. The letter follows, in part:

I had about the most miserable winter that I can remember. It was cold and wet and for months we didn't see the sun—not till May, which has so far been unusually fine, but even now the leaves are not full-grown and there was a white frost last night, or so I am told, as I can never find energy enough to get up before 8 or 8:30 and the sun rises some time in the middle of the night. To the physical misery is

CHAPTER FIVE: 1917–1919

to be added the mental one of feeling that the experiment I embarked so hopefully upon some two years ago here, shows even less promise of success than it did during the war. I mean the endeavor to resuscitate and enliven the product of the Press and to fix it in some sort of a groove at a higher level than it had been. During the first year, under war conditions, when little was being done, the prospects seemed good — as, from the Manager down, the people at the Press I actually had to deal with seemed at least interested and willing to try new plans of procedure. And I thought it only needed the return to more normal conditions to see a more or less complete revision of their policy — acquisitions of much-needed new material to work with, etc. etc. But now that almost the whole force is back and the place is going full speed ahead with accumulated and new work, no one has time any more even properly to consider new departures and the whole tendency is to drop back into the old rut, of rushed and half-done work — of the *easiest* way of doing things, whether they are very well done or not. . . .

As to equipment, Rollins's little Montague Press had a better one. I had always heard how much money the Press had at its disposal, to use regardless of business profit or how it was always ready to embark upon enterprises for the sake of scholarship whether they paid or not. And now I am told that the Press is very poor and that the utmost economy must be practiced as to paper, ink, and general expense of production. So there seems to be little or no prospect of any sacrifice to the god of excellent mechanical work — which is the only deity I know in the printing business — and though what I have tried to get the Manager to see may some time have some result, it is too far in the future for me to wait for. I passed my 49th milestone the other day and if I'm ever to realize some of my plans for book-making I can't afford to wait on the slow-going English temperament — nor can I find much sustenance for enthusiasm in it.

Burroughs wrote me such a glowing picture of life and work in Cambridge, that while I read it I could almost believe it — but the reality, as realities mostly are, is quite different.

> My plans, on coming home, are still somewhat vague—but I think the one I spoke of before—of an attempt to set up a small publishing business in connection with my friend Brown, will be the first experiment, as it promises to be the least expensive to embark upon. We shall not attempt to do our own printing at first, but will probably try Hopkins at the Marion Press, Jamaica, if he will consent to work out my designs. To save expense we shall probably not attempt to live in N.Y. Elizabeth will enter Radcliffe or some other college if she can get in, and Anne has many arrears of visiting to pay off, to members of her family and others—and I shall probably take a room somewhere convenient to Jamaica (if the Marion Press plan develops). After wartime diet in England, or even the present regimen, I can manage to put up with almost any kind of board, and I've long ago given over being particular about my lodgings. So I shall do well enough, no doubt. If Rollins was only still at Montague I'd go there direct, as I was happier working there than any other place I have tried. But I believe he has almost dismantled the mill, and neither Brown nor I have capital enough to risk putting in a plant at once....[13]

The time had come for Rogers to return to the United States. He completed his work at Cambridge at the end of June, but the sailing was delayed for a month due to a strike. Mr. and Mrs. Rogers and daughter Elizabeth finally left for home at the end of July.

Characteristically, Rogers underestimated his value to the Cambridge University Press. Shortly after he had left England, J. B. Peace had occasion to write to the Managing Director of the Monotype Corporation in London declaring that, "[Rogers'] work here was of the very highest value to us & it was with very great regret that we parted with him when he felt obliged on account of our country climate to make a shorter stay in England than he had at one time intended to make."[14] And in 1950, Brooke Crutchley, then University Printer, could write, "It was the example of his painstaking quest for perfection as much as the report itself that was to put new life into the University Press, and it is a pleasure, thirty-three years later, to acknowledge

CHAPTER FIVE: 1917–1919

once more the debt that Cambridge, as indeed the whole world, owes to a great craftsman and artist."[15]

After only a few months in the United States, Rogers began to look back to his Cambridge experience with a more roseate glow, and in turn found his own country to be rather less than he would have wished. On New Year's Day, 1920, he wrote to J. B. Peace, in England:

> I am also reminded of a passage in your last letter to me in London; in which you seemed to take upon yourself the responsibility for the lack of opportunity offered me while at Cambridge to make more interesting books. I assure you I came away from Cambridge with real regret, and with no feeling that perhaps more might have been done to use what talent I may have more advantageously. I don't see how anyone there (and you in particular) could have done more under the circumstances, or in fact under *any* circumstances. If there is any reason why we did not do more interesting and attractive books together I think it should be laid to my wretched health and lack of energy—certainly *not* to any want of sympathy or appreciation on your part. I shall always look back upon my stay in Cambridge and my association with you as one of the most interesting and (notwithstanding the physical discomfort) the pleasantest experience in my life—and after a brief re-trial of life over here in its present turbid state I'm almost tempted to set sail for England again—as, comparatively, a haven of sanity and repose. I thought we were an uninteresting lot of people before—gathered from all corners of the world—but the war and its aftermath seems to have brought all the most disagreeable and brutal elements on to the surface, and there is no escaping them, short of hiding oneself in some back-country village.
>
> You can walk for blocks in New York and not hear a word of pure English spoken—and our other cities are little better. With all the tremendous prosperity evident on every hand, we are yet a poverty-stricken nation in things of the imagination or spirit—and when the insane action (on the Treaty) of our politics-ridden Senate is taken

into the account, it makes me ashamed of being an American. I hope you will give a proportion of us credit for being heartily sick and disgusted with the present state of affairs in Congress. The ignorance of what has been done and is still being done in Europe, and the indifference to it all, is appalling, even amongst supposedly educated people here.[16]

Rogers ultimately returned to England, where he would produce some of his most honored masterpieces, but not until he had had an unusually productive nine years in the United States.

1920　　1929

The Affluent Decade

BRUCE ROGERS had come back to the United States with the hope that he could make the books he felt capable of making. He was now fifty years of age, at the height of his powers, with an international reputation as the pre-eminent master of his craft. Before we turn to the details of book production, of living and livelihood, let us take a brief look at the prosperous years in which Rogers found himself.

The 1920s was an affluent decade of conspicuous growth, productivity, and industrial expansion that also produced great men and women in literature and the arts. For the printed book it was an heroic period on both sides of the Atlantic.

The books that had been printed by William Morris at the Kelmscott Press in the 1890s were followed in succeeding years by volumes of true grandeur from private presses in England and on the Continent. Then a watershed in fine bookmaking was reached with a procession of superb books, of substantial literary content, issued by the Nonesuch Press in London from 1923 to 1935. They were designed by Francis Meynell, who readily acknowledged his debt to Bruce Rogers, his typographic "hero." Of historic importance was the fact that the Nonesuch books, following Meynell's direction, were composed and printed by machines in the best plants in England and Scotland, and including the Oxford and Cambridge University presses. Thus in the work of Rogers and Meynell, the transition was made from magnificent limited editions by inspired amateurs on the hand press, to noble books produced for a wider audience by dedicated professionals on power-driven machines.

THE AFFLUENT DECADE IN AMERICA

An unusual group of professional designers and printers in the United States, of scholarly stature, contemporaries of Bruce Rogers, added their gifts to the growing interest in fine printing. In addition to the familiar names of Rogers and Updike, we should recall the significant work of Frederic W. Goudy, Carl Purington Rollins, Will Bradley, Thomas Maitland Cleland, William Addison Dwiggins, Rudolph Ruzicka, John Henry Nash, William Edwin Rudge, and Dard Hunter. And during the twenties a number of new printing shops dedicated to the art and practice of typography at its highest levels were established on both the American east and west coasts by idealistic young men who were, nevertheless, competent professionals.

New type design flourished. New faces were cut for several private presses; but also in the wider world of general printing, commercial type foundries in Europe and America re-cut some of the classic types from the past, and commissioned new types by prominent contemporary graphic artists.

Book clubs had become active devotees and supporters of fine printing, and occasional publishers of books. Among the most prominent were the Grolier Club in New York, the Club of Odd Volumes in Boston, the Caxton Club in Chicago, the Rowfant Club in Cleveland, and the Book Club of California in San Francisco. Museums and special libraries collected and occasionally showed press books, including the French *livre de peintre*. Organizations of designers and printers in several large cities (typically, the American Institute of Graphic Arts in New York) attracted substantial memberships, with meetings and exhibitions. Among the many exhibitions nationwide, two in New York excited Rogers' special admiration, as recorded in two letters he wrote to Carl Rollins. On 19 May 1924: "You *must* see the [Metropolitan] Museum book show—Bill Ivins* has done himself proud—it is probably the most gorgeous exhibition of books ever got together...." And in 1928, "You *must* come down to see the two greatest exhibitions of printing that the present generation is likely ever to see. I mean, of course, the Kelmscott books at the Grolier Club and the Merrymount books at the Art Center.... The Kelmscott as the most magnificent

---

*William M. Ivins, Jr., was Curator of the Department of Prints at the Metropolitan Museum of Art, New York.

CHAPTER SIX: 1920–1929

specimens of *printing* from any one press ever existing, and the Merrymount [D. B. Updike] as the finest lot of *books* ever turned out by one man."[1]

The new prosperity brought with it an active market for press books among booksellers and new young collectors. The antiquarian book trade became world news when great library collections were being built, with consequent dramatic increases in book prices that were paid by bidders in the turbulent auction rooms. And a new young breed of publishing houses was established whose owners, following the example set by Alfred A. Knopf, employed professional typographers to design their books.

The widespread international concern with fine printing was manifest in the many periodicals published in England, France, Germany, and other European countries, as well as in the United States. The most significant among them, if one may select only two, would have been *The Fleuron* in England, and *The Colophon* in the United States. *The Fleuron* was a handsome, copiously illustrated, quarto volume of many hundred pages, issued annually between 1923 and 1930. The first four volumes were edited by Oliver Simon and printed at the Curwen Press in London, the remaining three by Stanley Morison and printed at the Cambridge University Press. Essays on a high level of research and scholarship were written on all matters of typographic interest, current and historical, design, type, illustration, calligraphy, biographies, book reviews, etc., etc. On this side of the Atlantic, the first issue of *The Colophon*, a book collectors' quarterly, appeared in 1930. Nevertheless, it was a child of the twenties in its scope and typographic elegance. About one half of the articles were printed by Elmer Adler at his Pynson Printers in New York; the balance of each issue was distributed among fine presses with complete freedom of design. Ultimately all the best American and European presses were represented, and *The Colophon* became a valuable repository of contemporary graphic art and printing at its best. *The Colophon* was published with interruptions and reincarnations until 1950. Anyone interested in the adventures to be met in writing, making, and collecting books—in bookmen's talk—will find enormous pleasure now as then, in the handsome quarto pages of *The Colophon*.

THE AFFLUENT DECADE IN AMERICA

In the multiplicity and diversity of his work, 1920 to 1928 was one of Rogers' most productive periods. Secure in his own studio during a congenial relationship that had been established at the Printing House of William Edwin Rudge in Mount Vernon (a suburb of New York City), Rogers was also employed as typographic advisor to the Harvard University Press in Cambridge, Massachusetts, and was on a monthly retainer as consultant to the Lanston Monotype Machine Company of Philadelphia.

As on other occasions in Bruce Rogers' life, time, place, and opportunity came together—logically and inevitably. The apparent fortuity of a casual luncheon meeting brought Rogers to William Edwin Rudge, the dedicated proprietor of the only printing house in the United States with the equipment, the staff, the skills, the pride in workmanship, and the love of craft that would give Rogers a solid base for eight fruitful years of significant bookmaking.

Included in an essay by James Hendrickson in the Typophile Chap Book, *B. R. Marks and Remarks* (1946), we are fortunate in having Rogers' own words describing his first meeting with Rudge, and something of the relationship that developed between these two distinguished men of the book:

> My first meeting with Will Rudge was, I think, in 1919, shortly after my return from a three years' stay in England. The place was the dining room of a business men's club on 42nd Street, and the occasion was some sort of conference of six or eight men. I have forgotten why I was included in it, as it was never my custom to attend business meetings, having at that time no professional affiliations of any kind.
>
> I was seated next to Rudge at the luncheon table and noted that he ate but moderately, and drank nothing but water. I was impressed at once by his quietness of manner and voice, in sharp contrast to the somewhat boisterous conviviality of the other men present. In after years I learned that much of that calmness was due to his extraordinary self control.
>
> After the luncheon was over he invited me to accompany him downtown to his printing works, then located on William Street, almost

CHAPTER SIX: 1920–1929

under the Brooklyn Bridge. There we went up several flights in a dingy building, to the floor that housed his office and printing equipment. At first glance it looked like the ordinary establishment of that period, a confusion of type-stands, presses, paper-cutters and all the other usual equipment. But as we walked about I sensed something out of the ordinary; it was partly in the character of the men themselves and partly in the manifest understanding between them and their employer. There was an atmosphere almost of a co-operative enterprise, as though they and Rudge were partners in the business (which, indeed, later they became at Mount Vernon).

On the way downtown Rudge had suggested that possibly we might collaborate on some basis or other, and later in his office we discussed the possibility again. I had, on my return to America, been asked by Harold Murdock, newly appointed manager of the Harvard University Press, to become the printing adviser to that press—a position that would occupy only a portion of my time but would require occasional visits to Cambridge. So I suggested to Rudge that it might be well to begin with a few single commissions, just to see how the arrangement would work out.

This he agreed to, and the first thing I planned for him was Carl Zigrosser's *Twelve Prints by Contemporary American Artists*, published by E. Weyhe [New York]. The text consisted of only a title-page, contents and a short introduction, to accompany the portfolio of prints. Garamond type was at that time the novelty of the day and at my suggestion Rudge at once got in the necessary large sizes. The work seemed to please everybody concerned, even the author.

During its progress I had an opportunity to make the acquaintance of the principal workmen in the shop, which only confirmed my original impression—that of a picked body of men.

Though to them a mere outsider I had never had more instant and thorough co-operation in carrying out my ideas. In the eight years of my connection with the press this feeling of friendly co-operation and helpfulness was continually confirmed and intensified.

THE AFFLUENT DECADE IN AMERICA

My engagement with the Harvard Press then required my presence in Cambridge for two or three months, to help reorganize the work there. On my return to New York I found that Rudge had acquired a stone building in Mount Vernon, only a short distance from his own residence, and was busily engaged in moving his whole equipment to that admirable location. It is well known how he afterwards developed it into the finest printing establishment of its size in any part of the country.

The prospect of working in such agreeable surroundings helped on my decision to accept his proposition and we speedily concluded the agreement. I was to give him the first three days of every week, or alternatives as occasion might warrant. This worked very well at first, but I soon found that it was not always practicable to work for half a week on a particular piece of work, then drop it, to take it up again the following week; so before long I was spending almost every day at Mount Vernon, whether engaged on the work of the press or on my own commissions; in fact there was never any strict accounting of time on either his part or mine.

At first my desk was in a room of moderate size, between the office and the work-rooms; but when the building alterations were made and the splendid, open-roofed reception room and library with its great fireplace was completed, Rudge urged me to use it as a studio. But that was emphatically *his* room and I demurred, feeling it was much too splendid a place to house my small affairs. So I was given an even larger work-room on the second floor, which was soon fitted up with drawing tables, filing and type cabinets, and a large antique armoire which I had bought at an auction house in University Place. This helped fill the room and provided an excellent hat- and coat-closet.

Later on, Frederic Warde, lately back from Europe, came in to occupy a desk at one of the large windows, where he pursued his own course of work. Still later, in 1928, when I returned to England for a residence which lasted four years, Warde succeeded to my position as designer for much of Rudge's work.

CHAPTER SIX: 1920–1929

In the meantime the press had taken on a new aspect — almost that of a school of printing. Young men from various parts of the country, and even one from England, began to drop in and ask Rudge for jobs; and in every instance he would say: "Well, take off your coat and go out to the composing room (or the press room) and the foreman will put you to work." I never knew the wage agreements, but most of them stayed — with or without wages.

It became almost a reversion to the old apprenticeship system, and the result was to assemble quickly a group of men, some of them just out of college, who really wanted to learn the profession and craft of printing in its best aspects.

It is perhaps invidious to mention names, but amongst them were the late Frederic Warde, Peter Beilenson, Edmund B. Thompson, Joseph Blumenthal, Earl Widtman, John Fass, Roland Wood, Ernest Morgan, Walter Kahoe, Melvin Loos, O. Alfred Dickman, Ralph Duenewald, Milton Glick, James Hendrickson, Edgar Wells, and Herbert Simon of London. It is significant that many of these newcomers in the printing trade now manage their own establishments successfully on something of the basis that they had learned at Mount Vernon.

All in all I spent eight productive years working with Rudge, and no collaboration could have been happier for me. He left me an entirely free hand and unhesitatingly backed up nobly even my most unpromising projects, with new types, papers, equipment — everything — whether they were likely to prove profitable or the reverse.

I have often speculated upon just what value the connection was to him; but if it was an unprofitable one he never so much as intimated it to me. Our association was from first to last a congenial one to me at least and, I trust, for him as well.[2]

At this point it may be permissible to introduce a personal note. As the reader may have observed, your present reporter was one of the young apprentices mentioned above. Thanks to the rare generosity of William Edwin

THE AFFLUENT DECADE IN AMERICA

Rudge to aspiring young men, I was sent to the composing room at the Rudge plant, there met metal type for the first time and there enjoyed my first sniff of a can of printer's ink. That was in 1926, and although I did not meet Bruce Rogers until several years later, I could boast that on my first job in printing I worked directly under the world's greatest book designer. The Rogers studio was on the second floor. The composing room was directly underneath on the first floor.

As the years slipped by, and some of us did indeed set up our own shops, we frequently met Rogers at various functions. Later, a warm personal friendship was established, especially in visits to his home in New Fairfield, Connecticut. Everyone in those years addressed him by his initials, or talked and wrote about him, as "B.R." In England, too, he was B.R. to his friends. Consequently in succeeding pages of this book he will often be referred to in that manner.

Until the middle years of the twentieth century, many of the long-established, large, American publishing houses and several of the prominent university presses owned their own printing plants. Shortly after Bruce Rogers returned from England, the Harvard University Press, with well-equipped book production facilities, asked him to accept an appointment as Printing Advisor to the Press. The starting date would be in January of 1920. His duties would call for the improvement of the regular Harvard trade books as well as some of the more important printed matter for the University. He would also be at liberty to use their plant facilities for occasional private clients. On acceptance Rogers spent much of the first few months of the new year in Cambridge. When he began to devote more time to Mount Vernon, he was nevertheless in Cambridge at least once each month. At first he had a desk in the general office, then soon moved to the shop floor where he could work more closely with the compositors and pressmen, to the benefit and pleasure of all concerned. The relationship with Harvard lasted until 1936. After Rogers returned to England in 1928 the association became only consultative and honorary.

Rogers designed about thirty books during his years at Harvard, as well

CHAPTER SIX: 1920–1929

as catalogues and other ephemera, and was available for general consultation and advice. According to David T. Pottinger, production manager at the Press, B.R. "gave each of his thirty or so run-of-the-mill Harvard books more detailed attention than most typographers would ever dream of giving to their prize items."[3]

Of the books designed and printed at the Harvard University Press, four of the limited editions were selected by B.R. among his "successful thirty." Of these, two volumes, *The Passports Printed by Benjamin Franklin at His Passy Press* (1925) and *Benjamin Franklin's Proposals for the Education of Youth in Pennsylvania* (1927)(plate 21), were printed for the William L. Clements Library in Ann Arbor, Michigan. One of Rogers' beautiful books was *The Wedgwood Medallion of Samuel Johnson, A Study in Iconography* by Chauncey Brewster Tinker (plate 22), a quarto published by the Harvard University Press in 1926. The fourth title among the selected thirty was a slender octavo volume, *John Barnard and His Associates*, printed in 1927 for The John Barnard Associates. These four books, and four others, were made during the 1920s in Cambridge, Massachusetts, hand set from type cast from the original Baskerville matrices. The story of the recognition and location of this type takes us back to Bruce Rogers on the other side of the ocean.

Browsing in a Cambridge bookstall shortly before he left England, Rogers found and purchased an original type specimen sheet of the Baskerville type printed in the eighteenth century by John Baskerville (1706-1775), its designer, who was himself appointed University Printer at Cambridge in 1758. From that sheet Rogers was able to identify the origin of a type (currently available from a French type foundry—Fonderie Bertrand) as having been cast from the original Baskerville matrices. Due to wartime restrictions, he was unable to order and import any of the type to England, but had a quantity shipped to the United States, which ultimately became the property of the Harvard University Press. Only the 14-point size was ordered. When a smaller size of type was needed for subsidiary matter, Rogers turned to Oxford type as a comfortable companion. (After the Second World War the original Baskerville matrices were generously donated to Cambridge University by Charles Peignot, typefounder of Paris. And Rogers had earlier donated the Baskerville specimen sheet to the University Printer.) Among other typographic refinements Rogers made at the Harvard University Press, he ordered fonts of Fournier type ornaments from France, and induced the Monotype Company in Philadelphia to cut long descenders for their Caslon type in use at the Press.

The limited editions which had been designed and printed for Harvard or for outside clients carried Bruce Rogers' name in the colophons in several variations such as "Typography by Bruce Rogers," or "Printed under the direction of Bruce Rogers." His own device, the thistle mark, appeared in only one book, *The Portraits of Increase Mather* (1924) by Kenneth B. Murdock. An elegant quarto, 250 copies of the volume were privately printed for William Gwinn Mather of Cleveland, Ohio.

In closing his essay on the Rogers years at Harvard, Pottinger wrote of being "thankful that we have been able to see genius at work even though we could not penetrate the heart of its mystery."[4]

The books and ephemera printed at the Rudge plant in Mount Vernon, the work done at Harvard, the elaborate type specimens made for the Lanston Monotype Corporation, and a few books done at other printing shops show an almost bewildering typographic dexterity. Of nearly one hundred titles, printed for an assortment of institutions, book publishers, and private clients, no two books were alike in design and in the manipulation of type. Rogers thus commanded an orchestration of subtle elements in the uses of type, ink, and paper, never before conceived.

Rogers' experimentation with type ornament and its uses reached full expression during these years. He found a natural affinity between the individual pieces of type ornament and the small pieces of type that make up the alphabet—those tiny units of lead with which printers have fashioned their books since the fifteenth century. Rogers enjoyed the infinite variety possible in the arrangement and juxtaposition of these individual units, as may be seen in reproductions in these pages. But reading about subtleties of book design and seeing reproductions are but poor substitutes for the real thing. Your present reporter hopes that these pages in your hands will provide the

CHAPTER SIX: 1920–1929

urge to see and handle the actual books themselves. The Bruce Rogers books were widely collected during his lifetime; they may be seen in major libraries in the United States and England.

Among the thirty books that Rogers said (in 1943) were outstanding among a lifetime's production, thirteen were produced between 1920 and 1928. Four of these, printed at the Harvard University Press, have already been mentioned. Of the nine titles from Mount Vernon, only two, the *Champ Fleury* and *Ancient Books and Modern Discoveries*, were of large format and of a substantial body of text. The remaining seven were relatively small or slender books, but each was a rare typographic gem. If time and space would allow, it would be instructive and a pleasure to write about all the books of this period. Instead, we will, briefly, describe below the nine which Rogers called "successful."

The Journal of Madam Knight, with an Introductory Note by George Parker Winship (plate 23), is a charming 12mo, completed in an edition of 525 copies during B.R.'s first year in Mount Vernon. The publisher was Small, Maynard & Company, Boston. The text is a sprightly account of a journey from Boston to New York during 1704 by an observant lady of good family, recently widowed. Rogers resisted the temptation to make this a quaint colonial period book. Instead, for the text, he chose the Garamond type, of French origin, which had been newly issued by the American Type Founders Company. The text was embellished by a few line drawings in the manner of the eighteenth-century French wood engraver, J. B. Papillon. Curiously, Rogers chose Caslon for the title page. But he never hesitated to mix typefaces or historical periods which, in the hands of lesser designers, would, to say the least, have been typographic misadventures.

Night and Moonlight by Henry D. Thoreau (plate 25) was made in 1921 for publication by Rogers' friend, Hubert R. Brown. It is a slender, small 16mo of only twenty-four pages—a typographical jewel set in Garamond type without decoration except for a lovely, two-color woodcut headpiece by Florence Wyman Ivins. In the prospectus for this little volume, Rogers announced that he intended to print several small books whose subject would be his own choice. Of *Night and Moonlight* he wrote, "Though one of the shortest, it is perhaps the most poetic of Thoreau's studies of landscape. He definitely intended to give it that quality, aiming as he himself says, 'to add to the domain of poetry'; and in turn, I have endeavored to make it an addition to the poetic side of book-making." The edition was four hundred copies including eighteen on Japanese paper.

In his bibliography, Frederic Warde wrote (pages 37-38) that, "The 'blonde' effect of *Night and Moonlight* is due in part to the use on the title-page of Goudy Open capitals and to the little crescent-moon brackets that surround the page-numbers. These brackets were made from open-face capital O's, which were cut in half."[5]

Priapus and the Pool (1922) by Conrad Aiken (plate 24) was one of several books Rogers made for Maurice Firuski, proprietor of the Dunster House Bookshop in Cambridge, Massachusetts. Rogers here had the challenge of designing a book of contemporary work, with uneven lines of verse. For the type he chose Linotype Original Old Style, a face of neither great beauty nor distinction, but here used with classic simplicity (proof again that the capacity to use a type with grace is of greater importance than the type itself). This is another of the few volumes without decoration produced by Rogers during this period. Its only embellishment is the Dunster House monogram in color on the title page. It is a beautiful book, worthy of honor among the "thirty" — an example of the magic possible with nothing more at hand than type and ink and paper. Designed as a square octavo, the edition was 425 copies, with fifty on handmade paper, signed by the author.

The Pierrot of the Minute by Ernest Dowson (plates 27/28), a small book, page 7 x 4½ inches, of only some fifty pages, completed in 1923 for the Grolier Club, was one of Bruce Rogers' greatest achievements. Its combination of type and ornament is, simply, a rare work of art.

In March of 1921 the Grolier Club invited six American designers and printers each to make a book "with a free hand," the title to be chosen from a list of rather short texts submitted by the Club. The final book was not to be taller than a royal octavo, the cost to the Club not to exceed $4.50 per copy for an edition of three hundred copies, printed and bound. After Mr. Updike apparently declined the invitation, the final list of printers and

CHAPTER SIX: 1920–1929

their books was: Bruce Rogers, *The Pierrot of the Minute*; Frederic W. Goudy, *Three Essays by Augustine Birrell*; Thomas M. Cleland, *The Compromise of the King of the Golden Isle* by Lord Dunsany; Walter Gilliss, *The Culprit Fay* by Joseph Rodman Drake; John Henry Nash, *Quattrocentisteria* by Maurice Hewlett; and Carl Purington Rollins, *A Lodging for the Night* by Robert Louis Stevenson. The six volumes as a series were offered to the Club's membership for a total of $30.

The reproductions in these pages of Rogers' *Pierrot* give but a faint hint of the ineffable charm of the book itself. For a description of the little volume the present writer defers with pleasure to James Hendrickson, a Shakespearean actor turned typographic designer, who, when a compositor at the Rudge plant, set some of the intricate pages of *Pierrot*. When later the two men became close personal friends, Hendrickson was responsible as "elicitor" for the ultimate completion of *Paragraphs on Printing*. On its page 50 he wrote a long and affectionate footnote about *Pierrot*:

> One cannot help thinking as he turns these exquisitely printed pages how delighted the hapless poet would have been to see his playlet made into such a completely charming little book. Here, if ever, a printer has succeeded in capturing the spirit of his author. Dowson spent much of his thirty-two years of thwarted life in France; so the Deberny types and Fournier ornaments make a pertinent setting for the story of Pierrot and his Moon Maiden in the *Parc du Petit Trianon*. But far beyond this the designer has caught the light and graceful rhythm of the poem itself. A small page size has been chosen and the author gives the cue for the size of the book in his scenic directions at the very outset: "... On the left a little Cupid on a pedestal ... Pierrot enters ... He is burdened with a little basket," etc. Even the binder's board used for the cover is thin and semi-flexible, so that in all respects the term "dainty" might be applied to this alone of B.R.'s work. The book is covered with a lacquered marbled paper, dark grey in color, suggesting the "summer night," with more gayly colored but still subdued mottles which might be summer garden lanterns or toy balloons; and the

title-label, printed on a natural colored paper, is wrapped around the backbone. The cream colored laid paper used for the text pages is sufficiently thin to fold and to turn easily in so small a book. The Ancien Romain types had been obtained from the Deberny Foundry of Paris in 8-, 10-, and 12-point sizes, the 10-point being employed for the text. It may be noted that the names of the speakers are in 12-point small capitals, letter-spaced; to have put them in 10-point capitals would have made them too prominent, and the 8-point capitals would have been too thin and light. The type measure adopted is of such length as to permit full lines of verse to be printed with only ten carried-over lines for the whole poem. As poetry, and especially a play in verse form, makes a very irregular type page, the ornamental borders have the practical value of giving the pages unity and continuity of appearance. Printing the borders in a dusty old-rose tint makes them sufficiently unobtrusive and yet it adds a certain gayety to the page. On title- and colophon-pages the Grolier arms have been worked into the border design. It should be pointed out that despite the invention displayed in arranging the tiny Fournier vignettes into patterns of sound design, the type matter is never obscured or even challenged, so skilfully reticent is the decorative element. The designer once humorously referred to his printing of *The Pierrot* as "just a bit of French millinery," but this is a description which the more determined of his followers may find it difficult to accept.[6]

The Construction of Roman Letters by Albrecht Dürer (plate 26) is another book in which Bruce Rogers showed his mastery of space — in this instance very small space — and his rare ingenuity in transforming a few typographic elements into a work of art. The edition of 350 copies was made for the Dunster House Bookshop in 1924. There are forty-two pages, 7⅝ x 4⅝ inches; the three-page printer's note was set in Centaur type with a few modifications in the lower case; there are thirty-four pages of the Dürer letters 1⅝ inches tall, each enclosed in thin red printer's rules. The paper is a superb handmade sheet of a subtle light grey; the presswork is especially

CHAPTER SIX: 1920–1929

fine with the Dürer letters printed in a rich velvety black ink of great depth. The lettering, which Dürer said was constructed for the guidance of architects, painters, and others, first appeared in his famous treatise on geometry, *Unterweysung der Messung*, published in Nuremberg, Germany, in 1525.

On Dry-Cow Fishing as a Fine Art by Rudyard Kipling was made in 1926 for the Rowfant Club of Cleveland, Ohio. It is a slender 12mo of twenty pages, 176 copies printed in Oxford type, with some Bernhard Script on the title page, and several decorations in brown and orange drawn by Rogers. In a note on the design, he wrote: "In planning these little decorations for Kipling's amusing fish tale, the color scheme was suggested by my recollections of moon-rises behind the pollard willows along the Cam, in the fens between Cambridge and Ely. One evening a stray red calf ran up and down the bank in the sunset light, bawling for company. . . ."[7]

It is rather strange that Rogers should have chosen this slight volume as one of the successful "thirty" from his large body of work in which there were many other more impressive books of scholarly challenge. Nevertheless, the members of a book club with a major interest in fine printing were no doubt gratified to publish and own this example of typographic virtuosity and charm. Indeed, it may be appropriate here to quote two sentences by Rogers from *Paragraphs on Printing* in justification of his choice: "Finally it may be said that the decorative value of a simple page of beautiful type, beautifully printed, is a value quite apart from the esthetic pleasure given us by any other of the graphic arts. So elusive it is that it becomes difficult to analyze or describe; printing in its essential simplicity occupies a compartment all its own amongst the graphic arts."[8]

Ancient Books and Modern Discoveries by Sir Frederic G. Kenyon of the British Museum (plates 29/30) is one of Bruce Rogers' major achievements—very properly one of the "thirty." Commissioned by the Caxton Club of Chicago, the edition of 350 copies was delivered in 1927. An elegant quarto (page 12½ x 9 inches), its ninety-two pages of text set and printed at the Rudge plant and its thirty full-page plates magnificently printed in collotype by Emery Walker in London, combine to record the epic story of the preservation of man's thought on clay tablets, papyrus rolls, leather, and vellum manuscripts, from 2200 B.C. to the years before the invention of printing.

The involved procedures by which the hand composition of type for *Ancient Books and Modern Discoveries* was finally completed were typical of the extremes to which B.R. would go to obtain his objectives. The details of its production are described in William J. Glick's biography of William Edwin Rudge, a chap book published in 1984 by the Typophiles:

> BR planned the book for Lutetia, a new design by Jan van Krimpen and available in foundry type from Enschedé. But BR did not like three of the lower case letters: the "m," "n," and "e." He chose as substitutes the equivalent letters from Linotype Caslon Old Face. Arrangements were made to have sorts of them cast, properly aligned and fitted to combine with the Lutetia. Because not enough Lutetia was purchased to set the entire book, the text was first set in Linotype Caslon for proofreading and casting off. As usual with BR's books, there was much recasting of lines, even whole paragraphs to avoid uneven spacing, "rivers" and "widows." Finally page proof was approved and the text reset in Lutetia. As the pages for one press signature were set up, they would be printed and the type distributed and the next signature set up. It was supposed that the Lutetia would set line for line with the Linotype Caslon; the Caslon had been chosen on this assumption. This did not always prove to be the case, and it was necessary to do further reworking of many lines.[9]

The decorations for the title page and chapter openings for *Ancient Books and Modern Discoveries* were made by Rogers from pieces of type ornament fancifully and ingeniously combined in clusters. There was even an attempt made to suggest papyrus, parchment leaves, etc. Units from all the headpieces were combined into a single design for the tailpiece. The inspiration may be traced to the arabesque ornaments seen in the books of Jean de Tournes, one of the great printers of sixteenth-century France, much admired by Rogers.

Champ Fleury by Geofroy Tory (plates 33/34), one of the great Renaissance treatises on letter forms, was reprinted by Bruce Rogers on commission

CHAPTER SIX: 1920–1929

from the Grolier Club and completed in 1927. It was a massive accomplishment in design and production, of first importance in the literature of the printed book. It is one of Rogers' most impressive volumes; its inclusion as one of the honored "thirty" can not be questioned.

As early as 1915 Rogers had submitted trial pages to the Grolier Club of a proposed reprint of the Tory work. The projected quarto volume that would run to several hundred pages, with copious illustrations, was considered too expensive by the Club at that time. Whereupon Rogers suggested instead the shorter treatise in the same field of scholarship, *Of the Just Shaping of Letters* by Albrecht Dürer, which he printed in London in 1917.

In 1922, when Rogers was settled in Mount Vernon, he again proposed the *Champ Fleury* to the Grolier Club, which then accepted it. Translation from the French was assigned to George B. Ives.

Geofroy Tory (1480-1533), artist, scholar, and humanist, was one of the major figures of the French Renaissance. Among his many gifts, he was also an illustrator and printer who played a major role in the transition of the physical book from the ponderous folios of the incunabula to the book as we know it today. The first edition of the *Champ Fleury*, written, designed, and illustrated by Tory, was printed in Paris, and published by him in 1529. It is a voluminous work written with abundant classical, philosophical, mythological, and allegorical references, "wherein is contained," according to its title page, "the Art & Science of the proper & true Proportions of Attic Letters, otherwise called Antique Letters, and in common speech Roman Letters, proportioned according to the human Body and Face."

The original Tory volume is divided into three sections or "books." The first contains "the exhortation to establish and order the French tongue by fixed rules for speaking elegantly in good and sound French diction." In the second book "the invention of the Attic Letters is treated, and their proportions are compared to the natural body and face of the perfect man. With many fine conceits & moral lessons concerning the said Attic Letters." In the third book "are drawn in their due proportions all the said Attic Letters in their alphabetical order, of their due height and breadth, each by itself, with instructions as to their right fashioning & correct pronunciation, both

Latin and French, as well in the ancient as in the modern manner." Finally, thirteen complete alphabets were drawn including Hebrew, Greek, Oriental languages, and variations such as *lettre de forme, lettre bâtarde* and others.

The volume that was finally completed in 1927 at the Printing House of William Edwin Rudge is a generally faithful reprint of the original sixteenth-century pages, but enhanced in every detail by Bruce Rogers. Five years were involved in translation and production of 390 copies of this large quarto of 240 pages (12½ x 8½ inches) printed on B.R. Wove Antique paper, with seven copies on a handmade paper in a special binding. The text was hand set throughout in Centaur type; the side notes and other subsidiary data were set in the American Type Founders Company Garamond; and Goudy Old-style was used for the two-line initial letters. There were 130 illustrations and diagrams for which photo-engraved line plates were made. Concerning the meticulous preparation of these plates, Rogers is quoted in the Club's prospectus for its *Champ Fleury* (offered to the membership at $75.00 per copy): "Instead of copying mechanically the imperfections due to over-inking and bad printing, which in the first edition must have caused Tory many a sigh of dissatisfaction, I have tried to reproduce the originals more accurately by re-drawing them over photographic enlargements. The results, while not strictly facsimiles, more nearly approximate the original designs as they were meant to appear, and as many of them did appear in the better-printed edition of 1549."[10] *Champ Fleury* is one of Rogers' greatest achievements.

The Sisters (1928), an unfinished novel by Joseph Conrad (plate 31), with an introduction by Ford Madox Ford, was made into a slender octavo of seventy-two pages, set in Monotype Scotch Roman type with long descenders. The edition of 926 copies on Glaslan paper and nine copies on a green handmade paper were made for Crosby Gaige, a successful producer of plays for the New York stage who had an avocational pleasure in fine books. (For a few years Gaige had his own Watch Hill Press at his Watch Hill Farm outside New York, where books were printed for him by James Hendrickson and Frederic Warde.)

For *The Sisters*, during his last year at the Rudge establishment, Rogers

CHAPTER SIX: 1920–1929

went so far as to make ingenious combinations of type units and type ornaments serve as illustration rather than limiting them to their more normal use as abstract decoration. The reproductions here on plate 31 show the narrow strips that formed the chapter headings. Rogers discussed their purpose in *Paragraphs on Printing*. He said, in part, "The type decorations proved unexpectedly difficult because of the limited space they were planned to occupy. With only about a quarter inch of depth and the width of the page as dimensions, it proved a matter of many days' work and many failures before adequate representations of Russian wheat fields, Paris, or the road in Spain were recognizable. There was not much in the text upon which to hang ornamental suggestions of it. In the Introduction the phrase in the first line, 'a beast from the jungle' required only a strange animal, some bushes, a stretch of rule simulating grass, and two little ornaments like pagodas to convey the hint of the East."[11]

Perhaps Rogers named *The Sisters* as one of his successful "thirty" because of the unusual and extremely adroit employment of type ornament which he must have considered appropriate to the text. The present writer appreciates the labor and skill involved in this typographic extravaganza, but finds it a *tour de force* to which Rogers never returned in such detail.

The President of the Lanston Monotype Machine Company of Philadelphia, J. Maury Dove, asked Rogers to design the March/April 1922 issue of *Monotype* (their bi-monthly house publication), which showed the Scotch Roman type with the newly added long descenders. The twenty-four-page brochure with its generous format (11 ½ x 8 ½ inches) gave him ample scope for an impressive type presentation. For the decorative borders, headings, and spots, Rogers used existing Monotype material. This issue began an advisory relationship, with a retainer, between Rogers and Lanston that resulted in several impressive type specimens.

In 1923 Rogers designed the brochure announcing the availability on the Monotype of the Garamont type, a new rendering by Frederic W. Goudy, the prolific American type designer. Goudy's version was an adaptation of the type then attributed to Claude Garamond, sixteenth-century French

THE AFFLUENT DECADE IN AMERICA

type designer. (Beatrice Warde's later researches demonstrated that the model for Goudy's Garamont was actually the type of Jean Jannon [1580-1658], which was, nevertheless, a derivative of the original Garamond design.)

The brochure as planned by Rogers consisted of twenty-eight handsome pages, 10⅜ x 7⅛ inches, and printed cover. Its text is an illuminating example of the serious scholarship that was an accepted part of much of the trade during those productive years. The issue contained a chapter entitled "Private Presses in England" by the English scholar Holbrook Jackson; "A Note on Claude Garamond" by W. M. Ivins, Jr., of the Metropolitan Museum of Art; and a "Printer's Note" by Bruce Rogers. In his bibliography, Frederic Warde wrote of this Garamont type specimen: "Mr. Rogers could find no ornaments of appropriate character for this face, which has a somewhat sharper appearance than the foundry version. Even had he wished to, he could hardly have drawn special decorations for a type specimen. Instead, he retouched and somewhat refined the drawing of 'flowers' he had brought from England, and had matrices engraved from these. . . . The whole pamphlet seems to have been done in high spirits."[12]

The very provocative "Printer's Note" by Bruce Rogers, reprinted below, bespeaks an articulate book designer's pleasure in his craft. It appeared as an extended colophon with a bit of characteristic whimsy at the end:

> In the first trials of a new type a printer finds one of the pleasantest adventures to be met in his profession. He has had the opportunity to study founder's proofs of the type in orderly alphabetic sequence, or arranged alternately with *H* and *O* and *m* to test its alignment. He has perhaps even pondered feelingly that cryptic command, "Pack my box with five dozen liquor jugs," which calls up the full resources of the alphabet, along with other pleasant memories; but he has yet to visualize the type as it will appear in actual composition; to try it in all its various possibilities, closely or openly spaced, leaded or solid; to find out and to humor its special peculiarities, its adaptability to rough or smooth paper, its partiality to light or heavy inks.

CHAPTER SIX: 1920–1929

The printer to whom all this does not appeal is hardly worthy of his calling; so it was with pleasure I accepted Mr. Dove's invitation to print an issue of "Monotype," using a trial casting of Mr. Goudy's new version of the sixteenth century design attributed to Claude Garamond. After having the present type before me for a month or more while testing it under all the conditions enumerated above, it seems to me one of the most successful reproductions of an early type that any modern designer has yet given us. Some characters, I am told, have been refitted, and a few modifications are still to be made; but to all intents the type as presented has assumed its final form and will soon be open to the use of printers everywhere. It only remains to add that, as an authority once said I was "still to be reckoned a limited edition man," I must bear out his classification, and incidentally give this note the characteristic colophonic flavor, by stating that this issue of "Monotype," printed from type that will be destroyed (not distributed) after printing, is limited to 20,000 copies.[13]

The industrious Goudy completed drawings for another new typeface, called Italian Old Style, which was inspired by the classic types in noble books printed in Venice during the late years of the fifteenth century. A complete series of sizes of the type in roman and italic was issued by Lanston Monotype in 1924. Again, an elaborate brochure, sixteen pages, 12 x 8½ inches, was planned to launch the type, and Rogers was again asked to design the twenty thousand copies that were to be printed under his supervision at the Rudge plant (plate 32).

For the text, Rogers turned to picturesque pages from the once-popular, three-volume edition published in London in 1817: *The Bibliographical Decameron: or, Ten Days Pleasant Discourse upon Illuminated Manuscripts and Subjects Connected with Early Engraving, Typography, and Bibliography* by Rev. Thomas Frognall Dibdin (1776-1847). Rogers produced a type specimen of extraordinary, even exuberant, attractiveness, including brilliant arrangements of Monotype units for decoration. His informative printer's note follows, with a delicious pun at the end:

THE AFFLUENT DECADE IN AMERICA

The conversation from Dibdin's Bibliographical Decameron, which I have here reprinted, was chosen partly for its own pleasant quality and partly because of its appropriateness to the purpose of this pamphlet. Later bibliographical research has no doubt superseded Dibdin's in accuracy and completeness, but to many of us the charm of his style is as engaging as ever and his taste in printing as unimpeachable; and this brief account of seven early Venetian printers, with its islands of text and oceans of commentary, supplies just the right material for displaying Mr. Goudy's Italian Old Style under various requirements of composition. The new type itself, though showing the study of several of the best early Italian faces, reminds me most strongly and admirably of Ratdolt's fine Roman. Single letters of the font are quite full and round enough to look well in lines of almost any length, and its close fitting makes it especially suitable for composition in narrow measures, as (I hope) the following pages will show. It was, too, an interesting problem to work out a title-page and initials reminiscent of the simple wood-cut designs of the great Venetians, and I found abundant material for them amongst the ornaments furnished by the Monotype Company, even though a few astronomical signs have been pressed into service. In the text initials only have I departed from conventional practice by making photo-engravings in reverse after the designs were composed, to give the black ground effect of the early Italian wood-cut initials.

The mention of islands, above, suggests to me that when my own time comes to be marooned on a desert island (by a party of no longer indulgent friends, whose books I haven't completed, or whose letters I haven't answered) instead of taking along the favorite volumes that most amateur castaways vote for, I think I shall arrange to be shipwrecked in company with a Monotype caster and a select assortment of ornamental matrices. The fascination and amusement—and the occasional happy result—that can be got out of the almost numberless combinations of a few simple units would enable me to cast away for an indefinite period with great contentment.[14]

CHAPTER SIX: 1920–1929

After administrative changes at Lanston, a new president, Harvey D. Best, requested Rogers to design a series of six double-spread advertisements which would appear in the trade magazines. In 1927 these advertisements were collected and reproduced in volume XXI, number 72, of *Monotype*. They provided a dazzling display of typographic originality with lavish and ingenious combinations of various types and ornamental units. In addition to showing Monotype's considerable resources, a few pages of the publication sketched the origins of the Monotype machine and, of course, its virtues. The invention of a machine that would cast its own individual pieces of type and set the type at great speed was the work of Tolbert Lanston, a lawyer working for the United States Pension Office. Patents were filed in 1890 and granted in 1896. (During the 1880s Ottmar Mergenthaler invented a machine that cast lines of type. Both the Linotype and the Monotype, each with its own special advantages, finally replaced centuries of laborious hand composition. In turn, metal type has been made obsolete in the present century by photo-composition on film.)

During the last of his eight years at the Rudge plant, Rogers was called on to make typographic plans for *The Private Papers of James Boswell from Malahide Castle*, prepared for the press by Geoffrey Scott and Frederick A. Pottle. It was an immense undertaking that finally required eighteen volumes issued from 1929 to 1933. The entire edition followed Rogers' detailed instructions, with much of the supervision conducted by mail after his return to England.

The amazing discovery of the private papers of James Boswell (1740-1795) and their acquisition by an American collector may well be the most important literary adventure of the twentieth century. For more than a hundred years the legend had persisted that the private papers, documents, and letters of Dr. Johnson's biographer had been destroyed by Boswell's heirs, who considered his profligate way of life a discredit to the family name.

In 1924 Chauncey Brewster Tinker of Yale edited a volume of Boswell's letters that had somehow turned up in France. In 1927 he placed a notice in

THE AFFLUENT DECADE IN AMERICA

the London *Times* requesting possible information concerning any existing Boswell manuscript. An anonymous reply led to Malahide Castle outside Dublin, where a Boswell great-granddaughter had, in 1873, married into the ancient and noble family of Talbot. The long and incredible story of how these papers were ultimately found hidden in remote cabinets and chests in Ireland and Scotland, how they were finally sold by a somewhat reluctant Lord Talbot and his wife to the American Lieutenant-Colonel Ralph Haywood Isham in 1928 and for several years thereafter, and their eventual acquisition by the Yale University Library was told in fascinating detail by Frederick A. Pottle in *Pride and Negligence, The History of the Boswell Papers* (McGraw-Hill Book Company, New York, 1982).

As soon as the Boswell manuscripts arrived in New York, Isham, who wanted a sumptuous format for this great acquisition, negotiated with William Edwin Rudge for printing and publication. Rudge agreed to participate in the editorial and production costs and to act as sales and distribution agent. Bruce Rogers was to be the designer. He chose Monotype Baskerville for the text. The many reproductions of Boswell documents were printed with great fidelity by Rudge in the use of his Aquatone process. The volumes as issued were magnificent examples of the arts of the printed book. They are, surely, the most impressive single monument of the Rudge/Rogers association (plates 35/36).

Production details were described by Rogers in the edition's prospectus: "The format and typography having been placed entirely in my hands by Colonel Isham, I have chosen a style flexible enough to accommodate the various papers, journals and documents comprised in the collection. No especial effort has been made to secure an air of antiquity, but by the importation of a recent English reproduction of John Baskerville's famous eighteenth century types it has been possible to present the text in a form typographically harmonious with Boswell's individual mode of expression. The size of the different volumes is determined, as a rule, by the dimensions of the facsimile documents. The format in most cases is a quarto (8½ x 11½ inches and 9¾ x 13⅛); but a number of the volumes will be in folio. Hand-

CHAPTER SIX: 1920–1929

made paper is used throughout; a Maidstone paper has been chosen for the quarto volumes and Ronneby for the folio. Five hundred and seventy copies only will be printed...."[15]

The eight years during which Rogers enjoyed the security of his studio in Mount Vernon had been very agreeable working years. However, his domestic situation was rather less successful. Late in 1919, some months after the return from England, Mrs. Rogers found spare living quarters in New York, which proved to be only temporary. In a letter of 21 October of that year, B.R. wrote to Carl Rollins that his wife had taken "a year's lease on three small rooms and a bath on the *roof* of the 10-story apartment building where Elizabeth is now boarding. They were servants' quarters but they form a little suite in themselves — and the manager has agreed to put in the bath, electricity for cooking — etc. etc... So Anne and Elizabeth at least are settled for the winter, and I'll try it for as long periods as I can stand N.Y...."[16]

As the decade unfolded, Mrs. Rogers' health was fragile and she was away from time to time visiting relatives. Meantime, daughter Elizabeth married a young man, Alan Burroughs, whom she had met when they were both students at the Art Students League in New York. In 1922 their child was born, but the marriage had failed, and Elizabeth became seriously ill. Mrs. Rogers, none too well herself, went to live with her daughter and infant grandson in Pennsylvania, where a practical nurse, Mrs. Pierson, was employed to be of help. But in 1924, Elizabeth died, only twenty-three years of age. Despite a family life punctuated with tragedy, Rogers seemed able to keep his private unhappiness separate from his work.

Because of B.R.'s need to move from country to country to fulfill his typographic missions, and because of his wife's continuing poor health, the security of a permanent home had never seemed possible. In 1925, however, he impetuously bought a house in New Fairfield, Connecticut, to which he did come from time to time, and where, after his wife's early death (in 1931) and his final return from England in 1935, he spent the last twenty-two years of his life. Having completed the purchase of the house, Rogers wrote in great glee, on 12 October 1925, to his friend Carl Rollins:

> But listen!! and this is most exciting! — we have bought a place in the country — !!! Though I don't see when we are ever going to live in it. It's 5 miles N.W. of Danbury. We saw it first on our return from a week-end with the Hardens and I went over it then. Drove up again the next week and closed the deal — it's an old house — corner-stone dated October [1817] I think — the former owner thinks 1777 — In excellent repair and almost perfect original condition. Sits high on a hill with view downwards on all sides and, to the eastward, almost to N.H. I should say, 16 or 17 acres with fruit, grapes and an excellent garden. Small hay-fields, divided by stone walls and quite a large forest of young birch trees. When we found the owner asked $5500 only, we felt we couldn't afford to let it go — so offered him $4500 and got it for $4750 — with several pieces of furniture, etc. I'll send you some photos of the house if they turn out well. — It is really an architectural gem of that period.[17]

During these years when much of the time Rogers was living alone in hotel rooms, there were close ties to friends, including some of his young associates. James Hendrickson wrote of one such relationship in an essay printed in *Heritage of the Graphic Arts*:

> Another venture of this period, to which BR was more or less a godfather, was your reporter's June House Press in the country back of Stamford, Connecticut. . . . The June House, so called for the June family, one of the earlier owners, was a small frame dwelling dating back probably to the close of the eighteenth century. It had a big fireplace with built-in Dutch oven. BR produced more than one excellent omelet before this fireplace, commenting as he did so, "Some of these days we will look back upon this as the happiest time of our lives". . . .
> BR took a lease on a water-mill on an adjoining property which he named Cuckoo Mill with the hope, never realized, of one day having

CHAPTER SIX: 1920–1929

a press there. Somewhere there must be copies of a New Year's greeting card with a charming drawing by BR of the Cuckoo Mill in winter. The implication of the name was BR's playful reminder that, like the cuckoo bird which is known for its custom of laying its eggs in the nest of other birds for them to hatch, he had never had a press of his own and his books were always produced in other men's printing houses.[18]

Concerning the mill, B.R. wrote to Carl Rollins on 16 November 1925 from his studio in Mount Vernon: "I've at last found a mill! as the enclosed snapshots will show is about 5 miles north of Stamford, about 1 hour from here, driving — and within a mile from where Wells and Hendrickson have set up their hand-press. I've been spending week-ends with them.... Can't you and Margaret run down to Stamford next Saturday — if it's a good day — and look it over — It has been used, up to within two years and *looks* as though, if you turned on the water it would go."[19]

Rogers' dream of a press and a water mill, together in sylvan surroundings, was never realized. Although he enjoyed brief possession of the mill, intuitively he never allowed himself to be burdened with possession of an active press and its responsibilities. He had an active and cultivated mind with many interests; nevertheless, he pursued his life in bookmaking with tenacity and singular absorption. Unlike Daniel Berkeley Updike, who deplored talk about printing during social gatherings, Rogers relished his typographic friendships and the discussions they produced. Rudolph Ruzicka, a scholarly graphic artist and friend, wrote in his reminiscences, published in 1986 by the Grolier Club: "And he was actually quite fascinating, Rogers. First of all, he had remarkable eyes. The pupils were very sharp and sort of green, unlike any other eyes I have ever seen in a man. Moreover, he was so entirely conscious of his craft — which was, of course, brought by him to the point of art — that he seemed never to talk about anything else. He talked quite freely about it. For example, at meetings of the Typophiles . . . he always brought examples of his work in progress, proofs and so on, to show people. However, at the same time, he had the effect of utmost modesty, almost withdrawn into himself. But that was merely a manner."[20]

THE AFFLUENT DECADE IN AMERICA

In 1928 Rogers began an exchange of letters with Lawrence of Arabia that ultimately blossomed into the printing of the *Odyssey of Homer*. The story of its progress from the original conception to its completion in London will be told in forthcoming pages.

The eight years in the United States had been a very busy period that left a large and varied body of work. Rogers' energies and talents had been on call from many directions. With the *Odyssey* in prospect, and with plans under way for the Centaur type to be cut for the British Monotype machine, he looked forward to his return to England. Much of the work done during the preceding decade had been rather decorative. In the forthcoming years, in congenial and less hurried surroundings, with the English countryside as a constant delight, Rogers would commit himself to a few undertakings of the greatest importance—volumes that would exhibit a classic austerity.

In June of 1928 he received an honorary degree of Master of Arts from Yale University. Soon thereafter Rogers closed his studio and brought to an end the fruitful years with Rudge at the rock-sequestered printing house in Mount Vernon. In the summer he and his wife sailed for Europe accompanied by their six-year-old grandson and Mrs. Pierson, the child's nurse.

The affluent decade came to an end late in 1929 with the calamitous arrival of the Great Depression. William Edwin Rudge died in 1931 in his fifty-fifth year. The printing house survived for only another five years, during which time it completed printing and publication of the Boswell papers with strict adherence to the original Rogers plans.

1928   1935

Homer · Pacioli · The Oxford Lectern Bible

At fifty-eight years of age Rogers arrived in England, where, in the years ahead, he would produce his ultimate masterpieces. Three books, *The Odyssey of Homer*, *Fra Luca de Pacioli*, and the Oxford Lectern Bible, would exhibit a purity and nobility of design free from historic influences and typographic decoration with which some of his earlier work had been associated. Furthermore, with few other demands on his time he was able, in the production of these books, to devote himself to the realization of supreme craftsmanship.

After leaving New York, before settling down to work in London, the Rogerses went to the Continent to meet English friends. Writing from the Hotel Danieli in Venice on 27 September 1928, B.R. told Henry Kent, "We have been here several days, having planned to meet Emery and Dorothy Walker and Sydney Cockerell, who are on an Adriatic cruise ship." At the end of this long letter in which B.R. wrote about what they had seen and done during a happy time with their friends, he added, "Travelling seems to agree with me, and I never felt better. I thrive on Italian food and wine, even the *vin ordinaire*. We avoid the hotel meals as we like the more regional cooking of the popular pavement restaurants."[1] After the Walkers and Cockerell left on their ship for the Dalmatian coast, Rogers and his wife went on to Florence, and after visiting a few other cities in Italy, returned to London.

Another happy interval came at Christmas. B.R. and his family were invited to spend the holidays at Daneway, the Walkers' country home. There were festivities which B.R. remembered as "a dip into rural Christmas festivities that few Americans see." The Walkers and their guests had been invited to spend Christmas eve at the neighborly, impressive home of Sydney Blow, the Duke of Westminster's architect. Blow had been a pupil of Ruskin and had acquired William Morris tapestries and wallpapers, and other works of art. B.R. wrote, "There was a great candle-lighted tree in the living-room and as we were late we found the presents being distributed to the tenants and their children. . . . After the tree was stripped we all adjourned to the dining-room and kitchens for supper — hams, turkeys, ducks, and a goose — all raised on the estate. It fairly outdid Irving's Christmas Dinner. After we had stuffed ourselves there was a dance in the parlor in which everybody joined, and then the party broke up. . . . We . . . reached Daneway about midnight."[2]

By February of 1929 the Rogers family had been installed in a small Elizabethan cottage in Slindon, a lovely area some fifty miles from London, with a southward view to the sea, northward to the woods and downs of Sussex. B.R. reported in a letter to Kent that they were not altogether comfortable, "but we are not accustomed to any high degree of that commodity, so we'll pull through." The household, in addition to himself, included Mrs. Rogers, who was in frail health, their grandson, and Mrs. Pierson. B.R. went to London every Tuesday morning and stayed until Friday at the Strand Palace Hotel.

The three days each week in London were becoming interesting and productive. In a long letter of 12 February 1929 to Kent, it was evident that Rogers was making headway with several projects. More important, perhaps, he revealed his genuine pleasure in the people he was meeting, and his obvious (if unstated) pleasure in being in England:

> I'm getting some work started, at last. It has been slow business finding out where to go for materials and assistance, as what I'm doing is so different from Walker's usual work that they can be of little help, at present.
>
> My work on the Monotype *Centaur* is nearly completed, and I have

CHAPTER SEVEN: 1928–1935

begun to plan the pamphlet with which it is to make its public bow —
(being Centaur it ought to make a kick — let's hope it will). The pamphlet's text is a paper by Pollard. I have lunch with him and Scholderer
(who is a particularly pleasant fellow) about once a week, when I can
get to the B. Museum. But I've recently discussed typography and other
things with two much more famous men. You'll think this great swank
— but I was invited to luncheon at Bernard Shaw's, and found him not
at all an arbitrary person — at least at his own house. Mrs. Shaw was
especially charming, and has a much keener eye for printing than G.B.S.
Walker and Cockerell and Dorothy Walker were the other guests and,
being old acquaintances of the Shaws, it was almost like a family party.
My invitation came by way of T. E. Lawrence, who had written Mrs.
Shaw of my being in London — and as he's a special friend of hers, I
suppose she wanted to see if I might possibly corrupt him on his return
to England.

You may have read that he is back now, and he came to see me last
Thursday. For two hours we both talked as hard as we could and I only
left in time to go to a luncheon at the Guildhall with Geo. W. Jones.
Lawrence isn't at all a disappointment — quite the reverse. He is small
& quiet and self-contained and extremely modest. His letters were so
interesting that I own I was almost regretful when I heard he was coming back to London — but he's a great success personally.

You already know about the *Odyssey* so I can write of it to you (sub
rosa). Lawrence has four books done and they are in my hands — a
whacking translation, I think — the best ever. He has two more books
pretty well roughed out, but he goes over it and re-writes 6 or 8 times.
He is delighted with my scheme for the book and hasn't a suggestion
of change to offer, and he is particularly pleased with the new Centaur
type. Bartholomew and Cockerell had both written me querying the
lower-case y — but almost the first thing T. E. said was, "What a
splendid y — the most difficult letter of the alphabet!" — so it stands.
[This y was re-designed for the Monotype version.]

He's coming in again on Thursday and hopes to be in civilian clothes so that he can lunch with me.

I was the guest of honor two weeks ago at a dinner of the Double Crown Club — of which I'm an Hon. Mem. Nearly everybody in the English printing world was there: Pollard (who rarely dines out), Hornby, Maxwell of R. & R. Clark, Chapman and Shand from Oxford, Roberts and Bartholomew and Lewis from Cambridge, Morison and Geoffrey Keynes and both the Simon brothers and a lot of others whose names I can't recall. Holbrook Jackson gave the address (on Burton's *Anatomy*) and showed all the XVII Cent. editions. The discussion afterwards was most amusing — particularly Chapman's contribution to it.

Lunched a day or two later at the First Edition Club — having finally agreed with Dr. Williamson on a date convenient for both of us, after trying to meet ever since we arrived in August. (Please tell Miss Granniss this.) They have a pleasant club house (perhaps you visited it) but it has a little too private a flavor to suit me.

Today being Shrove Tuesday I lunched on pan-cakes at the Oxford Univ. Press' London office in Amen Corner with Hubert Foss, their music editor, whom I met in N.Y. I was a little too late to see Milford, who was called away — but I hope to see him soon. They occupy an old house once belonging to Wren, and Milford's own office is one of the most beautiful rooms I've ever seen — all original work. From the roof of an addition to the old building is the finest view of St. Paul's that can be had.

Thus endeth the present chronicle of my activities — mostly eating and drinking, you'll say. But it's 8 P.M. and I haven't had any dinner yet — so must be at it again. Am going to Gow's in the Strand, in the next block, sit before an open grate and have a thick chop, a potato baked in its jacket, some celery and a large pot of ale or stout. Wish you were with me. Gow's was a favorite and constant eating-place of Goudy's when he was in London, and someone said it had been named for him—but as the English never say die they called it just Gow's.

Give my best regards to Miss Granniss and say I hope to write to her direct some day soon—when I feel that I've really got some work under way. Also my remembrances to all my friends you know (which about includes the whole number, I imagine).

You can share parts of this letter, if you choose, with any of them you may think would be interested.[3]

Due to Mrs. Rogers' failing health, the household returned in April to London, where B.R. rented a small furnished house in Golders Green, a suburb near Hampstead Heath. It was about a mile to the London Underground, then twenty-five minutes to the heart of London. "Although it is said to be very healthful," Rogers wrote some time later, "we have some of us been sick with colds or flu nearly all the time & Brucie has been out of school for nearly half the time since last Sept. But he grows, and grows stronger apparently."[4]

THE MONOTYPE CENTAUR

Rogers' first task since his arrival in London the previous summer had been supervision of the cutting of the Centaur design by the Monotype Corporation. The first printing of the complete font in sizes 10-point to 72-point appeared in a pamphlet of quarto size, in September 1929. It included an historical essay, "The Trained Printer and the Amateur, And the Pleasure of Small Books" by Alfred W. Pollard, and a "Printer's Note" by Bruce Rogers. In his opening paragraph Rogers reminisced: "In writing a short introductory note to this first piece of printing in my Centaur type as now made in various sizes by the Lanston Monotype Corporation, it is, first of all, a pleasure to record my vivid recollections of the friendliness and forbearance with which, many years ago at the British Museum, Mr. Pollard met the importunities of an unintroduced American visitor who had then only recently decided to become a printer. The store-houses, not only of the British Museum Library but also of Mr. Pollard's own richly varied knowledge of books and printing, were readily thrown open to me; and they have always remained open during twenty-five intervening years—a standard by which to measure work done and a stimulus to new endeavour."⁵

The paragraphs that followed described the origin and development of the Centaur type (already discussed, pages 27 to 37). Rogers closed his Note with expressions of satisfaction with the Monotype cutting and his reason for choosing an italic by another hand: "When, last year, in response to many appeals it was decided to have the type reproduced for machine composition I naturally turned to the 'Monotype' method of composition and casting, on account of the satisfaction I have had in the past with the results obtained by that method. Its flexibility, combined with its great range of type sizes, has enabled me to produce work that would have been difficult even for the hand compositor, and which could not, so far as I am aware, have been done successfully by any other system of machine composition. The care and skill with which the 'Monotype' has reproduced the Centaur design has resulted in a type approximating my first idea of it even more closely than the earlier cutting did.

"Being incapable of devising a suitable Italic letter I induced Mr. Frederic Warde to make a modified version of his beautiful Arrighi Italic to accompany my Roman characters. His type . . . seems to me one of the finest and most legible cursive letters ever produced."⁶

A few months after the machine cutting had been made available, Rogers wrote to Rollins in a letter of 9 February 1930, expressing annoyance at the time consumed:

> Having the Centaur type cut has meant 3 or 4 times the amount of work I anticipated—besides all the unlooked-for delays. It was necessary to make 4 sets of patterns to cover the great range of sizes—with individual modifications of certain letters, almost without number. The design called for so many departures from their usual practices that even after the first size was satisfactorily made, they were all at sea about the other sizes—and I was equally so, except by experiment. So really I've made *four* types.
>
> I don't at all feel that the design justifies all the trouble it took to

CHAPTER SEVEN: 1928–1935

make — but they were all enthusiastic about it and I had no choice but to go on. Thank goodness that's done with — or nearly so, for small details are still cropping up occasionally.[7]

Bruce Rogers was always vexed and impatient with the ever-present delays in his work, yet he seemed not to realize that he himself was the indispensable cause. Trial and error is an essential ingredient in the ultimate achievement of a work of art. Rogers' genius saw flaws and limitations to be overcome that were not apparent to lesser minds. In the multitude of details involved in the production of a book, he would never let anything go that he found less than right. Neither should he, nor could he, have done otherwise.

In the above-mentioned letter it is agreeable to find that after a year in England Rogers could again express his pleasure in living there: "The satisfaction of living over here isn't so much in the 'high spots' that I mentioned earlier as in the daily contacts with casual people, everywhere. They still are human and polite, and one's nerves are not continually being irritated by the man in the street. And in the country you can still find slow-going, almost 18th-Century, characters and conditions & they are still miles away from up-to-dateness. I must say I like it. It's almost like being a boy again in the middle west — or at Montague in 1910."[8]

After Rogers had agreed (early in 1929) to undertake design of a new lectern Bible he was drawn into close touch at the Oxford University Press with John Johnson, Printer to the University, with whom he soon formed a very warm personal friendship. At about the same time Johnson had completed reorganization of the Fell type series and wished to prepare a specimen showing. The series was acquired about 1670 by gift to the University from Doctor John Fell, Dean of Christ Church in Oxford. The bequest consisted of an assortment of matrices for complete alphabets, purchased from the Netherlands in a range of sizes for hand composition.

Johnson asked Rogers to design a type presentation that would "for the first time exhibit the truest value of the faces by founts specially cast for it."[9] It would seem that B.R. proposed "The Rime of the Ancient Mariner" —

a favorite since his college days—as a suitable text for a small book. The suggestion was accepted and in 1930 the Oxford University Press issued the famous poem in a slender volume of forty-eight pages, with an introduction by Sir Arthur Quiller-Couch, 750 copies printed. The prospectus announcing publication referred to the lyrical genius of the poem and stated, "It has been the aim to carry over something of the lyrical quality into the typography and decorations of the book itself . . . which in their design have a direct relation to the text."[10]

The high-spirited typography of the book is clear evidence that Rogers again enjoyed the use of type ornament—this time to interpret and decorate a haunting tale of the sea. Two units, including a dolphin he had originally planned for the *Odyssey*, were especially cut for him. For the *Ancient Mariner* he used the leaping dolphins in an exuberant border for the title page; elsewhere he arranged the dolphins and other units to suggest the sea, the sun, the flight of the albatross (plate 37). In a letter to Rollins (29 January 1931) Rogers wrote, "It may be sheer conceit—but I somehow think that this border will stand as long as anything I've done with type."[11]

The poem itself was set in 14-point Fell type, with the marginal commentaries and the colophon set in a smaller size of italic printed in brown. The introduction was set in a cutting that Stanley Morison identified as having been designed by Claude Garamond; pages vii and viii of the *Mariner* were set in an italic cut by Robert Granjon for Christopher Plantin, the great sixteenth-century Antwerp printer and publisher.

The strain of family illness and the responsibilities involved in the commitment to several books of great importance showed in letters B.R. wrote to his two close friends, Kent and Rollins. However, all was not gloom, and one rewarding evening should be recalled. St. John Hornby, who had produced and published the sumptuous Ashendene books, invited B.R. to dinner and asked him to bring T. E. Shaw if "Lawrence of Arabia" would care to come. Shaw, an admirer of the Ashendene books, was pleased to accept. Rogers wrote, "Hornby lives in Chelsea on the river in one of the two most beautiful modern houses in London, both by Edward Manson,

CHAPTER SEVEN: 1928–1935

the architect. The house is beautiful and its occupants equally so. Hornby and his son are both six-footers of the guardsman type and Mrs. Hornby and their daughter-in-law were of course exquisitely dressed. Lord Hambledon, one of Hornby's partners, was also there."[12]

By April of 1931 the Rogers family had been living in England for almost three years. Mrs. Rogers was critically ill, Mrs. Pierson had had a nervous breakdown, and grandson Bruce was not robust. With the financial situation, as always, extremely difficult, plans were under way to return temporarily to the home in Connecticut during the summer. It is not surprising that in writing to Kent, Rogers showed his not infrequent inclination to melancholy and self-doubt. In his long letter of 24 April he wrote:

> Your letter of Mch. 8 & Apr. 16 has just arrived, and shames me into an immediate reply—for I think it must be either the second or third letter you have written me since I last wrote to you. But I have been in no mood for correspondence, having nothing, or almost nothing, pleasant to chronicle—and a catalogue of illnesses (not my own), troubles with dentists, landlords and other creditors, does not supply a basis for happy epistolary performances. So I have practically written only the letters that had to be written, in the endeavor to keep matters from getting too muddled—in connection with my affairs—both here and at home. Even at that it is a fair guess that writing has taken 75 per cent of my time—which ought to have been devoted to pushing ahead the various projects on which I am engaged—though "various" is hardly the word, as they number but two. I have started others, carried them on for a little, and then paid the bills and shelved them. I think I am suffering from the same disability that you very shrewdly attribute to Rollins; though it attacks me from a slightly different angle. Whatever may be the merit of what we have accomplished, it doesn't satisfy that inner sense which insists that it isn't quite what we should have done—either in character or in performance—and that, on the whole, we have wasted a tremendous lot of time and effort, without any very tangible results to be really proud of. It didn't matter so much when

we were 35 or 40 — there was still plenty of time in which to do the perfect thing — but at 61 (which I reach next month) one begins to look backward rather than forward, and regrets form quite as large a proportion of reminiscence as do self-gratulations and pride.

I am quite in agreement with you, that I have had magnificent backgrounds (largely through sheer good-luck). One of the greatest of older American presses, three great University Presses, and one of the youngest and most modern & enterprising smaller establishments — no other modern printer has had such a *mise-en-scène*. But what have I done to fill in the foregrounds? That's where the failure is. I've done little better than "niggle" — concerned with trifling details and (more or less) meticulous technicalities. Consider, in contrast, the splendor of Bodoni's performance (against a background of his own creation, too) or the Whittinghams, or the Didots, or a dozen others — even Morris's, granting his taste.

The fact is I haven't been big enough for the job, preferring to do the pleasant thing and the easiest (at the time). Specimens, rather than correlated and progressive achievements. So that, notwithstanding some tons of fairly well-made books like the Houghton Mifflin subscription sets — Emerson, Thoreau, Hawthorne, etc. which I can fairly claim — my place in printerdom will always be that given me by Rollins himself — as "Play-boy" — and I'm getting too tired to play.

Life too has been a "niggling" performance — at least since 1912. I can honestly say that of all the years since then only 6 or 8 months have been spent in thoroughly satisfactory surroundings and with wholly congenial people (I mean as a daily routine) — and those were the months I lived in the old house — the Holley house — at Cos Cob. Greenwich Village and upper New York and New Fairfield and London are all equally alien to my ideal of pleasant existence — for various reasons, of course.

Your picture of my many interesting contacts — social and professional — in London, is amusing through its very falsity. I have never led so monotonous and hermetical an existence as through this past 1½ years. My only dinings-out have been at the four meetings of the Double Crown club, where the younger and more energetic men make me feel decidedly out of it, when I do go. I rarely see even Walker or Merton, and our last effort at entertaining at home was having Geo. W. Jones and his daughter to luncheon on their return from America, *last November*. No theatre, no music, a movie once a month perhaps and an occasional Sunday bus-ride, form the sum total of diversions. Not a glimpse of the country except from the train to Oxford—where I was last in October, I think. Compared with mine you live a hilarious life, I'm sure. The only men I see with any regularity are Morison—with whom I lunch about once a fortnight—and Johnson, of Oxford, who always asks me on Tuesdays, his day in town. *He* has been the great and interesting addition to my acquaintance during this stay in England, and (I venture to say) the interest seems to be mutual. I can't quite understand it, from his point of view. A man of great executive ability and scholarship together, he rather scorns "design" in printing and "special editions," for which I stand in his eyes. Yet he seems to thoroughly enjoy our meetings, which work together over the Bible inaugurated. You would never think, what is really the fact, that he himself holds the most influential position, the greatest power, for good or evil, in the English printing world, if not in the whole profession. He is using it wisely, on the whole, but it might be still further extended in my opinion (which I don't hesitate to express to him privately). The Bible, we both hope, is going to be the greatest extension of his principles, in one direction at least, and I am really sorry, for his sake, that I shall inevitably have such a large share in the attention it will doubtless attract—whether of approbation or condemnation remains to be seen. It will probably be a mixture, according to the point of view of Bible readers.

I have seen Updike's Prayer Book at the British Museum and am glad I did not have to print it (now that I have the Bible in hand). It is, naturally, a splendid piece of Updike's work, but I doubt if, from its very nature, the Prayer Book can be made really beautiful. At any rate no one else could have done it better (except the binding I saw). I have a letter about it to show you when we meet.

Which same will, I hope, be in July, if you are in or about N.Y. at that time. We are coming back on one of the slow (and cheap) American Merchant Line boats, about the middle of July. But I am not going to divulge the exact date—to avoid possible reception committees. I remember keeping one waiting four hours in 1919, while we got our ten trunks, etc. through the customs. Never again, for me.

You sent me a "Toast" from the N.Y. *Mirror* last autumn, which celebrated my suppositious birthday anniversary (or so you thought) so in return I am sending you a suppositious portrait (made at the request of the Monotype Co.) to celebrate my real anniversary (61st) next month. I consider the photographer's a marvellous achievement, considering the subject.

I do hope this finds you in better health than when you wrote; and that you won't suffer from such an over-dose of personalities as this letter contains. Yet where can we be personal if not in letters to one's oldest and dearest friends?[13]

That letter reveals one aspect of a complex personality. Rogers declared with some frequency that after work in hand was completed he would renounce forever the nagging details of the typographic process. On the contrary, to the last hours of his eighty-seven years he remained firmly committed to the vagaries, and enjoyed the satisfactions, of the printed page. Despite a natural diffidence, Rogers had a rich reserve of warmth and wit. Let us join him on a happy occasion when, surrounded by friends and associates for whom he had a profound affection, he showed his pleasure in the work that had brought him fame. On 24 June 1931, just prior to a return to the United States, with the Monotype version of the Centaur type completed, he was tendered a luncheon at the Savoy Hotel in London by W. I. Burch, Managing Director of the Monotype Corporation. Called on to speak, Rogers said:

Americans are very generally credited with a weakness, amounting

CHAPTER SEVEN: 1928–1935

almost to a mania, for after-dinner (or after-lunch) oratory. If this be true, I am far from being a representative American. Being of a sedentary habit, I have always been constitutionally unable either to think or to talk on my feet, or to speak impromptu to even so small and intimate a gathering as this one.

I have therefore been constrained to follow the example of George Washington and prepare a *Farewell Address*, a title which I warn you not to take too seriously; as I have every hope of coming back in the Spring —if you have one next year.

I cannot help feeling that in the minds of at least two or three of this company (I mention no names, but I mean the gentlemen who direct the fortunes of the Monotype Corporation), regret at my approaching departure (if such a paradox in terms may be used) must be tempered by a feeling of relief. As my ship casts off her mooring warps I can imagine them saying to themselves (and possibly to one another) "Now we can get on with our work without any more outside interference."

Last year, at a dinner in this very hostelry, one of the Directors of the American Monotype Company said that typographic cranks like Morison, Goudy and Rogers were called "Damn nuisances" by the practical men at the head of great businesses—but he had the grace to add that they had all come to recognize that we were more or less necessary nuisances, and, on better acquaintance, even sometimes rather agreeable ones. I hope I may be included with the latter class.

My friend Jones here successfully combines both functions (I mean of typographic crank and man of business), so his ideas on the subject are much more valuable than mine, and I leave the further development of it to him. I can only add that I have never in the least degree been allowed by our genial host and his staff to feel that I *have* been a nuisance to them—it is only my conscience that tells me so.

English visitors to America almost invariably bring back flattering tales of American hospitality. I can assure you that I am taking back across the Atlantic equally vivid memories of the hospitality of England. And not only of days, or weeks, or even months of it, but of nearly three years. This present occasion bears witness that after a stay of that length the cordiality of your natures still maintains its warmth. Where did this legend of the cold-blooded English spring up?

I have often been asked by American visitors what I have been doing all this time in England, and my invariable reply is "Developing a Corporation"—an incontrovertible fact, in which I have been largely aided and abetted by our accomplished host, who, as you know, is a genius in that line as well as in type production. In fact, one of his ideals seems to be the production of *Rogers Fat-Face* or *Rogers Distended*. Had I not possessed just enough will power to resist at least some of his blandishments, I should probably be going back, not in the cabin of a freighter, but in its hold—covered with placards: "Use no hooks."

One of my oldest and dearest friends in New York, whom most of you know—Harry Kent, the secretary of the Metropolitan Museum—himself a printer, the designer of all the distinguished work issued from the Museum Press, and the most civilized American I know—in one of his recent letters to me remarked that of all living printers (and most dead ones as well) none had more varied or more interesting backgrounds for their work than I have had. Kent meant, of course, my many fortunate associations with leading printers and with the presses of the great Universities on both sides of the Atlantic. And if, against such splendid backgrounds, my own performances have not always been worthy of the scene, I can truthfully say that my foregrounds have always been richly filled with men notable in their own diverse professions—men whom I am proud to call my friends, and of whom this little gathering is strikingly representative.

First of these, in time, was George Mifflin, head of the great printing and publishing house of Houghton Mifflin, under whose guidance my real apprenticeship was served.

While still at the Riverside Press, friendships were formed with two men, one of them happily here with us today, to whom I owe more than can ever be requited. I refer, of course, to Sir Emery Walker and

CHAPTER SEVEN: 1928–1935

to Alfred Pollard, my dear friends for twenty-five years, both of whom are still giving to younger men that invaluable counsel toward perfection by which I myself profited so largely.

Then, in 1917, came that pleasant association with the late J. B. Peace at the Cambridge University Press — productive of lasting friendships at Cambridge even if (in those difficult years) of no very considerable results in the form of books.

It was while at Cambridge that I first met Stanley Morison, then carrying on at the Pelican Press during the (I think enforced) absence of Francis Meynell. My friendship with Morison ripened rapidly later on in America — during one of our heat waves — when he found me apparently the only American sympathetic with his desire to lie in his shirt-sleeves on the floor of a waiting room in one of New York's largest hotels. I have since found him equally sympathetic with my preferences amongst the less pretentious luncheon places of Fleet Street and Soho, and my admiration for *John Bell* (untrimmed). I regret that I cannot yet follow him far into his enthusiasm over Ichabod Dawks and newspaper print — present example excepted.

In 1919 my fate led me to a connection with the Harvard University Press and with William Edwin Rudge, whose recent untimely death removes one of the great figures from printing in America — a man who for ten years was my staunchest friend and who was always ready to uphold and promote even my least practicable enterprises, never counting the cost to himself.

Then, in 1928, after ten years of steady work, resulting in something like over-production, I returned to England; to renewed association with Emery Walker and to new friendships with Burch and his associates of the Monotype.

George W. Jones, that Master of Master Printers, whom I had already met in New York, and whose kindness and hospitality have been boundless, to my family as to myself: Lewis and Roberts at Cambridge, splendidly carrying on the tradition which I had had the honour of assisting Peace to revive: John Johnson at Oxford — that remarkable example of scholar turned printer—with whom many of my pleasantest days in England have been spent—the latest no longer ago than Saturday last when, as guest of honor, I had my first experience of a printers' beano.

These noted names by no means complete the list, but they prove my contention, that the finest products of bookmaking may be not books but friendships. And when I reflect that in however small a measure I have been instrumental in causing Monotype, if not to lie down, at least to sit down with Linotype; Oxford with Cambridge; Typographic Crank with Expert Engineer . . . then in the words of the Psalmist (at any rate I hope they were his) "My cup runneth over"— as Burch is always mindful to ensure.[14]

The Rogers family returned to their home in New Fairfield, Connecticut, in June of 1931. Rogers called it October House because of the inscription on the cornerstone which indicated that the house had first been built in October 1771. During the summer a three-week vacation was spent on the shore near Boston and a week with the Rollins family at Montague—the Dyke Mill to which B.R. always returned with nostalgic pleasure. The remaining summer days were spent at October House where much time was given to the necessary restoration of an old house. B.R. complained about the motor traffic, as rural Connecticut became increasingly attractive to city weekenders.

After only two months in the United States, B.R. again became restive. In a letter to Emery Walker inquiring about the progress of the *Odyssey* translation, he closed with, "I find that I am already counting the months before returning to England. After having seen most of my friends here I shall be quite ready to come back. America has little to attract one that is not to be found in even greater measure in England—and I find my strongest sympathies are there rather than here."[15]

During the ensuing months there were visits by family and friends to October House. Rogers prepared additional drawings for the *Odyssey* roundels, and read and returned galley proofs with his comments. He remained

CHAPTER SEVEN: 1928–1935

in touch with the Rudge plant where the Boswell papers were on press, and where the eighteen volumes would be completed within another two years. *A Garland for John Donne* was designed for the Harvard University Press, and occasional trips to the Grolier Club in New York laid the foundation for another notable book, *Fra Luca de Pacioli*. It is probable that during these months a relationship was begun with George Macy of the Limited Editions Club. *Aesop's Fables*, the first volume Rogers designed for Macy, would be printed at the Oxford University Press in England and delivered in 1933. Ultimately Rogers designed twelve books for the Limited Editions Club that will be treated in later pages.

During the autumn Mrs. Rogers became critically ill and was taken to Danbury Hospital. B.R. wrote that his work was at a standstill, that he had been unable to do anything more than visit the hospital, take care of the marketing and other errands. After several operations for cancer, Mrs. Rogers seemed to improve, but died at sixty-four years of age on the thirtieth day of December 1931.

We have no means of knowing the depth of Rogers' grief. Inasmuch as he had spent so many of his years moving from place to place, and had himself lived alone in hotels so much of his life, he seems to have made the transition to a single existence with considerable fortitude.

In the spring he returned to England, where unfinished work called him back. His grandson and Mrs. Pierson (familiarly called "Pinky") remained at October House, where the local farmer and his wife stayed on for another year, and where Esther Davis, the faithful housekeeper, came daily for many years ahead. Rogers returned to October House in the autumn, and thus continued his transatlantic commitments each year until 1936.

Back in England without his family, Rogers found congenial quarters in London at the small, Dickensian Anderton Hotel on Fleet Street. His workroom was in Clifford's Inn, an old building, on the floor above the Emery Walker printing establishment. Now footloose, B.R. enjoyed the small special restaurants in Soho, frequent meetings with friends and associates, browsing in bookshops, and roaming the English countryside he loved. We can follow his activities in letters to Kent and Rollins—letters that were clearly less troubled than they had been before his wife's death. They told more about the amenities of his existence and were less concerned with the minutiae and drudgery of book production.

In July 1932 he visited the Walkers in Daneway, where he found his friend seriously ill. But before returning to London he enjoyed a four-day excursion to Saperton in the scenic Cotswolds, where he made drawings and watercolors of the "beautiful wolds, hills, valleys and streams."

During that summer, Henry Watson Kent was also in England, and the two friends spent many days traveling together. In an essay Kent contributed to the Typophiles' Chap Book, *B.R. Marks and Remarks* (1946), he wrote about his friend, "I never saw him with a guide book in his hand, or a gazetteer, or any of those who's who sorts of books to be found in the breakfast room of every English country house. How he got his wide knowledge of persons and places has always been a mystery to me. He knows his London with its Thames, Oxford, Cambridge and the counties, especially Gloucestershire, better, I'll be bound, than most of those who live in those places."[16] And about Rogers in Cambridge: "Among the happiest days spent with B.R. were those connected with the river Cam. Punting, you may not know, is one of his accomplishments. To be asked to sit in one of those shallow, flat-bottomed, square-at-both-ends boats, while he, standing, propels it with a pole in most correct form—as well as any reverend senior—past the backs of the colleges, was an honor and a delight."[17]

Rogers remembered with pleasure an evening he had spent on the Thames: "A little group of young men affiliated with printing, publishing or advertising (they call themselves The Galley Club) invited me to go down to Greenwich for a supper at the old Ship Hotel, where the Parliamentary whitebait dinners used to be held....

"We embarked at Westminster Bridge on my favorite little Thames steamer, the *Maldon Annie*. It took about an hour to reach Greenwich and on the trip I was able to point out so many docks and different kinds of ships we passed that, not being at all nautically wise, they made me the Club Admiral. Quite a title: 'Admiral of the Galleys'! I thus out-rank my own

CHAPTER SEVEN: 1928–1935

grandfather who was captain of a stern-wheel steamboat on the Wabash."[18]

Having come to England in the spring, Rogers remained until autumn. During those months he advanced work on the *Pacioli*, the *Aesop*, and the Bible. After four years of preparation and production, the *Odyssey* was brought to completion and publication in November 1932.

THE ODYSSEY OF HOMER

The initiative that made possible a new translation and a magnificent printing of an *Odyssey of Homer* came from Bruce Rogers. In a brief foreword to a collection of letters from Lawrence of Arabia, Rogers explained:

> It was in 1927, while reading Lawrence's "Seven Pillars of Wisdom" for the first time, that it occurred to me that its author was the very man to translate the Odyssey anew. It was a book that I had long wanted to print in a style fitting its splendor as a story, but I had never read any of the existing translations with complete satisfaction: they all lacked something vital. Here, at last, was a man who could make Homer live again — a man of action who was also a scholar & who could write swift and graphic English.
>
> But where was he? At that time he was to me a half-legendary person and I knew only that somewhere out east of Suez was an air-craftsman who had legally changed his name to Shaw. I casually mentioned my project & my perplexity to Col. Ralph Isham, who startled me by exclaiming, "The very thing for Shaw to do! I'll write him tomorrow — he's in Karachi."[19]

Isham did write and offered to finance publication. Shaw replied on 2 January 1928:

> When your letter came I took the Odyssey down from the shelf (it goes with me, always, to every camp, for I love it), and tried to see myself translating it, freely, into English. Honestly, it would be most difficult to do. I have the rhythm of the Greek so in my mind that it would not come readily into straight English. Nor am I a scholar; I

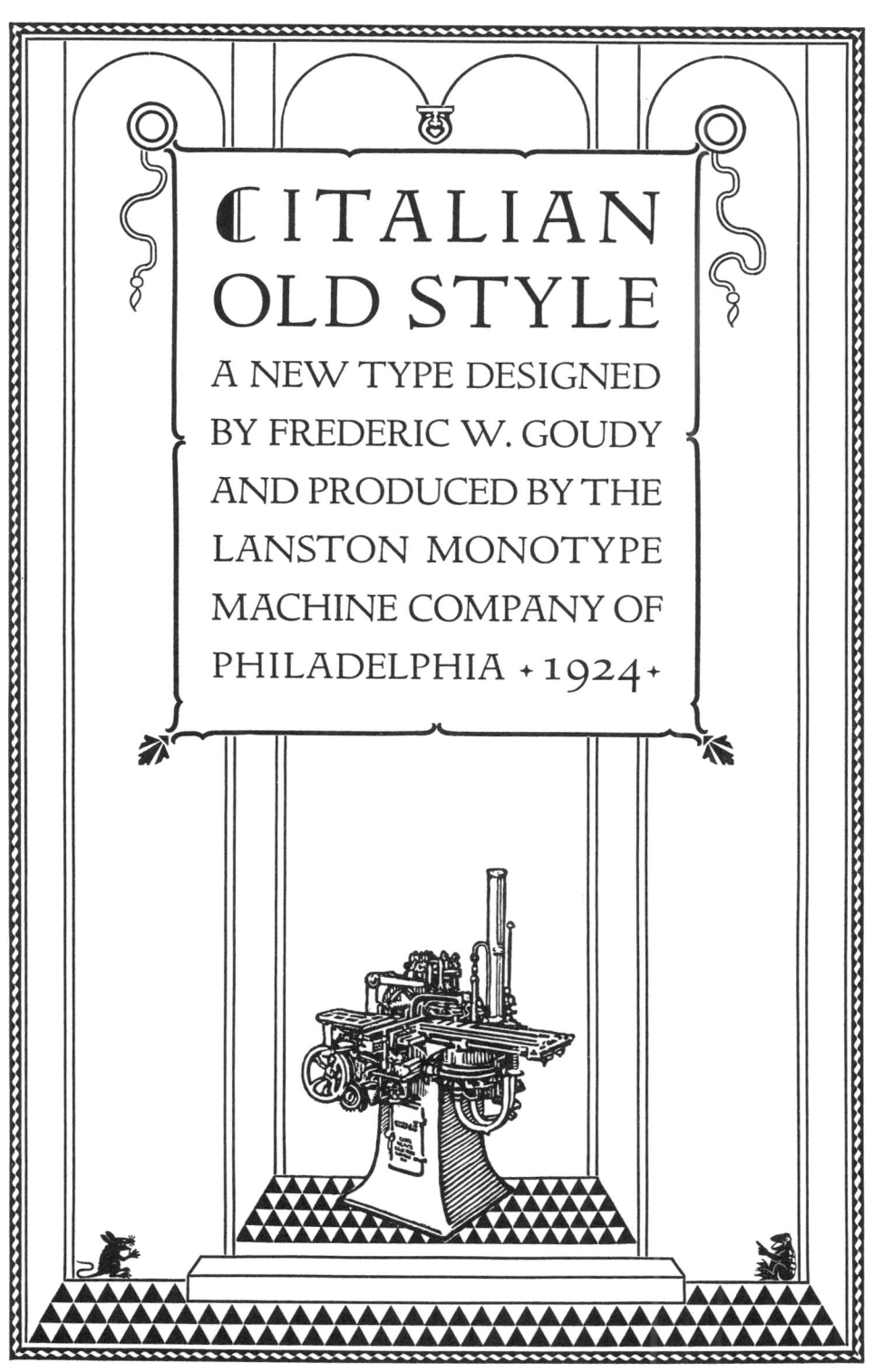

PLATE 32. (1924) Reduced

CHAMP FLEURY · BY GEOFROY TORY
TRANSLATED INTO ENGLISH AND
ANNOTATED BY GEORGE B. IVES

THE GROLIER CLUB · NEW YORK

1927

 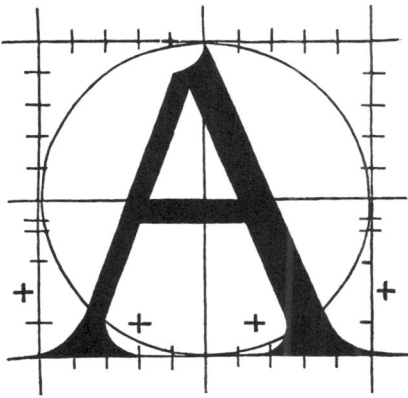

THE letter A, here twice drawn in its square, and formed of the I alone, is as broad as it is high, that is to say, of ten units* of breadth and ten of height, contained between eleven perpendicular & as many horizontal lines. To draw it properly, five turns of the compass are needed, for describing which I have marked the centres with the sign +, where the fixed foot of the compass should be placed, in order to describe the circumference. Observe, besides, that I place this same sign +, outside the square, on the perpendicular median line of the aspirate H, of the I, the O, the S, the X, and the Z, not for the foot of the compass to be placed thereon, but to show that there is the top of the said letters, which are almost the same at top & bottom. There is, however, & must be, some difference, except in the O, the outer circumference of which is entirely uniform. A is in shape pyramidal and triangular, in accordance with natural reason. We see that things built up to a point are more solid and durable than those which are as broad at the top as at the bottom. In another aspect, the A is somewhat in the shape of a compass; its two feet represent the feet of the compass, & the top the joint. The cross-bar of the A signifies a rule: a covert indication that, properly to design and draw Attic letters, the compass & the rule are necessarily required. Furthermore, A has its legs thickened & furnished with feet,—just as a man has his legs and feet for walking and passing on,—to tell us covertly that from it, the first letter in alphabetical order, we must pass on to B, & C, & all the other letters according to their arrangement. A must be pronounced with the mouth open, & as I have said before, where Martianus Capella is quoted—*sub hiatu oris congruo solo spiritu.* Which thing the Italians observe with care, not only

* *Corps.*

PLATE 34. *Champ Fleury.* Reduced

THE JOURNAL
OF
James Boswell
1775-1776

His Jaunts to London, Oxford, Birmingham
Lichfield, Ashbourne, Bath and Bristol

AND

His Meeting with
MARGARET CAROLINE RUDD
Spring, 1776

PRIVATELY PRINTED
MCMXXXI

JOURNAL IN SCOTLAND
1775-1776

Saturday 11 *November.*

MY intemperance was severely punished, for I suffered violent distress of body and vexation of mind. I lay till near two o'clock, when I grew easier, and comforted myself by resolving vigourously to be attentively sober for the future. There is something agreably delusive in fresh resolution. Reason tells me that I cannot expect to be better restrained now than by former vows; and yet, like a man who has had several blanks in the lottery and fancies that another ticket will certainly be a prize, I flatter myself that I shall have it to say that from the 11 of November 1775 I maintained an uninterrupted moderation in drinking. Indeed the horrid consequences with which my last night's debauch might have been attended may probably awe my mind. Sir Walter dined with us. I went to the New Church and heard Mr. John Gibson preach very well on "Glory to God in the highest." I drank coffee comfortably at home, and my Wife seemed to have quite forgotten my bad conduct. Her unhappy sister, Sir Walter's Mother, was still in Edinburgh, ill of a consumption, and preparing to go to France. I allowed my Wife to go and see her, as the feelings of natural affection may be indulged towards an unworthy object when dying. Her debasing herself by a mean marriage

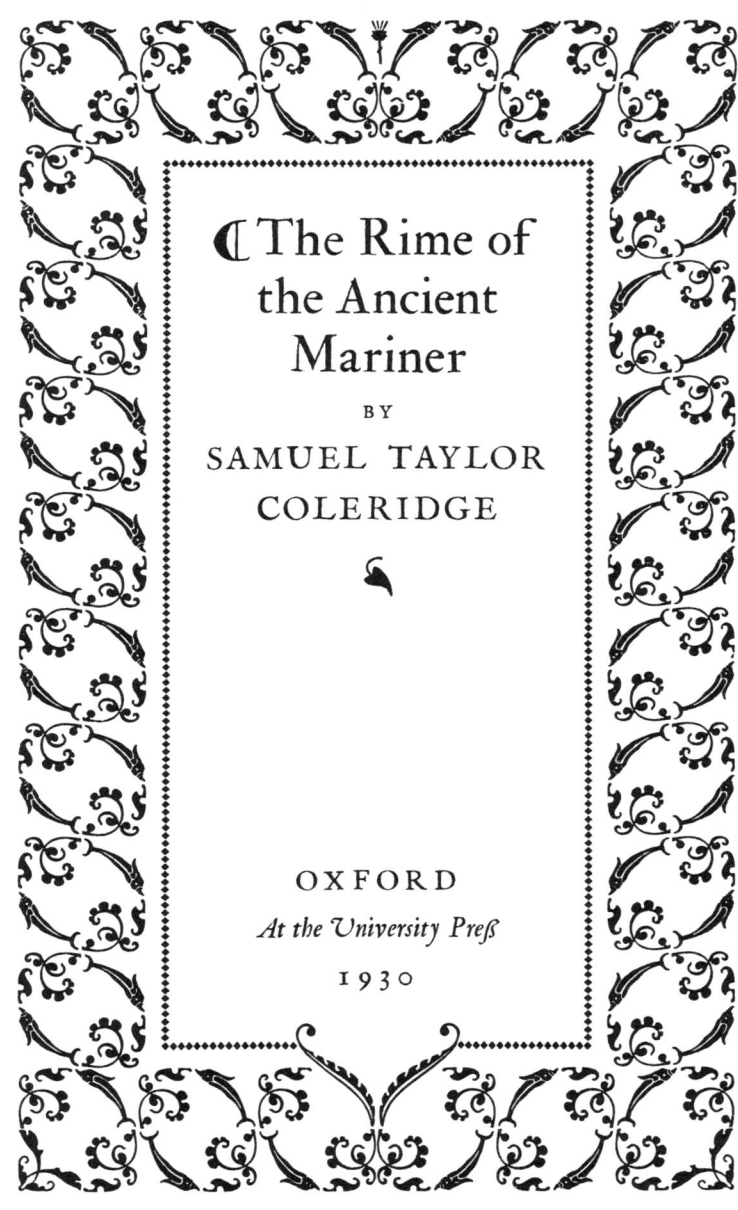

THE ODYSSEY OF HOMER

PRINTED IN ENGLAND

1932

O DIVINE POESY
GODDESS-DAUGHTER OF ZEUS
SUSTAIN FOR ME
THIS SONG OF THE VARIOUS-MINDED MAN
WHO AFTER HE HAD PLUNDERED
THE INNERMOST CITADEL OF HALLOWED TROY
WAS MADE TO STRAY GRIEVOUSLY
ABOUT THE COASTS OF MEN
THE SPORT OF THEIR CUSTOMS GOOD OR BAD
WHILE HIS HEART
THROUGH ALL THE SEA-FARING
ACHED IN AN AGONY TO REDEEM HIMSELF
AND BRING HIS COMPANY SAFE HOME

VAIN HOPE FOR THEM
FOR HIS FELLOWS HE STROVE IN VAIN
THEIR OWN WITLESSNESS CAST THEM AWAY
THE FOOLS
TO DESTROY FOR MEAT
THE OXEN OF THE MOST EXALTED SUN
WHEREFORE THE SUN-GOD BLOTTED OUT
THE DAY OF THEIR RETURN

MAKE THE TALE LIVE FOR US
IN ALL ITS MANY BEARINGS
O MUSE

BOOK I

By now the other warriors, those that had escaped headlong ruin by sea or in battle, were safely home. Only Odysseus tarried, shut up by Lady Calypso, a nymph and very Goddess, in her hewn-out caves. She craved him for her bed-mate: while he was longing for his house and his wife. Of a truth the rolling seasons had at last brought up the year marked by the Gods for his return to Ithaca; but not even there among his loved things would he escape further conflict. Yet had all the Gods with lapse of time grown compassionate towards Odysseus—all but Poseidon, whose enmity flamed ever against him till he had reached his home. Poseidon, however, was for the moment far away among the Aethiopians, that last race of men, whose dispersion across the world's end is so broad that some of them can see the Sun-God rise while others see him set.

PLATE 40. *The Odyssey of Homer*

THE ODYSSEY OF HOMER TRANSLATED FROM THE GREEK BY T. E. SHAW
[LAWRENCE OF ARABIA]

NE
OXFORD UN

O DIVINE POESY, GODDESS-DAUGHTER OF ZEUS! SUSTAIN FOR ME THIS SONG OF THE VARIOUS-MINDED MAN WHO AFTER HE HAD PLUNDERED THE INMOST CITADEL OF HALLOWED TROY WAS MADE TO STRAY GRIEVOUSLY ABOUT THE COASTS OF MEN, THE SPORT OF THEIR CUSTOMS GOOD OR BAD, WHILE HIS HEART THROUGH ALL THE SEA-FARING ACHED IN AN AGONY TO REDEEM HIMSELF AND BRING HIS COMPANY SAFE HOME.

VAIN HOPE — FOR THEM! FOR HIS FELLOWS HE STROVE IN VAIN; THEIR OWN WITLESSNESS CAST THEM AWAY. THE FOOLS! TO DESTROY FOR MEAT THE OXEN OF THE MOST EXALTED SUN: WHERE-FORE THE SUN-GOD BLOTTED OUT THE DAY OF THEIR RETURN.

MAKE THE TALE LIVE FOR US IN ALL ITS MANY BEARINGS, O MUSE!

PLATE 41. (1940)

The Hesperides Edition

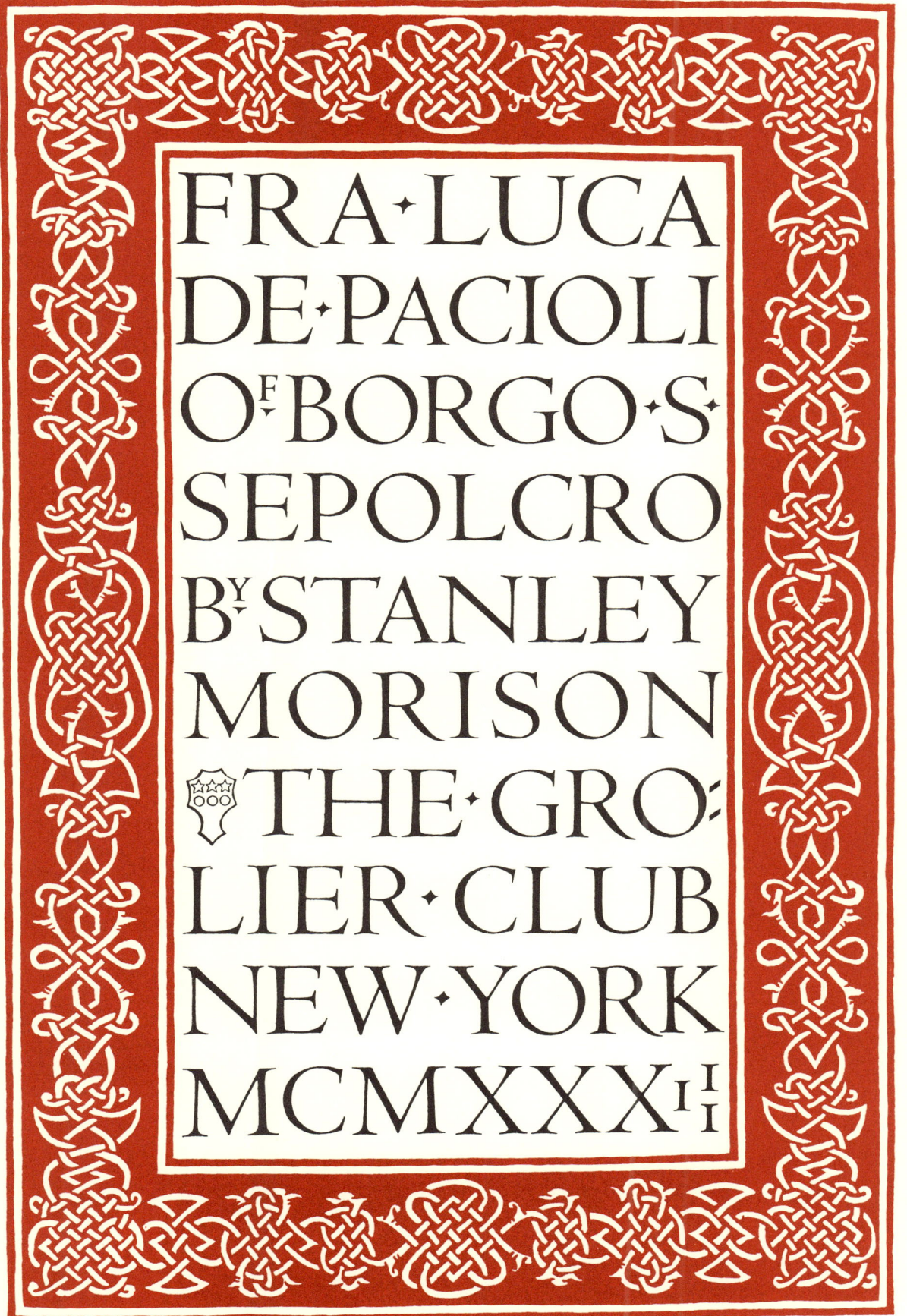

PLATE 42. (1933) Reduced

Fra Luca de Pacioli
OF THE SERAPHIC ORDER OF SAINT FRANCIS

UCA, ZUNIPERO and AMBROGIO were the religious names of the sons of Bartolomeo, surnamed Pacioli, or Pacciuoli (apparently the correct, or at least the earliest form of the name), or in Latin Paciolus, of Borgo San Sepolcro. This small, but not undistinguished, town lay within that part of Umbria which earliest came under the influence of St Francis and of his first companions. The Seraphic saint, having preached, was well received by the inhabitants; they gave him the ancient hermitage of Mont Casale nearby, and it was during a sojourn here that there took place the incident in which St Francis commanded Brother Angelo, a noble young follower, who had repelled three famous but out-of-luck brigands, to go after them and, kneeling, to offer them bread and wine. Brother Angelo found the three not far from the Borgo, as recounted in the *Fioretti* (chapter xxvi) by Brother Leo, who also tells of the subsequent conversion of the three. Brother Angelo became Guardian of the Convent of San Casale. Again, the first place to which the saint came, still in an ecstacy, after receiving the stigmata on Mount Alvernia, was the Borgo. Unconsciously and amid cries of "Ecco il Santo" he reached a leper house a mile beyond, and later came back to Mont Casale. All this was in 1224: Francis died in 1226. But the effect on Borgo San Sepolcro remained, and the fame of St Francis was carried through the world by eyewitnesses and

PLATE 43. Reduced

This letter is taken from B, its rounding extends to a half [thick] limb below the centre. The whole of this letter must be within the intersections except the curved limb, which must pass beyond the intersections to the corner of the square. The said curved leg is to be one-ninth thick, ending thinly in a point at the angle of the square after the manner of curved lines, as you see from the illustration.

PLATE 44. *Fra Luca de Pacioli.* Reduced

Æsop's fables

SAMUEL CROXALL'S TRANSLATION
WITH A BIBLIOGRAPHICAL NOTE
BY VICTOR SCHOLDERER AND
NUMEROUS FACSIMILES
OF FLORENTINE
WOODCUTS

THE LIMITED EDITIONS CLUB

1933

TABLE OF CONTENTS

The Fables furnished with Illustrations are
indicated by ☞ in this Table

☞ 1. *The Cock & the Jewel*   PAGE 1
☞ 2. *The Wolf & the Lamb*   2
    3. *The Two Frogs*   4
☞ 4. *The Frogs desiring a King*   5
☞ 5. *The Dog & the Shadow*   7
    6. *The Collier & the Fuller*   8
    7. *The Young Man & the Swallow*   8
☞ 8. *The Vain Jack-daw*   10
    9. *The Fox & the Goat*   11
    10. *The Man & His Two Wives*   12
    11. *The Fox & the Crow*   14
☞ 12. *The Ant & the Fly*   15
    13. *The Belly & the Members*   17
    14. *The Fox & the Grapes*   18
    15. *The Mouse & the Weasel*   19
☞ 16. *The Viper & the File*   20
    17. *The Peacock's Complaint*   21
    18. *The Countryman & the Snake*   22

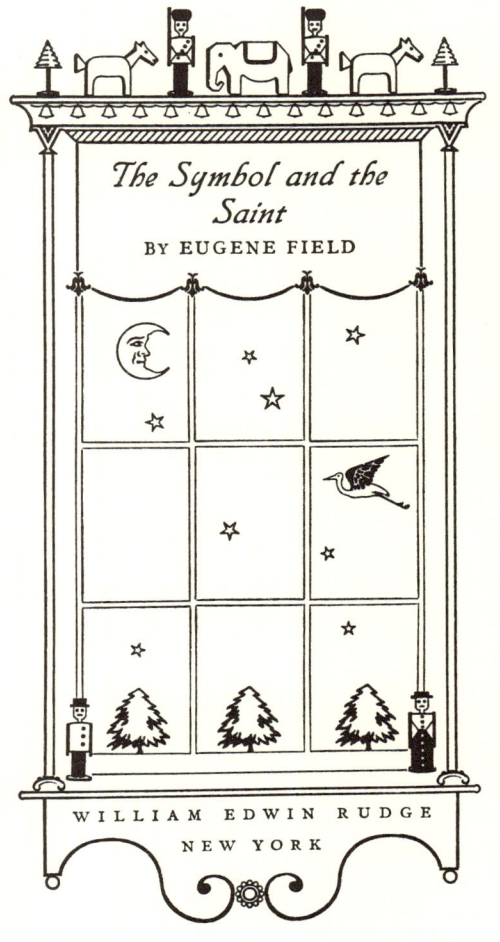

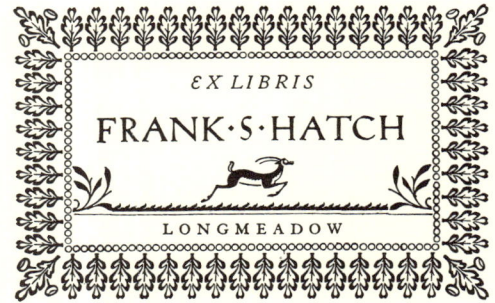

PLATE 47. *The Symbol and the Saint* (1924) and a few bookplates

THE COMEDIES
HISTORIES
& TRAGEDIES
OF

NEWYORK
The Limited Editions Club
1939

PLATE 51. (1939) Reduced

The Two Gentlemen of Verona.

ACTUS PRIMUS, SCENA PRIMA.

VALENTINE and PROTHEUS.

Valentine.   Cease to perswade, my loving *Protheus*;
   Home-keeping-youth, have ever homely wits.
   Wer't not affection chaines thy tender dayes
   To the sweet glaunces of thy honour'd Love,
   I rather would entreat thy company,
   To see the wonders of the world abroad,
   Then (living dully sluggardiz'd at home)
   Weare out thy youth with shapelesse idlenesse.
   But since thou lov'st; love still, and thrive therein,
   Even as I would, when I to love begin.
Pro.   Wilt thou be gone? Sweet *Valentine* adew,
   Thinke on thy *Protheus*, when thou (hap'ly) seest
   Some rare note-worthy object in thy travaile.
   Wish me partaker in thy happinesse,
   When thou do'st meet good hap; and in thy danger,
   (If ever danger doe environ thee)
   Commend thy grievance to my holy prayers,
   For I will be thy beades-man, *Valentine*.
Val.   And on a love-booke pray for my successe?
Pro.   Upon some booke I love, I'le pray for thee.
Val.   That's on some shallow Storie of deepe love,
   How yong *Leander* crost the *Hellespont*.

THE COMPLETE POEMS
OF
ROBERT FROST

WITH A PREFACE BY THE AUTHOR
AN APPRECIATION BY LOUIS UNTERMEYER
AND WOOD-ENGRAVINGS BY
THOMAS W. NASON

NEW YORK
THE LIMITED EDITIONS CLUB
1950

THE
TREMOLINO

BY

JOSEPH CONRAD

NEW YORK
PHILIP C. DUSCHNES
1942

THE ATLANTIC CHARTER

THE PRESIDENT OF THE UNITED STATES OF AMERICA AND THE PRIME MINISTER, MR. CHURCHILL, REPRESENTING HIS MAJESTY'S GOVERNMENT IN THE UNITED KINGDOM, BEING MET TOGETHER, DEEM IT RIGHT TO MAKE KNOWN CERTAIN COMMON PRINCIPLES IN THE NATIONAL POLICIES OF THEIR RESPECTIVE COUNTRIES ON WHICH THEY BASE THEIR HOPES FOR A BETTER FUTURE FOR THE WORLD.

I
THEIR COUNTRIES SEEK NO AGGRANDIZEMENT, TERRITORIAL OR OTHER.

II
THEY DESIRE TO SEE NO TERRITORIAL CHANGES THAT DO NOT ACCORD WITH THE FREELY EXPRESSED WISHES OF THE PEOPLES CONCERNED.

III
THEY RESPECT THE RIGHT OF ALL PEOPLES TO CHOOSE THE FORM OF GOVERNMENT UNDER WHICH THEY WILL LIVE; AND THEY WISH TO SEE SOVEREIGN RIGHTS AND SELF-GOVERNMENT RESTORED TO THOSE WHO HAVE BEEN FORCIBLY DEPRIVED OF THEM.

IV
THEY WILL ENDEAVOR, WITH DUE RESPECT FOR THEIR EXISTING OBLIGATIONS, TO FURTHER THE ENJOYMENT BY ALL STATES, GREAT OR SMALL, VICTOR OR VANQUISHED, OF ACCESS, ON EQUAL TERMS, TO THE TRADE AND TO THE RAW MATERIALS OF THE WORLD WHICH ARE NEEDED FOR THEIR ECONOMIC PROSPERITY.

V
THEY DESIRE TO BRING ABOUT THE FULLEST COLLABORATION BETWEEN ALL NATIONS IN THE ECONOMIC FIELD WITH THE OBJECT OF SECURING, FOR ALL, IMPROVED LABOR STANDARDS, ECONOMIC ADJUSTMENT AND SOCIAL SECURITY.

VI
AFTER THE FINAL DESTRUCTION OF THE NAZI TYRANNY, THEY HOPE TO SEE ESTABLISHED A PEACE WHICH WILL AFFORD TO ALL NATIONS THE MEANS OF DWELLING IN SAFETY WITHIN THEIR OWN BOUNDARIES, AND WHICH WILL AFFORD ASSURANCE THAT ALL THE MEN IN ALL THE LANDS MAY LIVE OUT THEIR LIVES IN FREEDOM FROM FEAR AND WANT.

VII
SUCH A PEACE SHOULD ENABLE ALL MEN TO TRAVERSE THE HIGH SEAS AND OCEANS WITHOUT HINDRANCE.

VIII
THEY BELIEVE THAT ALL OF THE NATIONS OF THE WORLD, FOR REALISTIC AS WELL AS SPIRITUAL REASONS, MUST COME TO THE ABANDONMENT OF THE USE OF FORCE. SINCE NO FUTURE PEACE CAN BE MAINTAINED IF LAND, SEA OR AIR ARMAMENTS CONTINUE TO BE EMPLOYED BY NATIONS WHICH THREATEN, OR MAY THREATEN, AGGRESSION OUTSIDE OF THEIR FRONTIERS, THEY BELIEVE, PENDING THE ESTABLISHMENT OF A WIDER AND PERMANENT SYSTEM OF GENERAL SECURITY, THAT THE DISARMAMENT OF SUCH NATIONS IS ESSENTIAL. THEY WILL LIKEWISE AID AND ENCOURAGE ALL OTHER PRACTICABLE MEASURES WHICH WILL LIGHTEN FOR PEACE-LOVING PEOPLES THE CRUSHING BURDEN OF ARMAMENTS.

14 AUGUST 1941   FRANKLIN D. ROOSEVELT
                                  WINSTON S. CHURCHILL

THE DIVINE COMEDY OF ⚜ DANTE ⚜ ALIGHIERI

THE PROSE TRANSLATION BY
CHARLES ELIOT NORTON
WITH ILLUSTRATIONS
FROM DESIGNS BY
BOTTICELLI

NEW YORK
BRUCE ROGERS & THE PRESS OF A. COLISH
MCMLV

PLATE 57. A selection from the many Rogers printer's marks

> read it only for pleasure, and have to keep a dictionary within reach. I thought of the other translators, and agreed that there was not a first-rate one. Butcher & Lang—too antique. Samuel Butler—too little dignified, tho' better. Morris—too literary. That only shows the job it is. Why should my doing be any better than these efforts of the bigger men?
>
> Bruce Rogers' dressing of the book will make it glorious, so that even an inferior version would pass muster. You are fortunate to be able to dine with him. I have for years admired him from ground level, and have even been able at intervals to buy books of his production; of course I've never met him: but you know, and he knows, that he's the ideal of all those who have tried to produce books. Or perhaps I should say, of all who have gone far enough in the direction of producing books to know what a job it is. It would be an awful thing if my share in the Homer did not justify its setting, in my own judgment.[20]

Nevertheless, the letter concluded with an expressed wish to make a start. Shaw hoped that he could complete the translation in two years, and made the strange but firm condition that his name must not appear in the completed book. And he reiterated his sense of inadequacy to be printed by Bruce Rogers.

On Shaw's acceptance, Rogers picked up the correspondence and wrote directly to him. Thus began a close relationship, at first by an extensive exchange of letters, later in a number of meetings in England. Among their several common interests was the coincidence that Shaw had had a hand in designing his own books and cherished the hope that on retirement he might produce some work himself on a small private press of his own.

Although Isham had offered Shaw a very generous sum to cover the translation, and had expected to finance its ultimate production and publication, Rogers felt the need to control all facets of the work himself. With great reluctance, Isham finally agreed to step aside.

Because Rogers had been looking forward to living in England for the next few years, he arranged with Emery Walker and his partner Wilfred

CHAPTER SEVEN: 1928–1935

Merton to have the *Odyssey* printed and published in London. A contract was drawn that provided for the Walker company (Emery Walker Limited) to finance production of the book, with payments to be made directly to T. E. Shaw as he delivered the translation in installments. Rogers would receive £1000 from the first sales and a one-third share in the profits. He would, of course, design the book and see it through the press in London. The colophon of this first edition read when completed, "Printed and published by / Sir Emery Walker, Wilfred Merton and Bruce Rogers / 16 Clifford's Inn, London / 530 copies." The copyright of the translation was vested in Bruce Rogers in anticipation of future editions by other publishers.

The progress of the translation, which consumed four years instead of the predicted two, may be traced in a first letter to Isham and, subsequently, thirty-nine to Rogers, between January 1928 and January 1932. These and a further thirteen letters written after the *Odyssey* was completed were later privately printed by Rogers. Together, they disclose a moving friendship between two rather enigmatic men of genius. A paragraph from B.R.'s introduction to the second group of letters bespeaks mutual regard: "When crossing to England I usually sent him a message from the ship the day before landing, and when we docked in Southampton he would arrive in one of his speed boats and take me off, perhaps for a trial run down Southampton Water and the Solent, or to East Cowes, where he was supervising the building of some of the larger craft for the Royal Air Force. Or we might have a luncheon of bread and cheese and strawberries in the garden of a little waterside inn near the boat-yard at Hythe and afterwards take out a new boat for an engine test. Once he took me round by Spithead to Portsmouth, to catch the London train from there."[21] And, finally, in a last letter to B.R. on 6 May 1935, anticipating Rogers' visit to England, the opening was, "Very welcome back! *Back*, you will notice, with a smile. You seem right, somehow, on this side."

Although Shaw had begun work early in 1928, it was not until the last day of June that he was able to send the first sample translation. "I see now," he wrote, why there are no adequate translations of Homer. He is baffling. Not simple, in education; not primitive, socially. Rather a William Morris of his day, I fancy.

There's a queer naivety in every other line: and at our remove of thought and language we can't say if he is smiling or not. Samuel Butler thought he was: and Butler's version lacks dignity, therefore, as much as it lacks poetry. Palmer is altogether the best, I think.

My version runs to 5000 words of this first book. I have tried to squeeze out all the juice in the orange; or what I thought was the juice. I tried to take liberties with the Greek: but failed. Homer compels respect. I confess he has me beaten to my knees. Perhaps if I did much more I might be less faithful.

The work has been very difficult: though I'm in a Homeric sort of air; a mud-brick fort beset by the tribes of Waziristan, on a plain encircled by the hills of the Afghan border. It reeks of Alexander the Great, our European fore-runner: who also loved Homer.

But, as I say, it has been difficult. This which I have sent is the sixth copying-out: so I shall not be a whit sorry (except in pocket) if your backers cry off the project, at sight of the sample.[22]

On the contrary, the proposed version was received with enthusiasm, and the work was to go forward. Shaw agreed to provide the translation in installments, each of four chapters — or "books" as they were known in the *Odyssey*. His script went to the Emery Walker office, where it was typed, then delivered to the Cambridge University Press for composition. Galley proofs were scanned by Rogers, who added occasional comments for consideration by Shaw to whom they were then sent.

Rogers believed that this new translation of one of the world's classics by one of the most noted Englishmen of his time deserved a monumental edition. Inasmuch as his partners in publication, as well as the translator, were all enthusiasts of bookmaking, it was unanimously decided to make as fine a volume as possible, "however expensive it might prove to be." Thus

CHAPTER SEVEN: 1928–1935

Rogers planned a generous page of 11½ x 8 inches, the type to be the recently completed 16-point Monotype Centaur. After several experimental page set-ups, 2-point leading was chosen to provide an open feel to the pages.

For decoration B.R. made drawings derived from figures on Greek vases for gold roundels that would be printed at the start of each of the twenty-four "books" and on the title page. In *Paragraphs on Printing*, where B.R. devoted several pages to the *Odyssey*, he wrote: "Both the Iliad and the Odyssey have been copiously illustrated in Greek vase painting, so there was much material to choose from. But only a few of the original compositions were followed at all closely; the others were made up from single Homeric figures in new combinations, illustrating some incident in each Book."[23]

Rogers sent specimen type pages and his sketches for the roundels to Shaw, who replied on 24 May 1929: "This is going to be a fine thing, this book—all except the inadequate translation, of course!" He expressed pleasure in the typography and most of the drawings, but had a few reservations. "The only figure I do not greatly love is the Zeus in '3'; and also the Athene who faces him. They are a little too 'social' to please me. Their excess of movement makes the drawing more an illustration than a decoration: and while I like decorated books, I do not like illustrated books. Some formalism; great dignity; and a rich line. Those are the things which would go well with the Odyssey, I fancy. The simplicity of 1; the vigour of 2; and the humour of 4: I approve of all those. But poor 3 does not seem to be happy."[24]

The magnificence of the gold roundels as they illuminate the finished volume was not achieved without ingenuity and great effort (plates 38/39/40). Each roundel was subjected to seven separate impressions through the press. Let us have the progression of their printing in Rogers' own words in *Paragraphs on Printing*:

> It took several months of experimenting with the difficulties encountered in producing the effects desired and making sure that the

work was permanent. The usual size of gold leaf as it is supplied to bookbinders was too small to cover the roundels, and it was likewise too thin. So a specially thick gold was beaten out for the job. To prevent the roundel showing through the sheet, two layers of printing ink, the color of the paper, were first applied; then the sizing for the gold was printed on the ink; then the gold laid on by hand. Once more through the press with the flat disc to fix it firmly on the paper; then a cloudy half-tone block with orange-red, to dull somewhat the surface of the gold and give a slight play of color; and finally the design in black: seven operations in all. But the method was apparently successful, as I have yet to hear of one that has peeled or rubbed off.[25]

As for all his books, Bruce Rogers selected the paper—the quintessential imperative in fine bookmaking—with utmost care. For the *Odyssey* he turned to Mr. Jack Green at the J. Barcham Green Mill to make a special handmade sheet in a slightly grey tone that would be a more suitable background for the gold-and-black roundels than a white or cream tint, and that would be equally kind to the 16-point type. The mill took great pains and turned out a magnificent paper of subtle, restrained eloquence, with an especially made watermark of a Greek galley.

For the ink Rogers found an old formula in William Savage's *Practical Hints on Decorative Printing* (London, 1822). Instead of the usual varnish-based inks, he called for "balsam of copaiba" an oily resinous substance. "It was somewhat slow in drying," B.R. said, but it had "a pleasant spicy aroma, on which many people have commented when opening the book." An added virtue of the ink was its capacity to print the roundels with a depth of black, without gloss. Inasmuch as the text arrived in installments, it was decided to print the pages on a small job press (not the same press on which the Dürer had been printed in 1917), two pages at a time. This was equally suitable for the roundels, which were separately printed. With the printing finally completed, the books were bound in a superb full black Niger morocco leather, with gilt tops and raised bands, with no decoration other than

CHAPTER SEVEN: 1928–1935

the title stamped in gold on the spine. The books were published in November 1932, at $50.00 per copy.

The present writer had the privilege of arranging an exhibition, "Art of the Printed Book: 1455-1955," for the Pierpont Morgan Library in New York in 1973. During the several years spent in selecting the 112 books finally shown, I handled every title reputed by historians of the printed book to be among the finest volumes made in the more than five hundred years since Gutenberg. I believe that the Bruce Rogers *Odyssey* is indisputably among the most beautiful books ever produced, including the widely acclaimed, illustrated *Hypnerotomachia Poliphili* of Aldus Manutius, issued in 1499.

It is difficult to describe a work of genius. In the *Odyssey*, with complete simplicity, without tricks or accessory decoration, with a classic austerity akin to the timeless proportions of the Parthenon, with only type and paper and ink, with consummate skill, Rogers created a masterpiece. It is appropriate here to recall that Sir Francis Meynell told me that he considered Bruce Rogers to have been "the greatest artificer of the book who ever lived." To which your reporter adds his enthusiastic accord.

The Oxford University Press in New York became the publisher of the forthcoming trade editions of the *Odyssey*. In order to protect copyright of the new translation, a preliminary issue of thirty-four copies was rushed through, printed in 1932 from type that was set for the regular trade edition to follow. These thirty-four copies (of which twenty-five were offered for sale) were printed on a handmade paper, with one gold roundel on the title page, and bound in full leather.

The regular trade edition was issued in November 1932. It was designed by Bruce Rogers as an octavo, set in 12-point Linotype Janson, printed and bound at the Plimpton Press in Norwood, Massachusetts. Only one roundel was retained, which appeared on the title page in dark blue. The only text change was the placement of the translator's note, which preceded the text in the new edition, whereas it had earlier been printed at the end. This first trade edition is a pleasant book of no special typographic distinction. As requested by the translator, Shaw's name did not appear.

As might have been expected, the text received a mixed reception from the classical scholars. The reading public responded with enthusiasm. The trade editions went through many printings, including a popular edition in 1934 on thinner paper and in a smaller format. Owing to Shaw's generosity, Rogers retained control of copyright and enjoyed the well-deserved royalties.

In 1935, the year of Shaw's death, the Oxford University Press in England published their trade edition, which Shaw had previously forbidden. The Press imported sheets printed in the U.S.A., with the added lines on the title page: "Translated by T. E. Shaw (Colonel T. E. Lawrence)." The roundel on the title page was printed in black over an ochre background.

A beautiful new printing of the *Odyssey* in the Hesperides Series was published in 1940 by the Oxford University Press in New York, the only one of the Series not produced in England. The text for this edition was set in Linotype Granjon and printed at the Walpole Printing Office in Mount Vernon, New York, on a splendid machine-made laid paper, page size 7¼ x 4¾ inches. The roundels were included throughout the text, redrawn by B.R. with a stippled background for printing in black ink with the type. The translator's name was included (plate 41).

The Hesperides volumes are among Rogers' notable achievements. During the years in England he induced Humphrey Milford, publisher of the Oxford University Press, and John Johnson, Printer to the University, to plan publication of certain literary classics in a series of small volumes which B.R. would design and which would be printed on superior paper, with closely supervised production. The back of the jackets, probably written by Rogers, explained the purpose of the series: "The Hesperides Series has been launched not so much with the intention of adding to the already over-large total of cheap reprints as with the hope that those who like their books to be typographically attractive as well as inexpensive may find in these volumes something they have long been seeking. There are various series that provide good reading cheaply, but it is hoped that the *Hesperides* will do something more. The price of each volume—$2.50 [in the United States]—is low enough to rank among the inexpensive luxuries of life, and the care given to

CHAPTER SEVEN: 1928–1935

the production and design of each will ensure them a place with their grander neighbours on the shelves of those to whom the appearance of books is not a matter of indifference."

The series began in 1935 with *The Poems of Robert Herrick* in two volumes, and closed with the *Odyssey* in 1940. These books — especially the *Odyssey* — show extraordinary skill in bookmaking. They are a joy to handle and to read. But even with the backing of a great university press, the hope of combining fine workmanship and superior materials at commercial levels of price has never been possible. After seven titles the Hesperides Series came to an honorable end.

With the printing of the *Odyssey* completed, Rogers sailed to the United States to accept in person on 15 October 1932 the honorary degree of Doctor of Humane Letters (the pun delighted him), conferred on him by his alma mater, Purdue University in Lafayette, Indiana. He then returned to October House, where he would remain for about six months before going back to England. In addition to fulfilling family obligations, he derived pleasure from his many American friends, especially Kent and Rollins, and enjoyed the warm admiration of a growing circle of young practitioners. He spent a week with Frederic and Bertha Goudy in Marlboro, New York, cutting "some mats and cast[ing] type while there." On his rather frequent trips to New York City, he made the Webster Hotel on West Forty-fifth Street his headquarters. Meetings with Frederick Coykendall, Chairman of the Publications Committee of the Grolier Club, brought the commission to produce another volume on construction of the letters of the alphabet, *Fra Luca de Pacioli*.

Rogers was responsible for the production of three books printed and published in the United States during his half-year in this country — the American editions of the *Odyssey* already described, *Letters from T.E. Shaw to Bruce Rogers*, quoted above, and *Champ Rosé*.

Shortly before Rogers returned to the United States he had spent an afternoon with T. E. Shaw in Southampton discussing some final points of the *Odyssey* translation then nearing completion. As he was about to leave,

Rogers asked Shaw for permission to print for their friends "some day" the letters that were the record of the making of their book and of a rare personal friendship. To which Shaw replied, "Why wait?"

Consequently, in 1932, B.R. proceeded with design and production of the letters. He first planned for composition in Bell italic, then changed to the more rugged Deepdene italic by his friend Goudy, whose wife Bertha then set the type by hand. The edition of two hundred copies, printed at the Rudge press in 1933, consisted of forty letters on eighty-four pages, 8¼ x 5⅝ inches. Three years later (the year after Shaw's tragic death in 1935) Rogers printed the thirteen letters that had been written after the *Odyssey*'s publication. An edition of three hundred copies, made with the permission of the Trustees of the Shaw Estate, followed the format of the earlier edition. Privately printed, no copies of either edition were sold. The present writer was among the fortunate recipients of both volumes, "With the compliments of Bruce Rogers."

The *Champ Rosé*, printed early in 1933 during the depth of the Depression, was, nevertheless, a light-hearted book. It was planned as a small volume in which, according to the subtitle, "may be discovered the Roman Letters that were made by Geofroy Tory and printed by him at Paris in his book called *Champ Fleury*." The printing throughout is in red ink. Its choice was explained in the introduction by Bruce Rogers, written with wit and humor in the archaic manner of sixteenth-century France: "And furthermore there came to me a harmless petty conceit, namely, that in these aforesaid days of hardship and depression much Book-keeping is being written down in red (or gules as the herald hath it, though not the times), perhaps it were better for Book-Selling too if Printing were done in that cheerful colour, to make some small semblance of gaiety in this dolorous world."

The book, which consisted of the introduction and twenty-four large diagrammatic roman letters, each on a separate page, was very well printed by B.R.'s young friend Peter Beilenson at his Walpole Printing Office in New Rochelle, New York, and issued by the Peter Pauper Press, the publishing imprint of Beilenson and his wife Edna. The Bruce Rogers printer's mark of Father Time and the thistle appeared on the colophon page, indicat-

CHAPTER SEVEN: 1928–1935

ing that he closely supervised the making of this slender book, which was done with forthright simplicity and charm.

In May 1933 Rogers sailed for London and returned to the three books of importance that were still in the course of production. The *Aesop* and the *Pacioli* would be completed during the year; the Bible would not be published until 1935. During his first weeks in England he was so busy that he had not found time to write. On the twentieth of June he sent a round-robin letter in the care of Miss Granniss at the Grolier Club requesting her to forward it in turn to several of his friends. The letter tells of an excursion into the country where he found a windmill that drew him back for a longer stay; about Oxford, John Johnson and the Bible; news concerning progress of the *Pacioli*; about meetings with T. E. Shaw and other English friends and visiting Americans; and exaltation about a forthcoming trip on a square-rigger. The letter, quoted in full, shows Rogers in high spirits:

> Not having written a single letter, except on business, since my arrival in England three weeks ago, I am so far in arrears that it is hopeless to now try to do more than send out a sort of a reversed round-robin — that can be circulated amongst those who might be interested in the diary of those three weeks.
>
> They have been spent mostly in London, with two visits to Oxford, and two to the place from which I am now writing: —Icklesham Mill near Winchelsea Sussex. It is a wind-mill, one of the few that are still going, and I discovered it two weeks ago, on Whitsunday. It was very hot then and I decided a trip by steamer down the Thames to Southend, the Coney Island of London, would be as cool an excursion as any. Leaving the Tower Pier at 9:30 the boat reached Southend at noon, but it had been so pleasant that I decided to stay aboard and go on to Margate, another 1½ hr. sail. From Margate I kept on to Ramsgate and then took a bus for Deal, Dover, Folkstone, Hythe, Rye and Hastings, reaching the last at 8:30 P.M. On the way from Winchelsea to Hastings I saw this wind-mill on the top of a hill overlooking the whole countryside and the Channel, and the next morning I came back

from Hastings to examine it more in detail, as it is a half-mile off the main road. I found the miller was also the neighborhood baker and that his sister took lodgers—at 6 shillings a day—including teas. So I came back the next week for a longer stay—and after another few days in Oxford and London, returned again yesterday evening, principally to write this letter, which I realized would never get done in London.

Here there is not a sound except that of the waves on the beach, a mile away, and the bleating of sheep and lambs. The country, as far as you can see, is dotted with them, thousands of them, and being mostly newly shorn they look at a distance like daisies on the green fields and hills. The only drawback is that they *will* bleat at unearthly hours right under my window, as the mill and house are set right in the midst of a field and are entirely surrounded by sheep. Amongst the country sounds I must include also larks and cuckoos and magpies. I am the only lodger at present and have the whole use of the sitting-room. As I look up I can see all over the Channel with red-sailed fishing-boats in shore and the big ships passing farther out, seven of them at present in sight.

And speaking of ships, I shall probably engage passage, next week, on one of the Australian grain ships, a big four-masted barque, now unloading in London. They go from here to their home-port in the Åland Islands in the Baltic off Stockholm, to fit out for their return to Australia in September. It is a trip of from 10 to 15 days, "according to the winds met with," as the circular reads. And I find that they nearly all take a few passengers. It takes about 3 days to return to London via Stockholm, railroad and boat. If it's good weather it ought to be a pleasant sail—at any rate I have always wanted to sail on a square-rigged ship, and this seems a good opportunity. I will attach the circular I got from the agents. The barque I shall probably go on is the "Viking." The "Herzogin Cecilia" sails about the same date so there may be a little racing even on this shorter trip than the Australian one. At any rate this practice in sailing the wind-mill on shore is a good apprentice-ship before going to sea.

In Oxford I stopped at Kent's favorite hostelry, the Golden Cross,

CHAPTER SEVEN: 1928–1935

and Johnson came with me for almost every luncheon and dinner while there. One day we were joined by Gilbert Murray and an American, Julian Price, who is staying there at present. Mr. Baddeley and Mr & Mrs Buckley (? Buckler) came for Sunday luncheon as usual—they all sent remembrances to W. K.—Johnson seems in better health than last summer and is still working 26 hrs. to the day. They had a field-day and (of course) tea, for the Press's Fire Brigade on Saturday afternoon, in the big court of the Press, and Johnson, as chief, appeared in a gorgeous uniform, with gold epaulettes and braid—but, alas! *not* a brass helmet. It was remarkably becoming to him and I advised his wearing it continually as it gave him a far greater air of authority than his usual clothes do.

He came up to London Saturday for dinner with me and the Henry Seidel Canby's, who are staying here at present, and they were delighted with him. He is really one of the most remarkable men in England. Just as we were leaving the restaurant Preston Remington came over from another table and gave me later news from N.Y. than I had had before. I happened to go to the same restaurant (the Quo Vadis, where Kent will remember that the Ancient and Mouldy Amalgamated Order of Quill and Engine Drivers held their first and last banquet) and Remington was there again, so we had another pleasant evening.

The Canby's are going to Oxford on Friday and I shall be going on the same train, as I have 1500 copies! of the Aesop to "autograph" for the Limited Editions Club. It will take two or three days—if I survive—and it is just as well to get this letter written first, as I shall probably never again "take my pen in hand" after that ordeal.

The Aesop is printing (and is going to be very handsome, I think). The Bible is half off the press—Johnson says a year from October for the finish—and they are starting another little book for me (of which more anon).

I haven't yet been to Cambridge, but Morison is now finishing his work on the Pacioli for the Grolier Club, all of which is now in type except his Preface—Miss Granniss in particular will be glad to learn the following particulars, for transmission to the Publications Committee.

It will make a volume of about 100 pages, the size of the Dürer and Champ Fleury. Binding similar to the Dürer. There is a frontispiece photogravure reproduction of the portrait in the Naples Museum, with Pacioli's autograph, which Morison has discovered. Also one or two facsimiles of portions of the fine MS. of the work, at Geneva. The letters themselves will be reproduced by line-cuts, instead of heliotypes, as originally contemplated. The book is all in type, the photogravures and other cuts are being made and the paper ordered from Batchelor. It ought to be ready to ship to N.Y. in September. I am having estimates of cost made, to send shortly to Miss Granniss. It has been impossible to get them before this, as Morison was not sure how much he would want to write, and we have had to discuss what to put in and how to arrange it, so there was no exact data to go on. But now it is in fairly complete form. The figures will be based on 300 copies of the ordinary edition, and I hope the Club will allow me to print at least 7 special copies on larger paper (as with the Champ Fleury). They will aid very materially in financing the book.

I have seen T. E. Shaw only once—at Clifford's Inn. When I reached England I had several addresses and sent a note to each of them. He turned up in a few days, in London. He spends most of his time at Cours, Isle of Wight, with occasional spells of work in Felixstone, on the east coast, inspecting and testing motor-boats as usual. He is looking very well and is in good spirits. Is revising the Odyssey somewhat, for the school edition. He says he is not resigning from the Air force—will finish his term there in about a year's time and will not re-enlist. Probably go to his cottage in Dorset, of whose location he drew a map on the inside cover of my copy of the "Letters"—writing on the title-page: "I only wish the originals had been half as legible." So he evidently approves that volume.

Canby saw Bernard Shaw at the opening of the Burne-Jones exhibition at the Tate Gallery, and asked him about his New York experi-

CHAPTER SEVEN: 1928–1935

ences. Shaw said he wasn't at all nervous during the ordeal, but that two days later, on the ship, he found that *all of his teeth were loose* (temporarily). So he must have been somewhat shaken.

I met again J. W. Mackail, Burne-Jones's son-in-law, at tea Sunday afternoon at Walker's. So I have, within a week, seen both outstanding figures in Greek and in Latin scholarship, and both asked me if T.E.S. was himself pleased with his Odyssey translation — implying, of course, that *they* didn't think much of it. But as it was designed to take it out of the hands of just such pedants as they, their coolness is only additional proof of its own peculiar merits.

I have left mention of Emery Walker to the last, as it is the least cheerful news I have to write. I have not seen him, as he can see no one except his most intimate old friends, and even the effort of talking to them wearies him unduly. His heart is reduced to almost its normal size, but he has had laryngitis which has gone very hardly with him. He can sit up in bed and has the *Times* propped up before him, pretending to read, but Dorothy says that she doesn't think he reads more than a few words at a time, and never asks to have the page turned. At times his mind is quite clear — at others he seems to be re-living the old Red Lion Square days, or other experiences of the past. He sleeps a great deal of the time, is in apparently no pain, and it is only his amazing vitality that keeps him up. They are fearful that his mind will go entirely blank. A week or two ago he was made a Fellow of Jesus College, Cambridge, which pleased him greatly — for a time.

I will enclose several addressed envelopes with this, to be mailed in rotation — if you will be good enough to do so — the New York ones first, the last to go to my family in Indiana.

And to all of you very affectionate regards.[26]

Nine days after writing the letter from Icklesham, B.R. boarded the square-rigger *Viking* in London and moved down the Thames to the open sea. During a stop-over at Mariehamn, Aaland Islands, in the Baltic, Rogers wrote to Kent on the first of September and told him in much detail about the voyage and of his great joy in being at sea:

> One of my early ambitions is now satisfied. I've had a voyage in a big square-rigger and though it was just a summer trip with no real hardships it was an experience I'll never forget. No more small-boat sailing for me—the bigger the better.
>
> When the Australian grain barques unload their annual cargoes of wheat, in London or somewhere in the British Isles, they then go to their home port in ballast to refit for their trip out in the fall. Down in the docks one day where one was discharging I got into conversation with the mate and asked him how it was possible to get passage across the North Sea and the Baltic. To my surprise he said to just go up to their London agent's and sign on as supercargo or steward, as they are not supposed to carry passengers. I put off immediately, found the office and met a fine Scot named Calder who managed the business for Erickson's ships (he owns a dozen or more of them). The one I had just come from would leave in a few days and there were seven or eight passengers already booked. No ship ever had so many "stewards" or "supercargoes," I'll bet.
>
> I found the fare was 10 shillings a day for a minimum of ten days, and the same for any longer voyage. Capt. Hagerstrand of the *Viking* which was in the dock came in before I left and said he would be glad to have me along; so I "signed on" at once. It was just as easy as that.
>
> I got a small kit together with some warm clothes, as it was sure to be cold at nights in the North Sea, and two days later we were all on board and the barque was warping out of dock. The passengers were four Americans, two English, one Australian and one New Zealander, all more or less sailors, including the three women. None of them had sailed in a big ship before. After a few days, when we had all got pretty well acquainted we began guying each other's mannerisms of speech. The Captain had a decidedly Scandinavian accent, one Englishman

CHAPTER SEVEN: 1928–1935

spoke Oxfordese, two (and perhaps three) of the Americans, Bostonese; but the Australian spoke the most exaggerated Cockney I've ever heard, even in Poplar. He protested that he spoke perfect English: "Oi sy lidy and yeow sy lidy — what the difference?"

We were towed by a big tug, not only to Gravesend where they usually cast off, but this time clear down to the mouth of the Thames. We found from the Captain that the crack ship of the Erickson fleet, the *Herzogin Cecilie*, which had left London the day before, was anchored off Walberswick waiting for a wind, and he meant to try to reach Mariehamn before her if possible.

It wasn't till nearly dark that we saw her at anchor and cast off the tug. The sails had all been set by then and though there was little breeze we were at last "under sail." The quiet that descended on us was marvelous and I don't think anyone went to bed, at least not till nearly morning. The breeze had freshened by that time and we were raising quite a wave under our bows. One of my favorite places on the ship is out on the bowsprit, where you have a view down the long deck of the whole ship. (The *Viking* is a flush-decked barque — about 320 feet long and with three square-rigged masts and the after mast schooner-rigged.)

Nothing of note happened for two or three days, when we saw the *Cecilie* hull down astern of us but heading over toward the Dutch coast. The next night I awakened to find us heeled well over (we had only a half-load of ballast) and I could tell before I went on deck that we were going some. It was about 11 o'clock.

There was only the light of the stars, but in clear weather in those latitudes there is a good deal of light at sea. I found the Captain near the wheel, and he said, "De *Cecilie* is back dere." With his glass I could just make her out.

We knew she could outsail us, as she had been cleaned in dry-dock in London and carried five more sails. In two hours the N.W. wind had increased to half a gale and the *Cecilie* was almost up to us. We split two upper sails but new ones were bent on at once. The *Cecilie* came up under our lee and so close that we blanketed her whenever she tried to pass. I could almost have thrown the traditional biscuit aboard, but I didn't happen to have one.

After a half-hour of this exciting race she gave up the attempt and went about under our stern. Apparently we could sail closer to the wind. At daylight the wind had gone down to a good sailing breeze, but the *Cecilie* was ahead off our port bow and already nearly hull down.

The next day being July 4, I made a kite out of two sheets of handmade paper (I don't know how I happened to have it along). The ship's carpenter made me some beautiful sticks and the Captain gave me a big ball of fine strong sewing twine. I soon used up all the red and blue in my water-color box but I fortunately had some colored crayons which would dissolve in water—so I painted the stars-and-stripes on my four-foot kite.

With the help of the Capt. and mate I finally got it into the air off the after deck, though the down-draft from the spanker sent it diving under the stern. Once the devilish thing wrapped itself round the log-line and we had to pull in the log to disentangle it. When it was up again I let it off several hundred feet where it flew beautifully, but while we were at lunch the steward came in and told us the kite was in the sea. So lunch was abandoned and we finally got it hauled in without any breakage. The color had all washed off, of course, and the two sheets of paper had soaked apart. But I repaired it and the next day we got it up again, without much trouble.

We were now pretty close in to the Danish coast, tacking to enter the Skagerrack. About this time the Captain told me that we were going about and that the kite would have to come down or be flown from the fo'c'sle. So he called two men and they passed the ball of twine outside all the shrouds and stays the whole length of the ship. It took about an hour and we were close in to the beach, with a big hotel on the bluff, before he put the helm up. But the kite didn't do so well and was soon down in the sea, this time a total wreck.

We rounded the Skaw light-ship that evening and turned south for Copenhagen. At Elsinore, with its modern castle, very little like that

CHAPTER SEVEN: 1928–1935

in *Hamlet*, the strait is only a mile or so wide, and there is nearly always a stiff tide flowing out from the Baltic. We were held up four days, waiting for a tug telephoned for from Elsinore. We all went ashore Sunday morning with the three mates and spent the day inspecting the town and shore resort a little to the north.

The tug arrived Monday morning and we learned that the *Cecilie* was still anchored off Copenhagen waiting for a larger tug. The next morning about four the Captain routed us all out with the call, "Ve are passing the *Cecilie*, ve are passing the *Cecilie*." We went up on deck in the cold dawn and cheered as we passed her, though she was at anchor a mile off—but the Captain was pleased.

We towed till off Falsterbö, the southern tip of Sweden, and then the tug cast off, taking two of our American passengers who had to get back to England. We were then in the Baltic and our course was again north-east. On the second day we again sighted the *Cecilie* coming up rapidly with a good wind. Again she passed us and disappeared ahead. Later we tacked through the strait between Oland Island and the mainland of Sweden, giving us two good views of the city of Visby with its completely surrounding walls.

Then early one morning we sighted the Älands and a little motor-boat with the pilot came off to us. The western entrance to the harbor is a winding channel through a lot of little islands, with the granite shores covered with pines, like the coast of Maine.

In the meantime I had made another kite with the Åland colors painted on it which I meant to fly as we came into harbor. Having no more paper I asked the Capt. if he had any thin cloth, and he appeared with one of his best white shirts which he insisted I should take for it. He giggled and said, "Dey will tink we are all crazy on dis ship!"

They had been clewing up the square sails as we got nearer, leaving only the stay-sails and a couple of jibs, and under these we rounded a sharp point into Mariehamn harbor. There were seven or eight barques already there at anchor and we sailed right in amongst them and dropped anchor just as though we were in a steamer.

All ships in harbor were dressed in gay bunting, as the President of Finland was to visit them that day. I had put up my kite, but it was too heavy for the calm harbor, so it soon came down again and I gave it to a little nephew of one of the mates.

We had passed the *Parma* at anchor outside the harbor, the barque in which Alan Villiers* owns a fifth interest, so I hoped to see him — but when I came ashore the harbor master told me he had gone back to London the night before — too bad, as I had wanted to meet him again.

The President arrived in a small steamboat and was duly entertained, but without much enthusiasm, as the Älanders are more Swedish than Finnish in their sympathies, and Finnish is hardly spoken at all in the islands.

All of Mariehamn can be seen in a day, as it is mostly one broad wooded avenue with the sea at each end and bordered with substantial houses — one of them Erickson's, where we had tea in the garden — though it was coffee and Danish pastries. There is a gay restaurant and casino at one end of the esplanade where we got excellent food and drink — though fiery aquavit will never be a favorite drink of mine.

Whew! What a whale of a letter, all nautical: but it's raining today and I'm writing in the lounge of the *Societeshuset*, as the casino is called. I want to put down some of the incidents of the voyage while they are fresh in my memory. I shall probably never take another one — at least it won't be a first one. I am now convinced that sailing a big ship is one of the finest arts in the world. But it is so common an art in Scandinavia that the captains in the Erickson fleet get only $75 a month! We leave tomorrow morning (about 3 A.M., in the steamer for Stockholm). I'll post this at Copenhagen.[27]

FRA LUCA DE PACIOLI

Discussions that had been held in New York with the Grolier Club in 1931 and early in 1932 led to one of Rogers' greatest achievements. He was com-

---

*Alan Villiers was a writer and sailor with whom Rogers developed a friendship.

CHAPTER SEVEN: 1928–1935

missioned to produce a new volume on the construction of Roman letters based on the seminal work, *De Divina Proportione* by Fra Luca de Pacioli, published in Venice in 1509. An erudite Franciscan friar and preacher, Pacioli was also a professor of mathematics at the Universities of Padua and Milan. He wrote the first treatise on double-entry bookkeeping, and claimed a professional friendship with Leonardo da Vinci.

This new publication was to be made as a companion volume to the Club's two earlier books on the construction of the alphabet — *Of the Just Shaping of Letters* by Albrecht Dürer (1917) and *Champ Fleury* by Geofroy Tory (1927). However, the Pacioli volume, unlike the earlier reprints, would have an added scholarly text by Stanley Morison on the author's life and on the importance of Pacioli's diagrammatic drawings.

In a letter of 8 February 1932 accepting the Club's proposal, Morison wrote to Frederick Coykendall, the Publications Committee Chairman, "There can be no doubt that the alphabet annexed to Pacioli's book on divine proportion forms the most spectacular of the several geometrically made models which were produced during the Renaissance, either in Italy or elsewhere." After discussing additional details of the forthcoming monograph, Morison closed his letter with his expressed devotion to the art of bookmaking: "On the subject of terms, I would like to see the book brought out in the finest possible way and I would go to considerable trouble here to effect a very handsome book. As a further help towards that end, I would be very pleased to accept, as a sole honorarium, a copy or two of the book itself."[28]

It is of considerable interest to learn of a passing thought by Rogers that the Pacioli volume might be printed by Giovanni Mardersteig, who was then producing magnificent books on the hand press at his Officina Bodoni in Verona. On 5 March 1932, while still in the United States, Rogers wrote to the Grolier Club: "Perhaps it would be pleasant to have it printed by Mardersteig, as he once gave me a standing invitation to make a book at his press; and this might be a very suitable one to produce in Italy — I would go to Verona to live, while it was in the press."[29]

But there were more compelling reasons to produce the book at Cambridge. Rogers explained in *Paragraphs on Printing*: "As I was living in England at the time it gave me an opportunity to work in pleasant collaboration with my friends, Stanley Morison, the author of the monograph, and Walter Lewis, Printer to Cambridge University. Philip Hofer, compiler of the bibliographical chapter in the book, was likewise in London while the work was in progress, and several of my friends in the Library of the British Museum were also consulted frequently; so it was naturally a great pleasure to work in close contact with such a learned and sympathetic group of bookmen. "As Morison had succeeded to my own short term of office (1917-1919) as Printing Advisor to the Cambridge University Press, and still held that appointment, it was inevitable that we make the book there; and it was interesting to renew my old contacts with the staff at the Press, though there had been many changes in the fourteen-year interim."[30]

The completed volume, similar in format to the Club's Dürer and Tory, is a noble tall quarto of 118 pages, 12¼ x 8⅜ inches, printed on a magnificent paper handmade by Batchelor in England, published in an edition of 390 copies with seven copies on "large paper." Rogers chose his Monotype Centaur and had the Morison essay of some nine thousand words set in 18-point. The text was followed by the twenty-three majestic Pacioli letters all on right-hand pages in their original 3¾-inch size, printed in an intense black ink of great depth. In a postscript Morison discussed the classical inscriptional letter and its relation to type, illustrated by four full-page reproductions of alphabets by Giovantonio Tagliente and G. B. Palatino. The line engravings were made by Emery Walker Ltd., and Frederic W. Goudy cast the small type florets that Rogers used for occasional spot ornaments. The initial letters and the title-page border printed in red were drawn from another Pacioli volume, *Summa de Arithmetica*, published in 1494. The binding of the Grolier Club edition was done in London, with a vellum spine and boards covered with an Italian figured paper that Rogers had selected in Florence (plates 42/43/44).

In order to have direct supervision of the printing (his invariable practice) Rogers moved to Cambridge in October 1933. He was especially pleased when Walter Lewis, Printer to the University, who was himself well known

CHAPTER SEVEN: 1928–1935

for excellent presswork, told the men on the pressroom floor to take their orders directly from B.R. and to give him what he wanted. Whereupon Lewis went on vacation and left matters in charge of his associate, Brooke Crutchley, who later also became Printer to the University.

In his autobiography, *To Be a Printer* (1980), Crutchley looked back to the printing of the *Pacioli*: "I had heard something of his methods from Nobbs but could hardly have grasped the full import."* After describing Rogers' long preparatory efforts, Crutchley continued, "Bruce Rogers is still with us, and so far I think we have printed four pages of his book! His paper is two-page size, and there has been endless trouble about damping it the right amount. He doesn't approve of sponging, but must have it laid between wet boards, with a moist blanket placed around them to keep the edges damp. First the boards are too wet and then not wet enough. The formes have to be double-rolled, and of course the ink has too much gloss in it, or is too blue, or too black. He goes over the blocks and initial letters with a tool, touching them up on the machine. We do what he wants and don't worry him. But I don't believe the book will ever be done." Nevertheless, Rogers knew what he wanted, and the work went forward to the ends he alone foresaw. "Today," continued Crutchley, "at B.R.'s instigation we have got in two racks for hanging his sheets to dry.... He has been spending the morning painting over the black parts of the printed sheets to get rid of the gloss and spreading them over Lewis's floor to dry.... The machine was standing all yesterday because the red ink wasn't right and he went to London to see the maker and supervise the mixing of a new supply to the exact shade he wanted."[31] A week later the ink had not dried. Here again, as he had done for the *Odyssey*, instead of using an ink with varnish, Rogers insisted on the use of balsam of copaiba.

The *Pacioli* title page is of special interest. The original type arrangement used for the book's prospectus was set in large sizes of Centaur capitals

---

*F. G. Nobbs, a compositor at the Press when Rogers was the advisor there in 1917–1919, was greatly impressed by B.R.'s working methods. In due course Nobbs became supervisor of the composing room and designer of much of the Press' book and ephemeral printing.

and lower-case letters. The decorative border was printed in red. As thus designed it was a handsome, monumental page, but at the last moment Rogers had an inspired change of mind. With a reduction in the number of words, the page was entirely re-set in 72-point capitals, with a few hand-drawn smaller sizes tucked in to accommodate date and design. But Rogers found the block of large capitals a little too bold, and proceeded to thin down all the serifs with a graver to approximate, he said, the finish of Pacioli's alphabet. The final printed design is a page of true grandeur tempered with grace—a beautiful title page unique in the whole history of the printed book. Indeed, it may be compared favorably with the most exquisite pages of illuminated manuscripts.

It is a pleasure here to quote an eloquent appreciation of this work by John Dreyfus, distinguished British practitioner and historian of the typographic arts: "Never in all his output did BR so successfully combine in one book such masterly handling of his Centaur type with his remarkable ability to redraw ancient ornamental material (and in so doing to make it entirely his own). Nor do I know of any other BR book in which format, paper, inks, and presswork were in such impeccable harmony. This volume fulfills BR's expressed hankering for a book that 'ought almost to be identified in the dark, merely by the feel or sound of it.' Turn off the light, touch it—and listen."[32]

During the spring and summer of 1934 Rogers was again in Europe. With the *Pacioli* completed and the Bible making good progress on press, Rogers joined Alan Villiers during a month in Denmark and spent ten days sailing back to England on Villiers' new ship. In a letter to George Macy from London on 6 October 1934 concerning the *Aesop*, then in production at the Oxford University Press, Rogers added that he was spending "most of my spare time since then in helping get the ship ready for her 1½ yrs. trip. I have painted her new name 'Joseph Conrad' on both bows and the stern and am now making a likeness of Conrad for a figure-head. Am modelling it in clay to be carved in wood later. It's considerably more than life-size. I worked on it steadily today from 11 A.M. to 6 P.M. without stopping for

CHAPTER SEVEN: 1928–1935

luncheon. We expect to leave Ipswich next Thursday or Friday and I shall go only as far as Plymouth. From there Villiers will take her to Nassau and then to Newport News and N.Y. arriving just before Xmas, but I don't want to spend all that time at sea."[33]

The *Joseph Conrad* reached New York on schedule. On a bitterly cold day in January 1935, Rogers was on hand at Pier A North River, where, swinging under the bowsprit of the small square-rigged ship, he bolted the figurehead in place. The ship with its crew and apprentices would soon leave on a voyage around the world under sail, the Bruce Rogers figurehead pointing the way. At the end of the winter B.R. returned to London and to the Bible then approaching completion.

THE OXFORD LECTERN BIBLE

Some years after World War I the Canadian government planned a memorial chapel for the battlefield of Ypres (pronounced "Wipers" by the soldiers), where so many of their young men lay buried. As a memorial from the British people King George ordered that a folio Bible, worthy of the occasion, be presented to the chapel.* But since no great pulpit Bible had been printed in England since the Baskerville folio of 1763, the Librarian of Windsor Castle could find only an inadequate substitute. (The Doves Press folio Bible, completed in 1905, is a work of considerable beauty, but its five chaste volumes are essentially a private press *tour de force* not suitable for daily church use.)

During the more than five centuries since the invention of printing, the Bible has been published in innumerable editions, in every conceivable size and shape and typeface, with and without illustration. There have been impressive polyglot folios and Bibles for special occasions, such as the Eliot

---

*There are conflicting reports concerning the origin of the need for a new Bible. The reason given above is recalled by the present writer as being current at the time the Bible appeared in 1935, and it was so told by Rogers in *An Account of the Making of the Oxford Lectern Bible*. But in the Bible's prospectus issued by the Oxford University Press on publication, it is stated, "A few years ago His Late Majesty King George v wished to give a handsome Bible for the Lectern of a new Cathedral in New York."

Indian Bible printed in Massachusetts in 1663, but since the appearance of the majestic Gutenberg Bible in the fifteenth century, only rarely have volumes been produced in which the beauty of the printed page was consistent with the significance of the words.

Humphrey Milford, publisher of the Oxford University Press, aware that the Press had failed to meet the King's request, suggested that they proceed at once with plans to produce an English Bible that would serve the needs of the church and at the same time achieve nobility of form. Early in January 1929, Milford, together with John Johnson, Printer to the University, invited the American Bruce Rogers, then resident in London, to undertake the design of a new Oxford Lectern Bible. The text would be that of the King James Authorized Version, first printed in London in 1611.

The specifications called for a folio (page size 16 x 12 inches) that would fit on the brass lecterns of most Anglican churches. The text would include the Apocrypha and the Translators' Preface, and the whole volume was not to exceed 1,250 pages in length. At a conference in January, Milford, Johnson, and Rogers were joined by Hubert Foss, designer of music publications issued by the Oxford University Press, who urged that the Monotype Centaur (then approaching completion) should be used for composition of the Bible.* Milford and Johnson were of the same opinion, but Rogers, unwilling to make a hasty decision, agreed to begin at once with the preparation of trial settings.

The 22-point Centaur, which seemed the most likely size, was found to be too extravagant of space and too open and light. For a page with more depth of color Rogers next tried Goudy's Newstyle, but saw it as "too striking in effect" and too typographic. B.R.'s purpose was, he wrote, "to produce a clear, legible page reminiscent of no particular period but as handsome as might be under the limitations."[34] He then tried Monotype Bembo, but Milford, Foss, and Johnson continued to prefer Centaur. In order to meet the need to stay within 1,250 pages, condensation of the Centaur would be necessary, involving re-design of many letters in the font. W. I. Burch,

---

*Hubert Foss, a founding member of the Double Crown Club (a group of committed English designers, printers, and publishers), was himself involved in typography.

CHAPTER SEVEN: 1928–1935

Managing Director of the Monotype Corporation in London, immediately agreed to make whatever changes might be needed. He supplied tracings of the 22-point Centaur patterns over which Rogers redrew all the ascending and descending letters, shortening their stems, compressing laterally the rounded loops of b, d, p, and q, and he reduced the widths of e, n, o, and u. The capitals, already slightly shorter than the ascending letters, were acceptable without change, but a new cutting of small capitals was necessary. These revisions made it possible to cast the 22-point type on a 19-point body. The space saved, horizontally and vertically, met the restriction not to exceed 1,250 pages. Thus Centaur became the final choice, and the Bible, completed five years later, contained 1,238 pages (plates 48 and 49).

With the decision made for the type of the main text, Rogers proceeded to cope with the many other typographic problems inherent in a work of such complexity. Almost a full year was consumed in setting up trial pages and in the design, cutting, and casting of new type for the special needs. Verse numbering was retained for which Rogers preferred Monotype Plantin figures (as printers designate numbers) rather than those in the Centaur font. He then made drawings for a new paragraph mark to accompany the figures. Centaur type was used for all book and chapter headings, running heads, and other details. The Arrighi italic was used on some pages of the front matter. New capitals drawn by Rogers, somewhat bolder than the regular Centaur font, were cut for the three-line initials throughout the text; for the five-line initials that appear only at the beginning of each book, new capitals were drawn and photo-engraved. These and many other details were described by Rogers in a comprehensive and extraordinarily interesting illustrated twenty-four-page quarto pamphlet, *An Account of the Making of the Oxford Lectern Bible*, written at the request of the president of the Lanston Monotype Machine Company of Philadelphia. Designed by Rogers, it was printed in the Bible types by John Johnson at the Oxford University Press shortly after the Bible's publication.*

---

*The spelling of a few words such as "form" and "forme," and a few minor transpositions in phrasing, were adjusted to conform with English and American usage. The text here quoted has been taken from the American edition.

Rogers' approach to the design of the Bible, and especially the account of the steps in the development of the title page (included in the above-mentioned pamphlet), is very revealing of his methods.

> I had decided in the beginning that notwithstanding its size of page the composition should not be ponderous or too formal—"monumental," I believe, is the word for the appearance I wished to avoid. I wanted this book to appear as though I were accustomed to knocking off large folios daily, or at least weekly, as mere routine work.
>
> So my first sketch for the title-page was as conventional as that of any ordinary octavo Bible. It was made merely to get the copy on the page and as a point of departure. To avoid the formal monumental effect mentioned before I decided that as the headings throughout the book were to be composed largely of lower-case type the title-page too should be set mostly, if not wholly, in that form of letter. It would be wearisome to detail the various transformations through which the page went on its way to its final form. At one point I even abandoned lower-case and sketched a page entirely of capitals. (I shall never be quite sure it wouldn't have been better than the existing one.) The words HOLY BIBLE were drawn and re-drawn six or eight times— in outline letters, in shaded letters, in red letters. They were photo-engraved on copper, they were cut on wood and finally on brass. No size of Centaur was exactly the right size for the large block of lower-case, so it was set in 60-point and reduced by photo-etching to its present dimensions. (The practised eye will note that the final word "Command" was placed out of center to avoid the unpleasant proximity of the d to a y in the line above.) The letters for the one italic line were cut especially in that size from the Arrighi italic patterns; though the swash letter at the beginning of the line was furnished later by the Ludlow Typograph Company from one of their italic founts, as it seemed to have just the right decorative quality to relieve the more rigid effect of the Roman type.[35]

CHAPTER SEVEN: 1928–1935

A further passage in the *Account* should be quoted because it reveals one of the hidden problems in the practice of typography as an articulated craft, i.e., the importance of the image of words in their infinite combinations. On seeing the first completed pages of Genesis set in type, Rogers wrote:

> My first sight of them was a distinct disappointment. They lacked the even and solid effect of the trial pages we had set in the same type at the Monotype works, and for a time I was puzzled as to where the discrepancy lay. But on going back to the earlier Monotype proofs I soon found the reason.
>
> The passage I had chosen at random for the text of our first trial lines, and which we had gone on repeating in each succeeding trial, was from II Chronicles, and it happened to be one made up largely of exceptionally long words and sentences, which when composed looked almost like a paragraph of Latin; whereas the opening chapter of Genesis contains many words of one syllable, with numerous short verses and other interruptions of its continuity. (The words "And God," usually preceded by a verse mark and number, occur twenty-nine times in the first page.) So it was futile to expect the same evenness of line and color that we had achieved in the trials. By going over the spacing carefully we were able to improve it, but throughout the Bible there are pages where the many short verses or the enumeration of many proper names, with their necessary capitals, preclude the possibility of smooth composition.[36]

Two years after the meeting at which Rogers had been approached with the request to design the Bible, preliminaries had been completed and final composition had begun. Having seen the first thirty-two pages in type, and having a promised schedule of eight new pages every fortnight, Rogers could express his satisfaction on 29 January 1931 when he wrote to Carl Rollins that the Press was doing remarkably well with the spacing, "and I have very little to alter in the proofs. Johnson is delighted with my praise of their work on it and although my supervision of the spacing was to cover only Genesis and I was to exit with Exodus, he may let me go on with it, at least as long as I'm over here. . . . The Oxford Press is as pleasant a place to work with, and in, as Cambridge was—but I don't suppose they ever before let an outsider get directly at the workmen, or run around the press loose."[37]

During the years involved in the production of the *Odyssey*, the *Pacioli*, and the Bible, Rogers had divided his time between Europe and America. After the usual winter in the United States, and as the Bible approached completion, Rogers returned in April 1935 to supervise its binding.

Because he had earlier found that the 16 x 12-inch page allowed only rather cramped margins, Rogers had proposed that a limited number of copies be printed with a more ample page, on handmade paper, for the larger cathedral lecterns and for collectors and others interested in the book as a work of art. Finally, one thousand copies of the standard size were issued on Wolvercote paper, bulking about 3½ inches, bound in leather and sold at fifteen guineas per copy at a time when the exchange value of a guinea was approximately five dollars. And two hundred copies were produced, with magnificent presswork (damp printing) on a superb Batchelor handmade paper, page 18¼ x 13 inches, bulking 4½ inches, hand-sewed and bound between boards covered with a fabric made to Rogers' specifications.* Of these, 180 copies were offered for sale, of which forty copies were allotted to Rogers for sale in America. The large-paper edition was sold in England for fifty guineas per copy, in the United States for $265. (At this writing, in 1987, a copy was sold by an American bookseller for $12,500!)

Some years earlier, at the Barcham Green & Son paper mill in England, Rogers had seen a small lot of an especially beautiful paper made from an unusual fiber imported from Japan. With considerable reluctance the Messrs Green agreed to sell the paper of which there was only enough for one copy of the Bible. This copy, an inch taller and wider than the handmade-paper copies, was intended by Rogers for the Library of Congress in Washington. Its presence there, handsomely bound in full leather, was made possible by the generosity of sixty of B.R.'s friends, whose names were printed on a leaf of the book.

*It was anticipated that many of these single volumes would be rebound more elegantly in two volumes.

CHAPTER SEVEN: 1928–1935

In the final pages of his account of the making of the Bible, Rogers paid tribute to the men at the Oxford University Press who set the type and printed the sheets. His words of appreciation are now a nostalgic reminiscence of the processes of direct impressional printing of metal type on paper, called letterpress, since superseded in a changed technological and computerized society:

> So I venture to say that I believe this Bible, from beginning to end, to be the finest and most consistent example of composition and make-up that has been produced in our day. I may say this, as I had very little to do with it. It was done by the man at the keyboard, the man at the stone, the man at the head of the Monotype composing room, and the man in the proof room. And when the forms of type passed out of their hands to the press room the same care and skill were exercised by the head of that department and the man on the press. For over four years this vigilance was maintained, so that in the finished work no deviation is observable from the standards of color, impression, and register that were set in the beginning, beyond those slight variations inevitable when printing on hand-made paper.[38]

The Oxford Lectern Bible was the last book that Rogers would make on English soil. The last paragraph in the *Account* seems to the present writer to have been a symbolic summation of his years of achievement in England, of his congenial relations with the printing houses that produced his books, of his love of the English countryside, and the depth of pleasure in the many personal relationships he would leave behind:

> Back of these skilled workmen were, of course, John Johnson, Printer to the University, and his staff of executives, giving effect to my various requirements; and these requirements must have seemed to them, at least at the outset, somewhat wayward and arbitrary. But even in those early days of the work their coöperation was whole-hearted and unstinted, and as we settled down into the gradually evolved method of treatment (which nevertheless allowed reasonable latitude for the variants we were to encounter later on) my occasional visits to Oxford for

inspection of progress made and discussion of problems still to be met became, to me at least, the most pleasant associations I can recall in all my varied experience of printing houses. And no less delightful were the long evenings after work hours when the Printer would take me out with him to see some splendid old country house, or some church or alms-house in a neighboring village, where he was sure to know the leading dealer in antiquities or the Mayor of the town—perhaps both in one person. Then we would drive homeward through the long twilight to his own pleasant house and gardens at Old Headington for another talk on the next day's work. Surely no book has ever been produced under happier or more auspicious circumstances.[39]

The Oxford Lectern Bible represents the full flowering of Bruce Rogers' genius as a designer of books. In the grandeur of its conception, in its classic severity without ornamentation, in the smooth flow of words across the page, and in the mastery of the subtle depth of impression of type on paper, the Oxford Bible takes its place among the noblest works done since the invention of movable type.

After completion of the Bible Rogers returned to the United States and spent the twenty-two years remaining to him at October House in Connecticut. He enjoyed a vacation trip to Europe in the summer of 1936 visiting friends and renewing his old haunts in England. (His close friend James Hendrickson later reported summer visits to England until 1939, but the present writer finds no correspondence in substantiation.)

The many books and ephemera of those late years were produced in the United States. To the last days of his life B.R.'s commitment to the printed page was undiminished, and his pursuit of every detail of manufacture was never less thorough. Nevertheless, he would not again reach the heights of his earlier work.

1933 1954

Limited Editions Club Books

Bruce Rogers designed twelve substantial books for the Limited Editions Club of New York. The first of these, *Aesop's Fables*, published in 1933, was produced at the Oxford University Press during the years when Rogers was in England; the others were produced in or near New York under his close supervision. The last, *L'Allegro* and *Il Penseroso*, was completed in 1954, when B.R. was eighty-four years of age.

George Macy was the founder and director of the Club that published a limited edition every month for its fifteen hundred members. His announced purpose was to make beautiful books — the classics of literature edited with introductions by prominent scholars, illustrated by leading artists, and produced by the best typographic designers and printers in Europe, America, and occasionally elsewhere. Organization and plans began in the booming twenties, but the first book did not appear until October 1929, the black month on the New York Stock Exchange that ushered in the Great Depression. Nevertheless, Macy maintained his extraordinary monthly schedule through the Depression years and until his death in 1956. (The Club continued for some years under family direction, followed by several changes of ownership.) Macy, who combined the capacities of a productive idealist with the acumen of a successful business entrepreneur, issued more than three hundred exceptional volumes during his twenty-seven years as publisher. Many of these books were examples of typographic elegance and sophistication; many were made to please those subscribers who were primarily interested in the appearance of the titles on their living room shelves. Correspondence between Rogers and Macy reveals a professional relationship of respect between publisher and designer; of their intention (not always realized) to achieve significant bookmaking; and evidence of Macy's support (if reluctant at times) of B.R.'s costly pursuit of infinite detail.

An edition of fables by Aesop had been planned in London by Rogers and Wilfred Merton (Emery Walker's associate) to consist of forty-five fables with early Italian woodcuts. In 1931 Rogers showed experimental pages to Macy, who promptly took over the project. He increased its scope to 198 fables translated and edited by the British bibliographer Victor Scholderer, with forty-two Florentine woodcuts that were redrawn or retouched by Rogers. As always, B.R. was fully involved in all of the planning and editorial decisions.

Aesop's Fables (1933), hand set in the Fell types at the Oxford University Press, became a book of 232 pages, 10¼ x 7⅛ inches, printed on Barcham Green handmade paper, bound at Oxford with a vellum back and marbled paper sides. A printer's "fist" was especially designed by B.R. to point the moral for each tale. In this volume (plates 45/46) he brought together antique Greek fables, early Italian woodcuts, a Dutch typeface, modern English scholarship and craftsmanship, to make a joyous book of rugged charm. Deservedly chosen by him as one of his successful "thirty," the *Aesop* was made in the years when Rogers was at his typographic peak, in the surroundings he most enjoyed.

Utopia by Sir Thomas More, the second book designed by Rogers for the Limited Editions Club, was sent to the membership a year after *Aesop's Fables*. Originally written in Latin and printed in Louvain in 1516, the text, translated into English by Ralph Robynson, was first printed in England in 1551. The Club's edition, with an introduction by H.G. Wells, and two sixteenth-century woodcuts, retouched by B.R., was set in Linotype Janson and produced in Mount Vernon at the Printing House of William Edwin Rudge —a tall octavo on an English handmade paper, bound with a vellum back and Frederic Warde's patterned paper sides. In the *Utopia* Rogers returned to the use of typographic ornaments that he composed by ingenious angling of the type units to achieve a lavish colored border for a brilliant title page (plate 50). With the same type units he made ingenious combinations for headpieces, initial letters, spot ornaments, and the colophon page, reminiscent of book decoration during the sixteenth century, the period of *Utopia*'s first publication.

THE PLAYS OF WILLIAM SHAKESPEARE

During 1934-1935 when Rogers was still spending several months each year in England, George Macy offered him the commission to design an imposing new edition of the complete plays of Shakespeare, each play to be printed and bound separately in a total set of thirty-seven volumes. Macy proposed a large format (page 13 x 8¾ inches) to match that of the 1623 Shakespeare First Folio. The text, with the original spelling and punctuation retained, would be edited by the English Elizabethan scholar Herbert Farjeon, who believed that the pungent vigor of the original had been dissipated in modernization. Rogers accepted the assignment with enthusiasm, and looked forward to the work as of major importance.

In addition to the fifteen hundred copies to be made for the Club's subscribers, Macy planned the printing of an additional 450 sets for sale to the public. For promotional purposes he issued an impressive cloth-bound brochure in 1938, also in folio size, entitled "Shakespeare: A Review and a Preview." It contained brief essays on Shakespeare's life and works, an account of earlier printings, notes on the text by editor and publisher, a discussion by Rogers on its design, and specimens of type pages with a few forthcoming illustrations. Each play as issued would have full-page illustrations for a frontispiece and for the opening of each act — a different artist to be chosen by Macy for each play. The full-page illustrations would not affect the typography.

In planning for the tall folio pages, Rogers wrote that he wanted a type that "should be bold and vigorous enough to convey to the reader's eye something of the rugged Elizabethan quality of the text. The publisher's generous conception of the undertaking allowed a large format, and therefore a correspondingly large type."[1] The first experiments were hand set at the Oxford University Press in the Fell types, and in 1936 John Johnson provided Macy with an estimate for complete production. When, however, it was decided to print this large undertaking in the United States, since hand setting was out of the question, it became necessary to find an acceptable machine type.

After experiments with several machine faces Rogers finally turned to the type then incorrectly attributed to the Dutch letter designer Anton Janson, who lived less than a hundred years after Shakespeare. (The type was actually designed by Nikolas Kis, a Hungarian punch cutter who lived in Amsterdam.) The Lanston Monotype Machine Company in Philadelphia agreed to make a new cutting of an 18-point size in close facsimile of the original type, "preserving all the slight irregularities of cutting and alignment which help to give it life and vigor." Not satisfied with the 18-point Janson italic, Rogers preferred a new cutting that had been made by Sol Hess, Art Director of the Monotype Company in Philadelphia. Several characters were, as usual, corrected by B.R., and a few swash capitals added by him. Italic small capitals were needed for the text, and those were made by re-cutting the italic capitals of the Monotype Garamond Bold. Concerning these procedures, James Hendrickson added a footnote in *Paragraphs on Printing*: "The brief description of this partial re-cutting of the Janson type sounds quite simple here, but it was anything but that. To accomplish it B.R. had to conduct a detailed and almost daily correspondence with Mr. Sol Hess . . . for some weeks, a reading of which would be an eye-opener for anyone who may fancy that fine printing is principally a pleasant pastime."[2]

The first experimental pages in the United States were set to Rogers' specifications by D. B. Updike at the Merrymount Press in Boston during October and November of 1937. Apparently Macy found Updike's estimates for continuation of the work unfavorable. The next set-ups and trial proofs were made by Ted Bailey, Manager of the Printing Office of the Yale University Press in New Haven. In the end, Macy turned to the Press of A. Colish in New York City, where the type was finally set and the thirty-seven volumes were printed (plates 51/52).

Rogers' meticulous involvement in the text of his books and details of production is again revealed in almost a dozen long letters he sent to Macy

CHAPTER EIGHT: 1933–1954

when Macy was abroad. The first of these was typical and may well be quoted in full. On 28 January 1938 B.R. wrote from his hotel in New York:

> I had hoped to hear from you before this about the titles, the front matter to Vol. I, etc., but I suppose you've had your hands full of more important things.
>
> I now think I would like to do this: (if Farjeon agrees.) Print the titles in short form *in caps* on the title pages—in modern spelling (as the page is modern in its remaining wording—your imprint); and at the head of the text the longer titles exactly as they are in the 1st Folio—mostly in large lower-case, but *not* following the typography of the folio as to words in caps, etc. Many of the plays have: THE Merry Wives of Windsor and things like that—which we can disregard, as this is not a facsimile in any sense.
>
> I hope, too, that Farjeon agrees with the author of that article in *The Colophon* about the old forms of shortened words, like "listening," "stolen," "most" etc. etc.—which the *Colophon* article approves. Also the various spelling of proper names and the capitalization of abstract nouns—Plenty, Justice, Death, etc. as given. I would like to have as much variety from the standard practice of modern spelling and usage as is consistent with ease of reading—that is, as Elizabethan as possible. That will help justify the use of an antique type and style. But of course these matters are entirely in Farjeon's hands.
>
> Everything is going as well here as could be expected. Bailey comes down to N.Y. almost every week and we lay plans. Sol Hess has been over once. I expect to have proofs of the Roman type, perhaps tomorrow. I have drawn swash letters for the italic and otherwise modified some of the other letters—small caps, etc. Bailey now has founts of the larger sizes, ready to experiment with the headings as soon as copy is received.
>
> I have spent a good deal of time investigating Shakespeare's arms for the title-pages. So far as I can find they have *never* been correctly drawn according to the description in the grant of arms to S's father.

LIMITED EDITIONS CLUB BOOKS

Carl Lohmann, Secretary of Yale, has been making investigations for me, as he is an enthusiast on heraldry. Tucker Brooks is also advising, especially about the wall-decorations at the tailor's shop in Oxford, of which I hope to make cover-papers. I got a piece of the linen which purports to reproduce the colors, from George Carter, but I doubt if it is accurate. Henry Canby also has a piece which he is going to send me. But I don't think any of the linens reproduce the colors very accurately. Couldn't you (or Johnson) get some one to go to the painted room and color a section of the photostat which I enclose, of my sketch for the cover, matching the colors as accurately as possible. Not *every* flower, but enough to bring in all the main tints used. There will probably be four printings, the fifth color being the paper on which the printing will be done (the lightest tints of the wall—high-lights on the interlacings, etc.)

And particularly the colors used in the frieze at the top and the band across the bottom, which are not represented in the linens printed.

The lettering is only roughly drawn and will be improved—but I think it must be Gothic to match the rest of the design, instead of matching the typography inside. I don't know yet how we can letter the backs, as most of the books will be so thin. I had thought of plain linen for the backs, with very little showing on the sides—not more than ½ in. Could we use that cheap kind of binding vellum (called "forel" in England) or the parchment such as we imported for the "Utopia"? Or would it be too expensive? Meynell will know the stuff I mean, I used it on the backs of Morison's "Fra Pacioli" and it came from a firm in Newcastle-on-Tyne—I can't think of the name at present—something like Nickerson. Any London binder will know.

The paper is causing me the most trouble. Gorham Bliss came down and after his return made another trial run, but it wasn't as satisfactory as the first one.* I didn't know that you had had a special dandy-roll made, to match the Æsop paper. I don't like the roll, as the chain marks

---

*Gorham Bliss was president of the Worthy Paper Company, a small mill in Massachusetts committed to making excellent paper by machine.

CHAPTER EIGHT: 1933–1954

are too close together for so large a page, and they are so heavy that when the sheets are finished they have distinct glossy stripes up and down. I want him to re-cover the roll with a bolder pattern of weave — the color and texture of the Æsop paper is all I care to duplicate, *not* the laid marks. If I had known you had ordered a roll I could have given Gorham the exact specifications. He says the roll cost $115 and the alterations will cost about $75, but I would very much like you to authorize the change, as I am certain we will get very tired of the irregular and prominent chain marks when we see them in book after book. If you will authorize the improvement will you just cable me "Yes" to the Royalton — or your office, and I will see it is done at once. There will be no delay, as we shall not need paper for a couple of months yet, at least.

I have also suggested that it would be a good thing to have about a ton of the paper made slightly heavier for use on title-pages and lining papers, where there will be need for opacity and added strength. Do you approve of that? The title-pages will all be printed on a job-press as a single fold, on account of registering the gold & silver of the arms. Enough can be run off at one time for all 37 vols., as the arms will always occur in the same position, so the process will not be an extra expense. I am investigating various foils to use.

This, I believe, covers all the points up to the present.[3]

Some of the editorial and typographic details discussed in the above letter were changed as the work moved into production. After a day at the Worthy Paper Company mill in April, Rogers wrote to Macy, "We all think that we have turned out perhaps the finest sheet of paper ever made in America — certainly for the price — and everybody at the mill got quite excited — the Bliss's, the machine men and even the office clerks."[4] The Shakespeare arms were ultimately drawn by Rogers and printed from photoengraved line plates in black and a tint, not with gold or silver as first anticipated. The tall, slender volumes were finally bound with gilt tops, the backs in binder's linen stamped in gold. The boards were covered with paper made especially for this edition. Its interesting derivation and pertinence was told by Rogers in *Paragraphs on Printing* (pages 71-72):

> Twelve years ago [in 1930] a remarkable discovery was made at Oxford. The premises at No. 3, Cornmarket Street, were in occupation of John Davenant, a vintner, from about 1592 to 1614. Shakespeare was a close friend of Davenant's and stood godfather to his son, William, and he "was wont to go into Warwickshire once a yeare, and did in his journey lye at this house in Oxon, where he was exceedingly respected."
>
> One of the rooms in the existing house was beautifully decorated in color and partly panelled, but all this interesting work, dating from about 1550, had been long lost sight of, and was not rediscovered until 1930 when some minor alterations were in contemplation. When some canvas and about a dozen layers of wallpaper were stripped from the walls, an interesting painted decoration was revealed in all its original brilliancy.
>
> A drawing was made from photographs of this wall, and sent to Oxford to be colored on the spot by a careful artist. The working drawings for four colors were then made, zinc plates produced from these and printed in the same tints as the original. The title, "The Plays of W. Shakespeare," was substituted in a panel at the top, in lettering modeled on that of the pious exhortations painted within similar panels as a frieze in the room that the Poet himself possibly may have occupied in his friend's house.[5]

The thirty-seven volumes of the Shakespeare plays, published in 1940, were followed a year later by *The Poems of William Shakespeare* in two companion volumes to the plays, in the same folio size, set in the same type, admirably printed at the Press of A. Colish on the same paper. Whereas the comedies, tragedies, and histories were illustrated by thirty-seven artists in their differing interpretations and techniques, the two volumes of poetry were decorated by Rogers with typographic flowers and ornaments. All the section headings and headpieces were painstaking and elaborate combina-

CHAPTER EIGHT: 1933–1954

tions, each in a different two-color arrangement of soft tones unusual in Rogers' earlier work. The cover paper was an overall pattern combining the units used on inside pages.

The edition, which was limited to fifteen hundred copies only, for the Club's normal membership, was edited by Herbert Farjeon and contained an introduction by Louis Untermeyer. It is B.R.'s final choice among his "successful thirty"—a decision with which the present writer would respectfully disagree in favor of many other books; not the least, surely, would be the remarkable Boswell Papers.

In the attempt to make a reasoned evaluation of these volumes one should consider the impact of the whole set, its weight in the mass, and the space occupied on collectors' tables and shelves when large ancestral homes are no longer of our time. Clearly it was the publisher's intent to issue Shakespeare's imperishable words in sumptuous form. In Rogers' design, and with his usual commitment to the spirit of the undertaking, he met the publisher's wishes in full. Although it can be a considerable pleasure to read a single volume of Shakespeare's works on a generous page in a large, rugged type, the introduction of constantly differing illustrative interpretations from volume to volume is disruptive. In this matter it is of more than passing interest to see in a letter to Macy of 28 February 1938, that B.R.'s own personal set would at his request be bound without the illustrations.

During the years when Rogers was at work on the Shakespeare, Macy asked him to design *The Wind in the Willows* by Kenneth Grahame, with an introduction by A. A. Milne, illustrated by Arthur Rackham. It was a special publication outside the regular annual series for members, for which the holders of the copyright (Charles Scribner's Sons) imposed a limitation of two thousand copies. The watercolor drawings by the very popular Rackham were the main selling feature, and Macy stated that he could have sold ten thousand copies. The illustrations were reproduced in full color by The Sun Engraving Company in London; the text of the ample quarto volume was set in Rogers' choice of Linotype Baskerville and printed by Peter

Beilenson at his Walpole Printing Office in Mount Vernon, New York — a gay and colorful quarto volume.

The Essays of Francis Bacon, with an introduction by Christopher Morley, and a bibliographical note by A. S. W. Rosenbach, was issued in 1944 during the Second World War. It was handsomely designed by Rogers as a stately Elizabethan folio without illustrations; with initial letters by B.R. and an occasional spot use of a typographic floret. The type was the Shakespeare Janson on a page 12¾ x 8¾ inches, printed at the newly established press of William E. Rudge's Sons, New York, in an edition of eleven hundred copies for a somewhat reduced wartime Club membership. The binding was made from an overall design by B.R. in blue ink on a gold paper.

Plato: The Republic, translated with an introduction by Benjamin Jowett, also issued in 1944, was planned as a modest tall octavo (9⅝ x 6¼ inches), straightforward in design. For the chapter headings Fritz Kredel provided medallions cut in wood and printed in black and brown. Linotype Granjon was used for the text; the edition of twelve hundred was produced by William E. Rudge's Sons, New York.

The Federalist, papers by Alexander Hamilton, James Madison, and John Jay, with an introduction by Carl Van Doren, was completed in 1945. Set in Linotype Original Old Style, page 9⅝ x 6¼ inches, the book was produced at the American Book-Stratford Press, a manufacturing printing plant in New York, in two volumes on a pale green paper. The books were embellished by Rogers with type ornaments reminiscent of early Americana.

The Extant Works of Epicurus (publication suggested by B.R.), a comfortable octavo in Greek and English, was completed in 1947. The left-hand pages in Greek were set in Intertype Lambrakis at a Greek-American printing shop in New York; the Cyril Bailey English translation on facing pages was set in Intertype Garamond; initial letters were in the Eve type and printed in red. For the section headpieces, suggestive perhaps of a Greek frieze printed in gold, Rogers used the stylistic type ornaments of humans and animals designed by Howard Trafton for the American Type Founders Company. The edition was produced by Aldus Printers, New York. The attractive cover in

CHAPTER EIGHT: 1933–1954

a simulated crushed black goatskin was blind-stamped in a Greek pattern drawn by B.R.

Gulliver's Travels, the satirical work by Jonathan Swift, sent to the membership in 1950, was conceived by Rogers as two sharply contrasting volumes. *A Voyage to Lilliput*, about the country where the residents were tiny, he made into a miniature volume, page 3½ x 2¼ inches, with the text set in a very small 6-point Monotype Garamont. For *A Voyage to Brobdingnag*, about the country inhabited by giants, the volume itself was gigantic, page 18½ x 13¼ inches, set in 42-point Ludlow Garamond. For title pages, headpieces, and initial letters, Rogers employed typographic ornament. Printed by Aldus Printers, New York, each volume was covered with an appropriate map of the voyages, drawn by B.R. The large, heavy slipcase for the giant volume was constructed so that it would also contain its tiny companion.

The Gulliver books in the two volumes — one difficult to read because of excessively small type, the other cumbersome because of its huge size and weight — were whimsical devices despite Rogers' normal respect for literature and its presentation. Perhaps he thought that the members of the Limited Editions Club, for whom these books were made, would enjoy a bizarre typographic solution to a work that itself was written with mischievous humor.

The Complete Poems of Robert Frost, with a preface by the author and an introduction by Louis Untermeyer, was published in 1950. The Limited Editions Club periodically awarded a medal to, and printed the work of, "that [living] American writer who shall have published the book considered most likely to attain the stature of a classic." Macy chose the Frost opus as the work they wished to honor in 1950, and asked Thomas W. Nason (who was already associated with the Spiral Press as an illustrator of Frost books) to make a number of wood engravings to embellish the new publication (plate 53).

Frost, whose poetry had been printed by some of the best American presses, was pleased that Bruce Rogers had been chosen for the new edition and added a note in a letter to Macy of 30 June 1950, stating, "It has always been of the greatest importance to me who designed the books I wrote."[6]

Showing his respect for Robert Frost's poetry, Rogers designed two splendid volumes. The verse was set in Linotype Scotch Roman for a generous page of 10½ x 7⅛ inches, with Bulmer for the title page, printed at the Marchbanks Press, New York, and bound in an appropriate handsome blue denim.

L'Allegro and *Il Penseroso* by John Milton, with introductory essays by W. P. Trent and Chauncey B. Tinker, and with twelve watercolors by William Blake illustrating the poems, appeared in 1954. The text was composed by Mackenzie & Harris, San Francisco, in Monotype Van Dijck, printed by the Thistle Press, New York; the watercolor drawings were reproduced in monochrome by the Photogravure and Color Company, New York. Bound dos-à-dos in green buckram, the edition consisted of the usual fifteen hundred copies for the Club's membership, plus an additional 280 copies for the Pierpont Morgan Library, with whose permission the Blake illustrations were reproduced.

1935   1957

October House: The Late Years

The eight years during which Rogers produced his great books in England (1928-1935) were years of special enjoyment in his work, his associates, and the cultivated environment in which he moved. The remaining two decades of his life, when he was at home in October House, were busy years, with a very substantial volume of work accomplished, with new honors received, and with several important exhibitions. As he settled into life in America, B.R. renewed old friendships, invited people to October House, attended meetings of the Grolier Club, the American Institute of Graphic Arts, the Typophiles in New York, the several book groups in Boston and elsewhere. He was elected to membership in the distinguished Century Club and frequently enjoyed two or three days midweek in the city at a nearby hotel.

His domestic situation was somewhat less than happy. Mrs. Pierson, who had been the grandson's child nurse, and who kept the household together when Rogers was spending much time abroad, remained as his housekeeper and hostess, and outlived him. In addition to the growing boy, an aged cousin was given refuge for a few years until her death. Those of B.R.'s friends who visited him with some frequency at October House were aware of discord in the home. Yet as always, Rogers never allowed personal difficulties to intrude on his typographic commitments. In his study at October House he always responded with pleasure and animation to talk about books and printing—including his own.

After long absences in England, the return of Bruce Rogers, with the intention of remaining in the United States, seemed to his American friends, and especially to his many young admirers, to be cause for celebration. In mid-November of 1935 the Typophiles, an informal group of printers, designers, bookbinders, paper manufacturers, librarians, and others dedicated to the printed page, who met from time to time at informal luncheons, invited B.R. to be their guest of honor at a dinner in New York. For the occasion a chap book called *Barnacles from Many Bottoms*, covering many phases of the Rogers career, was "scraped together for the man who loved sailing." It was written, illustrated, printed and bound *con amore* by the more than fifty men and women who also came to dine.

Late in 1935 Rogers designed an insert, *The Journal Up the Straits* by Herman Melville, for *The Colophon*. In the same year he prepared an autographed edition for Houghton Mifflin Company of *The Novels and Stories of Willa Cather*, published in 1937-1938.

The first bibliography of Bruce Rogers' work, prepared by Frederic Warde, described books produced until 1926. In 1936 a new bibliography compiled by Irvin Haas recorded titles completed between 1926 and 1936, and included books until 1926 overlooked by Warde. Printed at the Peter Pauper Press in Mount Vernon, New York, in the Centaur and Arrighi types, the volume contained a note by Rogers and a spirited introductory letter by Beatrice Warde of the English Monotype Corporation.

A distinguished joint committee of the American Institute of Graphic Arts and the Grolier Club organized a comprehensive exhibition of the work of Bruce Rogers that was mounted at the Grolier Club in New York and shown from 16 November 1938 to 8 January 1939. A total of 768 items were on display — from first boyhood efforts, graphic work for college publications, early lettering and book design, and of course the books printed over the years at the Riverside, Montague, Rudge, and other presses in the United States, culminating in the volumes made at the Mall Press and the great university presses in England. In addition there were bookplates, broadsides and other ephemera, studies and drawings for type, preliminary layouts for book design, and Rogers' landscape sketches in black-and-white and watercolor.

The two opening nights at the Grolier Club house were great events for the typographic community — one evening for the American Institute of

CHAPTER NINE: 1935–1957

Graphic Arts, a second for members of the Club. Speeches were delivered by Daniel Berkeley Updike and John T. McCutcheon, and an extended address, which has frequently been quoted in these pages, was delivered by B.R. himself with considerable detail about his career and his philosophical attitudes toward his work. The speeches and bibliographical listings of the 768 pieces in the exhibition were printed in an invaluable volume, *The Work of Bruce Rogers*, published by the Oxford University Press in New York in 1939.

In the same year Rogers received his third academic honor (after Yale and Purdue) from an American university. On 22 June 1939 Harvard conferred an honorary Master of Arts degree with the citation, "Bruce Rogers: A skilled designer of the printed page, adviser to the Press in both this University and in the ancient Cambridge across the sea."

The Second World War, 1939 to 1945, caused difficulties in all phases of production, but Rogers was able to accept commissions and found it possible to keep work moving. In 1940 he finished the design, begun by Frederic Warde, of a three-volume catalogue of the books in English literature in the Carl H. Pforzheimer Library. He was also responsible for three timely wartime broadsides: "We Shall Go On To The End" by Winston Churchill in Centaur type, printed on his own Albion handpress; "The Atlantic Charter" set in Goudy's Hadriano capitals, printed by William Edwin Rudge's Sons (plate 55); and "The Oath of a Freeman," from the first printing done in the United States. And B.R. contributed his design to a Typophile Chap Book, *Bombed But Unbeaten* (1941), a war commentary by Beatrice Warde.

In 1941 Rogers designed *Before Life Began*, for the Rowfant Club of Cleveland, Ohio, an autobiography by Dard Hunter, historian and practitioner of papermaking by hand. The book was printed at the Press of A. Colish on paper handmade at Hunter's own mill in Lime Rock, Connecticut, set in Bulmer type (page $8\frac{3}{4}$ x $5\frac{7}{8}$ inches). The attractive cover paper was made by Veronica Ruzicka. In 1942 Rogers designed *The Tremolino* by Joseph Conrad, a slim 12mo made for publication by the bookseller Philip C. Duschnes, New York, 1942. Dedicated to H. Watson Kent, "Chief instigator of this printing of his favorite sea tale," one thousand copies in Mono-

OCTOBER HOUSE: THE LATE YEARS

type Bulmer type were printed at the Press of A. Colish, New York, with three charming woodcuts in color engraved by Edward A. Wilson. It is one of Rogers' small books of typographic simplicity and elusive charm (plate 54).

Most of the books designed during these late years at October House were printed at the Press of A. Colish, where Rogers had the good fortune to find a friend in Abraham Colish, at whose substantial plant (first in New York, later in its own building in Mount Vernon, outside the city) B.R. was welcomed, with permission to supervise his own work.

Starting in 1940, James Hendrickson induced B.R. to hold meetings, and to talk about his attitudes and methods, that eventually made possible *Paragraphs on Printing*, an informative tract on the art and practice of the printed book. Printed and published in 1943 by William Edwin Rudge's Sons, this quarto volume of some two hundred pages, with full-page reproductions of most of the important Rogers books, provides a rare insight into the mind of a master at work. Hendrickson described its realization in a lecture reprinted in *Heritage of the Graphic Arts*:

> Meetings were arranged once or twice a week between Mr. Rogers, my wife and myself. These meetings would be wherever convenience permitted, in BR's hotel, our own hotel, or perhaps in A. Colish's printing shop, or in the Duschnes bookshop. (There were the occasional jollier get-togethers at dinner or tavern.)
>
> The procedure, in theory, was for J. H. to engage BR in discussion of typographic matters, and for C. B. [Mrs. Hendrickson] to make a short-hand record of these conversations. However, when the notes were translated, the resulting copy all too often was found to be confused and repetitious. . . . The "elicitor" [Hendrickson] would then edit material as necessary, and mail the corrected draft to New Fairfield for the author to approve or rewrite as he might see fit.
>
> This went on for some months with the elicitor treading a delicate path wherein he was swayed between a duty to the publisher to obtain as many words of text as possible and a determination not to lose a

CHAPTER NINE: 1935–1957

highly valued friendship in the process. Periodically BR would put his foot down, as it were, and announce that he was through—"not another word!" Then would come a period of jockeying for more copy until the author's interest could be again aroused. Thus the daily tally of words in hand became an increasingly anxious game. It was a great day when BR lighted upon the word "elicited" for the title-page. His author's eye regained its lustre and the project immediately took a strong tack to windward.

It need hardly be pointed out that the title of *Paragraphs on Printing* came of our artist's seemingly infallible knack of making the most of his materials—in this case a mass of fragmentary and somewhat compromising copy.[1]

The story of Euclid's *Geometry* goes back to the summer of 1930, when Rogers was still in England. Bennett A. Cerf, President of Random House, publishers in New York, wrote and proposed that Rogers design a limited edition of Euclid's *Elements of Geometry, Book I*. Cerf and his partner, Donald S. Klopfer, although general publishers, were also American sales representatives of the English Nonesuch Press, and themselves had commissioned limited editions that were made at several American fine presses.

After some exchange of correspondence, Rogers finally declined the offer on the grounds that he was fully occupied with the Oxford Bible, the *Odyssey*, and other commitments. As a further reason he added in his letter to Cerf of 23 September 1930, that he believed that "any book which is designed with as much care, and after as many trials and rejections, as I give to mine, and which is followed through the whole course of manufacture personally, can *not*, in the very nature of the job, yield profits to two or three middlemen (if you will permit me to call publishers and booksellers by that term, without offense). . . . I doubt if books *ought* to be treated with so much care and consideration of details as I have to give them. But the habit of years is too strong to break now, and I had rather not do a book at all unless it meets my approval down to the last final detail." Cerf closed the correspondence in January 1931 with a letter to Rogers: ". . . bitterly disappointed

OCTOBER HOUSE: THE LATE YEARS

of course, at your final decision that the proposed reprint of Euclid was out of the question. If ever you change your mind on the subject or get some new ideas for such a publication, I hope you will let me know."[2]

A dozen years later, in the United States, Rogers did remember and approached Cerf, who authorized him to proceed with design and to supervise production. In 1944 Random House published a sumptuous tall octavo, Euclid's *Elements of Geometry, Book I*, with an introduction from an essay by Paul Valéry, in an edition of five hundred copies. It was printed at the Press of A. Colish, New York, on an English handmade paper; the decoration in silver and blue on the title page was based on a woodcut by Gordon Craig; the text was set in Goudy's Deepdene italic; some fifty line-engravings of the diagrams were printed in a dozen different colors; and the cloth cover was stamped in silver. Rogers said that this edition was his attempt to atone for having failed geometry in college.

Surviving correspondence between Rogers and the production head at Random House indicates that Rogers did some free-lance designing for the publisher on one or two of their special trade books.

The second half of the 1940s, when B.R. was in his late seventies, continued to be a very active period. On his own initiative he began to plan for another massive folio Bible, this time to be printed in the United States. From 1945 to 1949, in addition to the Bible and a book almost every year for the Limited Editions Club, Rogers produced another half dozen books for other clients. In 1946 the Typophiles issued a biographical chap book (described below); in 1947 he suffered a heart attack; in 1948 he was honored by the American Academy of Arts and Letters.

B.R. Marks & Remarks, a small volume of 150 pages, 7 x 4½ inches, was a compilation of essays on the many phases of Rogers' career, written by his associates and friends, J. M. Bowles, Carl P. Rollins, David Pottinger, Christopher Morley, James Hendrickson, and Frederic Warde. In addition, it contained reproductions of thirty-five of Rogers' printer's marks in their many variations. Edited by Paul A. Bennett, the text set in Emerson type at B.R.'s request, the volume was designed by your present reporter and printed at the Spiral Press, New York. When B.R. was asked when he might

CHAPTER NINE: 1935–1957

write his memoirs, he replied that he found *B.R. Marks & Remarks* an adequate substitute.

At its annual ceremonial on 21 May 1948, the American Academy of Arts and Letters in New York bestowed on Bruce Rogers its gold medal for distinction in the graphic arts. It was gratifying that this group of writers, painters, architects, and musicians should have recognized a book designer. After the presentation by Professor Chauncey Brewster Tinker of Yale University, Rogers concluded his acceptance remarks with: "Printing has had many great days—when Gutenberg (or somebody) pulled his first proof from movable types; when Caxton set up his press in Westminster; when Jenson first used his beautiful Roman type in 1470; when the King James Bible was finished in 1611; when *The Freeman's Oath* and the Bay Psalm Book came off the press in Cambridge in 1639 and '40; when Franklin issued his handsomest book, *Cato Major*, in 1744—these are a few of printing's great days. And now, by your formal recognition of the art and its admission to the company of the other arts which this Academy so eminently sponsors, another great day has been added to the printer's calendar."[3]

A selection of the smaller volumes produced during the later '40s should be mentioned—books that were worthy on their own, but not a fair showing of Bruce Rogers at his best. They represented a considerable dispersal of his time and talents as opposed to earlier years of concentration on a more limited number of carefully chosen commissions.

In 1945, for Alfred A. Knopf, the American publisher who pioneered in issuing attractive trade books, Rogers designed *Poems of Alcman, Sappho, Ibycus*, rendered from the Greek by Olga Marx and Ernest Morwitz. An octavo, set in Greek and English type, studded with stylized type ornament, was printed at the Press of A. Colish in an edition of 956 copies. During the same year the University of Texas Press in Austin issued *Between the Lines*, an octavo volume of letters and documents from the Pforzheimer Library that involved the famous Thomas J. Wise literary forgeries. Set in Times Roman type, 525 copies were printed at Colish. For the New York Public Library B.R. designed a small octavo concerned with material in its George Arents tobacco collection. Entitled *A Few Words About Pipes, Smoking & Tobacco* (1947),

OCTOBER HOUSE: THE LATE YEARS

its ninety-six pages contained an unpublished manuscript written about 1840 and profusely illustrated by Alfred Forrester. The text throughout was set in the unusual Cochin italic and printed by Colish in an edition of five hundred copies. In 1948 the Yale University Press issued *The Arms of Yale University and Its Colleges at New Haven*. Coats of arms of the twelve colleges were reproduced in many colors in an extremely attractive small volume of thirty-two pages, 6½ x 4 inches. In the same year, Rogers designed a quarto volume, *John McCutcheon's Book*, with an introduction by Vincent Starrett, for the Caxton Club of Chicago, in an edition of one thousand copies printed by the Lakeside Press.

During the 1940s B. D. Zevin, president of the World Publishing Company of Cleveland, Ohio, wanted to add an American folio Bible of noble proportions to its already long Bible list. During the same period and entirely on his own, Rogers had been contemplating a new folio Bible very different from the one he had already done at Oxford. He tried to interest the Grolier Club without success. In a letter of 14 September 1944, the Chairman of the Publications Committee wrote: "I am . . . sorry to tell you now that after going over the whole project, our people have decided that we cannot undertake to publish the BIBLE."[4] With the cooperation of A. Colish, B.R. had already set some trial pages, and with the hope of interesting a publisher, had a complete bound dummy made which he deposited temporarily with the bookseller Philip C. Duschnes in New York.

During a routine business trip to New York in 1945, Abe Lerner, Art Director at World, visited the Duschnes bookshop, where he learned of Rogers' hopes for a new Bible. Zevin was receptive when told of the news, a meeting with Rogers soon followed, and he was authorized to proceed without delay. The Press of A. Colish was chosen for the type composition and printing.

Rogers' approach to the new Bible was totally different from the classic austerity with which he had designed the Oxford Lectern Bible. In a cloth-bound descriptive announcement, "The Making of the Bruce Rogers World Bible," the publisher quotes B.R. as stating, "The Bible has always been a book on which much decoration and illustrations have been lavished, and there is no reason in tradition why it should be treated solemnly in that respect. . . . So we have a good precedent for a decorated treatment — if any were needed."⁵ For the large 18½ x 13¼-inch page, Rogers chose the rugged Goudy Newstyle type for Monotype machine composition. With Goudy's permission Rogers modified a number of the characters; for display and other auxiliary needs he also used Goudy designs — Forum, Goudy Oldstyle, and Deepdene italic.

Concerning ornamentation, Rogers added in the prospectus that the World Bible "will be fittingly decorated, with headings to the sixty-six books, initial letters, and a bordered title-page made up from type ornaments or flowers. These, together with the type selected, are intended to give a slightly oriental flavor to the volume, indicative of the Syriac and Hebrew sources of the text on which the King James translators based their classic version."⁶

After four years in production, the World Bible was completed in 1949 in an edition of 975 copies. In one twenty-four-pound volume the Bible was bound in a sturdy red library buckram made to Rogers' specifications.

In a widely held judgment, shared by the present writer, the World Bible was not a successful esthetic solution. Nor was it financially rewarding to the publisher. Despite a well-designed text page, the superficial decoration, however ingenious, was a distraction rather than an enhancement of a work of monumental significance.

As a first step in the newly developing typographic technology, the electric typewriter, with proportional spacing, offered an inexpensive substitute for type composition. Its capacity to set texts for reproduction brought the need to make typewriter faces that looked like printers' type. Manufacturers of the new machines adapted conventional typefaces or attempted new designs. The Commercial Controls Company, makers of the Justowriter, turned to Rogers to make an adaptation of his Centaur within the limitations imposed by these machines. Called "Justowriter Rogers," its merits have long since been lost in the overwhelming changes brought on by photo-composition.

Rogers accepted another assignment—this one not concerned with the impression of ink and type on paper. He designed the lettering cut in stone high on the south wall of the Hunter College building on Sixty-eighth Street in New York City. Rather modern in conception, the letters have a slight swelling at the terminals, almost without serifs. In good weather and bad B.R. climbed the workmen's scaffold to supervise the carving. The inscriptions, in capital letters, are the words of Ralph Waldo Emerson: WE ARE OF DIFFERENT OPINIONS AT DIFFERENT HOURS BUT WE ALWAYS MAY BE SAID TO BE AT HEART ON THE SIDE OF TRUTH.

Early in 1949 Rogers was approached by Miss Helen Clay Frick, daughter of Henry Clay Frick, the collector, to bring to completion the massive multi-volume catalogue of the great Frick collection of paintings, sculptures, and other works of art. The catalogue had been begun in 1928 by Porter Garnett and by 1932 he had set and printed 164 pages at the Laboratory Press of the Carnegie Institute of Technology in Pittsburgh. (The Press was closed in 1935.)

Rogers agreed to revive the project where Garnett had left off, and to use the Lutetia type, imported from the Netherlands, for which a few characters were modified by the designer (van Krimpen) at Garnett's request. The beautiful English handmade paper was still available, stored in Pittsburgh.

For the actual production, Rogers called in two very talented young men, Bert Clarke and David Way. The work was begun in Pittsburgh, then a year later, composition and printing were continued during the next five years in New York, where Clarke and Way established their Thistle Press. The completed catalogue consisted of twelve massive volumes of text and plates (page 18 x 12 inches), in an edition of 175 copies. Rogers supervised the work throughout. In a small pamphlet, "Two Views of the Mountain," printed at the Thistle Press to celebrate Rogers' eighty-fifth birthday in 1955, Clarke looked back to the collaboration: "Never at a loss for a sound solution, BR took the Frick Catalogue in his stride, picking up the design problems from

CHAPTER NINE: 1935–1957

where Porter Garnett had left off fifteen years earlier. Title-page, front matter, ornamental headings for the several sections, binding plan, treatment of plates and interleaves—all flowed surely and rapidly, blending perfectly with what Garnett had done, yet adding, unobtrusively and unmistakably, the special stamp of BR's genius."[7]

In 1950 Rogers reached his eightieth year. During the remaining seven years he produced a considerable volume of work. His sustained attachment to the pleasures and vagaries of bookmaking may be seen in an introductory note he wrote for *The Twelve Monaths and Christmas Day* by the Elizabethan author, Nicholas Breton. He designed a colorful octavo, abundantly illustrated, printed and published by Clarke and Way, New York, in 1951, in an edition of one thousand copies on handmade paper. In the note he wrote:

> This book had its origin in a whim of mine to make an entire volume "with my own hands," as the private printer sometimes phrases it. To that end I borrowed from the Riverside Press some of their Riverside Caslon, which I had cut many years ago. With a type case, a galley and a stick I set the pages in the loft of my barn—an operation which lasted all summer. My intention was to print it on my 6 x 9 hand press, and I even contemplated making enough paper for three or four copies.
>
> In the intervals of type-setting I had composed the decorations from Howard Trafton's calendar cuts in the pseudo-Greek style, together with a few other odd ornaments. Howard even drew for me a stylized peacock and a hound.
>
> But by the time I had the book in type my ambition languished—and so did the pages.
>
> Thus the project lay dormant until David J. Way urged me to let it be printed at The Thistle Press in New York—which has now been done, as you see.
>
> The choice of Greek figures to illustrate a bit of XVII century English literature is of course an anachronism, but as we are the heirs of all the ages, in printing as in other arts, and the designs as composed

do illustrate Nicholas Breton's "Moneths," I do not feel it necessary to apologize for the anomaly.[8]

Two active members of the Society of Typographic Arts of Chicago, E. Willis Jones and R. Hunter Middleton, spent a long weekend in December of 1947 as guests of Bruce Rogers. Jones wrote an ardent account of the visit, published five years later in a slender volume of some thirty-two pages entitled *A Visit to October House*. The colophon reads: "The book arranged by Bruce Rogers; with title-page designed by the author, using a drawing by Rudolph Ruzicka. Printed in December, 1952, at The Thistle Press, New York, with photographs and collotypes by Arthur Jaffé, in an edition of 800 copies, of which 125 are imprinted for friends of The Thistle Press."

In 1953, in a volume entitled *PI*, the World Publishing Company issued a trade book whose subtitle described its contents: "A Hodge-Podge of Letters, Papers, Addresses, Written During a Period of 60 Years by Bruce Rogers." Its two hundred pages, set in Monotype Van Dijck, provide a fair selection of the writing over a long lifetime of a wise and articulate manipulator of the printed word. Rogers concluded his brief introduction with: "The pieces are arranged in chronological order; but were they not, even I could not distinguish the earlier from the later writings. This may be looked at in two ways: either I *didn't* advance or else I sprang, like Minerva, fully armed, from the head of Jove. The latter thought is of course the more flattering to my vanity."[9]

Among other work, two limited editions appeared in 1953. *The Indiana Home* by Logan Esarey, illustrated by Franklin Booth and Bruce Rogers, was published by the Indiana University Press. Of this attractive quarto volume in Janson type, 1,550 copies were printed at the Marchbanks Press in New York. *Selections from the Life and Writings of St. Francis of Assisi*, a tall octavo designed for the Rowfant Club of Cleveland, contained seven illustrations redrawn by B.R. from paintings by Sassetta.* Three hundred copies in Centaur type were printed at Marchbanks.

*Stefano di Giovanni Sassetta (d. 1450), Siennese painter. Panels of the legend of St. Francis are in the National Gallery of Art, London.

CHAPTER NINE: 1935–1957

In a letter of 10 October 1953, B.R. wrote to tell his friend Carl Rollins about books in work and projects he hoped would be realized. He closed the letter with, "So you see I have my hands full. As a diversion I am concentrating on [a] perpetual motion machine, to be driven by powerful magnets. It is so simple that I'm pretty sure there is a catch in it — or it would have been discovered during the hundreds of years that various people have worked on the project. If it *does* succeed I shall be a multi-millionaire, as it will furnish free power for railway engines, ships, automobiles, trains, factories, etc. etc."[10]

Will Bradley (1868-1961), a major graphic artist whose work included printing and the design of type and books, spent an autumn day at October House early in the 1950s, when host and visitor were themselves in their own autumnal years. Bradley wrote about his visit in an article printed in the February 1955 quarterly news sheet, *Hoja Volante*, of the Zamorano Club of Los Angeles. Included was a long paragraph about B.R.'s working quarters:

> On the north side of the "new" library are two large windows which furnish ideal light for a drawing board placed, atilt, at that end of an oak refectory table which provides ample room for reference and drawing material convenient at his right. On the east wall, at the corner, and in front of Bruce as he works, there is a window giving a view of Concord grapevines, now well fruited, a glimpse of Candlewood lake, and a panorama of distant hills. On the north wall between the east-wall window and the north-wall windows there is a floor-to-ceiling bookcase shelved to accommodate books of various sizes, some old and some new and doubtless many of the smaller volumes created by Bruce. Other bookcases, from wainscot to ceiling, occupy the east, south and west walls except for space taken by the east window, a doorway, to the diningroom, in the south wall and a doorway, leading to the original front-corner library, in the west wall. These cases are all built in and are shelved and filled about the same as the one in the north wall as described above. It would be difficult to plan a more ideal workroom or one more sympathetic and inspiring to the kindly and gentle

spirit of this loveable artist—so happily expressed in all of his work. "Here is my great pride"—or words to that effect, said Bruce, and from the top of his west-wall bookcase he unrolled a map of Fairfield. It was on paper mounted on cloth and of a size I judged to be about six feet by six feet, beautifully delineated with Higgins black and colored inks, watercolor and tempera. "I did this for the air wardens," Bruce said.[11]

L'Allegro and *Il Penseroso*, the last of the books designed by Rogers for the Limited Editions Club, appeared in 1954. The year 1955 marked B.R.'s eighty-fifth birthday and saw the publication of four of his books: *Old Bedford Days*, a privately printed volume of the "Recollections of Eloise Payne Luquer," was set in Scotch Roman type with two thousand copies printed at the Thistle Press. *The Happy Hypocrite, A Fairy Tale for Tired Men* by Max Beerbohm, a playfully decorated 12mo, was distributed by The Chiswick Book Shop, New York; the imprint on the title page was "Bruce Rogers, October House, New Fairfield, 1955"; the Centaur type was set by William E. Rudge's Sons, New York; six hundred copies were printed at the Stinehour Press in Lunenburg, Vermont. *Printing as an Art* by Ray Nash, a history of the Society of Printers of Boston, a trade book published by the Harvard University Press, was reviewed in *Printing and Graphic Arts*, February 1955, by Carl P. Rollins, who wrote that "skilful use of black-letter heads and red rules on every page suggested some of the features that gave distinctive character to the printing of the nineties. This touch of nostalgia is pleasant and appropriate."[12]

Finally, the fourth book to appear in 1955 was the large one-volume *Divine Comedy*. As early as the turn of the century, when Rogers was at the Riverside Press, and again in the 1920s when at the Oxford University Press in England, he had made trial pages for a folio edition of the Dante. He had been inspired by the Charles Eliot Norton prose translation published in 1902 by Houghton Mifflin, and by reproductions of drawings for the Dante by Botticelli. On first reading the Norton translation, Rogers was deeply moved by the masterpiece that became a lifetime's devotion. He studied

CHAPTER NINE: 1935–1957

Italian in order that he might, at the least, enjoy the cadence of the Dante cantos in their original tongue.

Over the years, no publisher had ever come forward with a commission to print the book. But now B.R.'s generous printer-friend, A. Colish, offered to produce the work and to finance publication. Whereupon Rogers immediately set to work on what he said would be "the most important book of my life."

The elaborate prospectus for the volume that was ultimately published in 1955 stated that "the idea to do a great edition of *Dante* first came to BR almost fifty years ago when he first saw Lippmann's* reproductions of the superb silverpoint drawings which Sandro Botticelli had created for the *Divina Commedia*" and that "it occurred to BR that a magnificent Renaissance book could be created around them."[13]

The illustrations that dominated the Rogers/Colish volume consisted of thirty double-page and seven single-page reproductions that B.R. had drawn over the facsimiles in the Lippmann book. He strengthened some of the faint lines, and rendered Dante's robe in black throughout although it was in black in only one of the originals. Photo-engraved line plates for printing were then made from the Rogers drawings.

When completed, in an edition of three hundred copies, the Dante consisted of 376 pages, 14 x 9½ inches; the text was set in 18-point Centaur Monotype with a large Renaissance initial at the opening of each canto; the paper was especially made at the Fabriano mill in Italy; the binding was in full morocco leather (plate 56).

In the end it must be said that during these late years when B.R. made the redrawings that were the outstanding feature of his Dante, his hand had lost the steadiness needed to convey the beauty of the Botticelli originals. If Rogers had planned the *Divine Comedy* without illustrations the volume would have been one of his impressive accomplishments. It is unfortunate that he had never been given the opportunity in earlier periods of his life to make an edition worthy of the epic he knew so well.

*Friedrich Lippmann (1839–1903), European scholar and museum curator, edited the volume that contained the reproductions from which Rogers made the drawings.

OCTOBER HOUSE: THE LATE YEARS

In 1955 the New York Public Library held a retrospective exhibition: "Books Designed by Bruce Rogers Exhibited in Honor of His Eighty-Fifth Birthday." The catalogue, compiled by Louis M. Stark, the Library's Curator of Rare Books, contained a brief biographical introduction and bibliographical data for the seventy-six books and miscellaneous items on display. Exhibited were examples drawn from the long years of Rogers' typographic career—from his student days at Purdue University to work currently produced. The catalogue included a pertinent statement by B.R. that had been printed in a review in *Publishers' Weekly*, 4 June 1955: "The books [exhibited] at the New York Public Library represent the endeavors of sixty years—endeavors to make an ideal book. . . . I long ago concluded that there was no such thing as an ideal book—or rather that there were innumerable ones. Every book that fulfills its purpose perfectly is an ideal book, even if not a beautiful one."

In his eighty-sixth year B.R. made plans that would assure him of work ahead over which he would have complete control. He wrote to a few of his wealthy collectors suggesting that they might wish to join a small group to be known as B.R. Associates, and thus to take part in financing the publication of a few books. "I have planned a series of old English literature," his letter explained, "to be called October House Classics. It includes Beowulf, The Life of St. George (from Caxton's Golden Legend) . . . Robin Hood Ballads, Malory's Morte d'Arthur, Julian Bernier's Blazing of Arms, and Chaucer's Canterbury Tales."[14]

Rogers prepared bound dummies and issued a printed prospectus for the series. He received some promises of financial backing, but only the first title was completed before he died less than a year later. *The Life of St. George* appeared in 1957. Three hundred copies printed at the Thistle Press were published by Bruce Rogers. It was a very attractive slender octavo, twenty-four pages 9¼ x 6 inches, in Goudy Thirty type, with a large roundel by Valenti Angelo in red over gold on the opening text page.

During the late years of Bruce Rogers' life some thirty to forty of his friends and admirers gathered faithfully at October House to spend a Satur-

CHAPTER NINE: 1935–1957

day during the middle of May to celebrate his birthday. The event was arranged each year by Edna Beilenson (of the Peter Pauper Press), who collected five dollars in advance from each visitor to cover the cost of a pre-arranged luncheon at a nearby inn, and (in those pre-inflation days) enough was left for an appropriate birthday gift. In May of 1957 arrangements had already been made when word came that B.R. was ill. The date was first postponed, then cancelled. It seems that a few days earlier, while bending over to arrange the flowers, B.R. had fallen into the shallow lily pond in front of his house and had caught a chill. The next day the doctor recognized pneumonia and telephoned for a room at the hospital in Danbury. With work on his desk that wanted attention, B.R. refused to be moved. He died the next day, the eighteenth of May, 1957.

Thus in history, Bruce Rogers of Indiana joined Nicolas Jenson, Aldus Manutius, Geofroy Tory, and other immortals of the printed page whose works graced the centuries in which they lived.

Notes, Bibliography & Index

Notes

Chapter One — The Early Years

1. Bruce Rogers, *The Centaur Types* (Chicago: October House, 1949), 1–2.
2. *B.R. Marks & Remarks* (New York: The Typophiles, 1946), 16.
3. *The Work of Bruce Rogers* (New York: Oxford University Press, 1939), xliv–xlv. This important publication presents the complete catalogue of an exhibition held at the Grolier Club in New York in 1938, arranged by the American Institute of Graphic Arts. The excerpts included here are drawn from the address made by Rogers.
4. Frederic Warde, *Bruce Rogers, Designer of Books* (Cambridge, Mass.: Harvard University Press, 1925), 7. Warde's bibliography, which is frequently quoted in these pages, was written when Rogers and Warde were in close touch. Furthermore, Rogers designed the book and supervised its production at the Harvard University Press, where the bibliography was printed and published. There is every reason to believe, therefore, that Rogers was consulted throughout, thus giving authenticity to its data and statements.
5. Ibid., 8–9.
6. *The Work of Bruce Rogers*, xlvi.
7. Bruce Rogers to Carl Weber, 22 November 1943. Special Collections, Colby College, Waterville, Maine.

Chapter Two — The Riverside Press: Massachusetts

1. *B.R. Marks & Remarks*, 26.
2. *A Portrait Catalogue of the Books Published by Houghton, Mifflin and Company* (Cambridge, Mass.: The Riverside Press, 1905–1906), 240.
3. Rogers, *The Centaur Types*, 2.
4. Ibid., 3, 6.
5. Bruce Rogers, *Paragraphs on Printing* (New York: William E. Rudge's Sons, 1943; New York: Dover Publications, Inc., 1979), 22.
6. Ellen B. Ballou, *The Building of the House* (Boston: Houghton Mifflin Company, 1970), 539–540.

NOTES

7. *The Work of Bruce Rogers*, xxxiii–xxxiv.

8. Bruce Rogers to Thomas Wood Stevens, 4 March 1903. Bruce Rogers Papers, The Newberry Library, Chicago, Illinois.

9. Bruce Rogers to Alfred W. Pollard, 24 October 1907. William Andrews Clark Memorial Library, University of California, Los Angeles, California.

10. John Dreyfus, *Bruce Rogers and American Typography* (New York: Cambridge University Press, 1959), 8.

11. Bruce Rogers to Henry Lewis Bullen, 7 October 1910. Typographic Manuscript Collection, Rare Book and Manuscript Library, Columbia University, New York, New York.

Chapter Three — Free Lance: The Centaur Type

1. Bruce Rogers, "Progress of Modern Printing in the U.S.," originally published in the London *Times* in 1912; reprinted in *PI* (Cleveland and New York: The World Publishing Company, 1953), 24–25.

2. Rogers, *Paragraphs on Printing*, 22.

3. *The Work of Bruce Rogers*, xxxiv–xxxv.

4. Rogers, *The Centaur Types*, 7.

5. Alfred W. Pollard, *Modern Fine Printing in England and Mr. Bruce Rogers* (Newark, N.J.: The Carteret Book Club, 1916), 16.

6. Rogers, *The Centaur Types*, 8.

7. Ibid., 8–9.

8. Rogers, *Paragraphs on Printing*, 3–4, footnote.

9. Rogers, *The Centaur Types*, 63.

10. Ibid., 13.

11. "Type Reviews," *The Fleuron*, no. VII, London, 1930, 171–172.

12. Alfred W. Pollard, "The Work of Bruce Rogers, Printer," *Bibliographical Society Transactions*, vol. 14, 1919.

Chapter Four — The Mall Press: London

1. *Typographical Partnership: Ten Letters Between Bruce Rogers and Emery Walker, 1907–31*, ed. John Dreyfus (Cambridge, England: Printed for The Carl H. Pforzheimer Library at the University Printing House, Cambridge, England, 1971), 2.

2. Ibid., 3–7.

3. Ibid., 8–19.

4. Ibid., 19–23.

5. "Letters from Bruce Rogers to Henry Watson Kent," ed. James M. Wells, *Printing and Graphic Arts*, vol. III, no. 1, February 1955, 3–8.

NOTES

6. Bruce Rogers to Ruth Shepard Granniss, 4 March 1917. Grolier Club, New York.

7. Bruce Rogers to Henry Watson Kent, 23 December 1917. Grolier Club, New York.

Chapter Five — The Cambridge University Press

1. Bruce Rogers to John Cotton Dana, 9 November 1917. Typographic Manuscript Collection, Rare Book and Manuscript Library, Columbia University, New York, New York.

2. *Printing and Graphic Arts,* 9–12.

3. Bruce Rogers to J. B. Peace, 27 December 1917. Cambridge University Library, Cambridge, England.

4. Bruce Rogers, *Report on the Typography of the Cambridge University Press* (Cambridge, England: The University Printer, 1950), 1. The complete 1917 Report, from which the passages in these pages are reprinted, was printed by Brooke Crutchley at Cambridge in 1950 as a Christmas presentation for the Friends of the University Printer. The Report was also published by the Wynkyn de Worde Society, London, 1968.

5. Ibid., 31–33.

6. Francis Meynell, *My Lives* (New York: Random House, 1971), 135.

7. John Dreyfus, *A History of the Nonesuch Press* (London: The Nonesuch Press, 1981), 19.

8. Meynell, *My Lives,* 138–139.

9. Ibid., 139.

10. Ibid., 138.

11. Ibid., 140.

12. Ibid., 141.

13. *Printing and Graphic Arts,* vol. III, no. 2, May 1955, 46–48.

14. David McKitterick, "Bruce Rogers at Cambridge, 1917–19," *The Book Collector,* vol. 29, no. 2, 237.

15. Rogers, *Report on the Typography . . . ,* ix.

16. McKitterick, "Bruce Rogers at Cambridge," 238.

Chapter Six — The Affluent Decade in America

1. Bruce Rogers to Carl Purington Rollins, 19 May 1924 and [April–May?] 1928. Arts of the Book Room, Yale University Library, New Haven, Connecticut.

2. *B.R. Marks & Remarks,* 63–72.

3. Ibid., 95.

4. Ibid., 100–101.

NOTES

5. Warde, *Bruce Rogers, Designer of Books,* 37–38.
6. Rogers, *Paragraphs on Printing,* 50–55.
7. *The Work of Bruce Rogers,* plate following page 46.
8. Rogers, *Paragraphs on Printing,* 181.
9. William J. Glick, *William Edwin Rudge* (New York: The Typophiles, 1984), 22–23.
10. Prospectus for *Champ Fleury* (New York: Grolier Club, 1927).
11. Rogers, *Paragraphs on Printing,* 166–169.
12. Warde, *Bruce Rogers, Designer of Books,* 40.
13. Bruce Rogers, "Printer's Note," *Monotype,* vol. 9, no. 6, published by the Lanston Monotype Machine Company, Philadelphia, 1923.
14. Bruce Rogers, "Printer's Note," *Italian Old Style* (Mount Vernon, N.Y.: Press of William Edwin Rudge, 1924).
15. Prospectus for *Private Papers of James Boswell* (Mount Vernon, N.Y.: Printing House of William Edwin Rudge, 1928).
16. Bruce Rogers to Carl Purington Rollins, 21 October 1919. Arts of the Book Room, Yale University Library, New Haven, Connecticut.
17. Bruce Rogers to Carl Purington Rollins, 12 October 1925. Arts of the Book Room, Yale University Library, New Haven, Connecticut.
18. James Hendrickson, "Bruce Rogers," *Heritage of the Graphic Arts,* Chandler B. Grannis, ed. (New York: Bowker, 1972), 70–71.
19. Bruce Rogers to Carl Purington Rollins, 16 November 1925. Arts of the Book Room, Yale University Library, New Haven, Connecticut.
20. Rudolph Ruzicka, *Speaking Reminiscently* (New York: Grolier Club, 1986), 109–110.

Chapter Seven
Homer · Pacioli · The Oxford Lectern Bible

1. *Printing and Graphic Arts,* vol. III, no. 3, September 1955, 63, 65.
2. Ibid., 66, 67.
3. Ibid., 67–70.
4. Bruce Rogers to Carl Purington Rollins, 9 February 1930. Arts of the Book Room, Yale University Library, New Haven, Connecticut.
5. Bruce Rogers, "Printer's Note," pamphlet issued by Lanston Monotype Corporation, Ltd., London, 1929.
6. Ibid.
7. Bruce Rogers to Carl Purington Rollins, 9 February 1930. Arts of the Book Room, Yale University Library, New Haven, Connecticut.
8. Ibid.

NOTES

9. Prospectus for *The Rime of the Ancient Mariner* (Oxford: Oxford University Press, 1930).

10. Ibid.

11. Bruce Rogers to Carl Purington Rollins, January 1931. Arts of the Book Room, Yale University Library, New Haven, Connecticut.

12. *Printing and Graphic Arts*, vol. III, no. 3, September 1955, 71.

13. *Printing and Graphic Arts*, vol. IV, no. 2, May 1956, 46–49.

14. Bruce Rogers, "B.R.'s Farewell Address," *PI* (Cleveland and New York: The World Publishing Company, 1953), 58–61.

15. *Typographical Partnership*, 34.

16. *B.R. Marks & Remarks*, 103.

17. Ibid., 119.

18. *Printing and Graphic Arts*, vol. IV, no. 3, September 1956, 67–68.

19. *Letters of T. E. Shaw to Bruce Rogers* (privately printed by Bruce Rogers, 1933).

20. Ibid.

21. *More Letters from T. E. Shaw to Bruce Rogers* (privately printed by Bruce Rogers, 1936).

22. *Letters of T. E. Shaw to Bruce Rogers.*

23. Rogers, *Paragraphs on Printing*, 149.

24. *Letters of T. E. Shaw to Bruce Rogers.*

25. Rogers, *Paragraphs on Printing*, 156–157.

26. Bruce Rogers to Ruth Shepard Granniss *et al*, 20 June 1933. Grolier Club, New York.

27. *Printing and Graphic Arts*, vol. IV, no. 3, September 1956, 70–75.

28. Stanley Morison to Frederick Coykendall, 8 February 1932. Grolier Club, New York.

29. Bruce Rogers to Frederick Coykendall, 5 March 1932. Grolier Club, New York.

30. Rogers, *Paragraphs on Printing*, 160–162.

31. Brooke Crutchley, *To Be a Printer* (Cambridge: Cambridge University Press, 1980), 74.

32. John Dreyfus, "Fra Luca de Pacioli," *BR Today* (New York: Grolier Club, 1982), 23.

33. Bruce Rogers to George Macy, 6 October 1934. Harry Ransom Humanities Research Center, University of Texas, Austin, Texas.

34. Bruce Rogers, *An Account of the Making of the Oxford Lectern Bible* (Philadelphia: Lanston Monotype Company, n.d.), 4.

35. Ibid., 9–11.

36. Ibid., 12–13.

37. Bruce Rogers to Carl Purington Rollins, 29 January 1931. Arts of the Book

NOTES

Room, Yale University Library, New Haven, Connecticut.

38. Rogers, *An Account of the Making of the Oxford Lectern Bible*, 14.

39. Ibid., 15.

Chapter Eight — Limited Editions Club Books

1. Bruce Rogers, "The Format of the New Shakespeare," *Some Notes upon a Project for an Illustrated Shakespeare* (New York: Limited Editions Club, 1938); reprinted as "A Note upon the Format of Shakespeare," in *PI* (Cleveland and New York: The World Publishing Company, 1953), 90.

2. Rogers, *Paragraphs on Printing*, 66, footnote by James Hendrickson.

3. Bruce Rogers to George Macy, 28 January 1938. Harry Ransom Humanities Research Center, University of Texas, Austin, Texas.

4. Bruce Rogers to George Macy, 15 April 1938. Harry Ransom Humanities Research Center, University of Texas, Austin, Texas.

5. Rogers, *Paragraphs on Printing*, 71–72.

6. Robert Frost to George Macy, 30 June 1950. Harry Ransom Humanities Research Center, University of Texas, Austin, Texas.

Chapter Nine — October House: The Late Years

1. James Hendrickson, "Bruce Rogers," *Heritage of the Graphic Arts*, 73.

2. Bruce Rogers to Bennett Cerf, 23 September 1930; Bennett Cerf to Bruce Rogers, 13 January 1931. Random House Papers, Rare Book and Manuscript Library, Columbia University, New York, New York.

3. Bruce Rogers, "Acceptance of the Gold Medal of the American Academy of Arts and Letters," reprinted in *PI* (Cleveland and New York: The World Publishing Company, 1953), 137.

4. Grolier Club to Bruce Rogers, 14 September 1944. Location untraced.

5. William Targ, "The Making of the Bruce Rogers World Bible" (Cleveland and New York: The World Publishing Company, 1949), 11.

6. "A Prospectus Giving Particulars and Specimen Pages of the Bruce Rogers World Bible" (New York: printed by A. Colish for The World Publishing Company, Cleveland, Ohio, 1948).

7. Bert Clarke, "Two Views of the Mountain" (New York: privately printed at the Thistle Press, 1955), 8.

8. Bruce Rogers, "Note to *The Twelve Moneths*," *PI* (Cleveland and New York: The World Publishing Company, 1953), 152.

9. Rogers, *PI*, vii.

10. Bruce Rogers to Carl Purington Rollins, 10 October 1953. Arts of the Book Room, Yale University Library, New Haven, Connecticut.

NOTES

11. Will Bradley, "A Visit with B.R.," *Hoja Volante*, no. xxxiv, February 1953, 4 (published by Zamorano Club, Los Angeles, California).

12. Carl P. Rollins, "Printing as an Art," review in *Printing and Graphic Arts*, vol. III, no. 1, February 1955, 21–23.

13. Prospectus for *The Divine Comedy of Dante Alighieri* (New York: Bruce Rogers & The Press of A. Colish, 1954).

14. Bruce Rogers to Stanley Marcus, 23 June 1956. Stanley Marcus–Bruce Rogers Collection, Bridwell Library, Southern Methodist University, Dallas, Texas.

Bibliography

The literature concerning Bruce Rogers and his work is large, diverse, and of uneven quality, and no attempt has been made to list here every piece written about him. The following compilation is restricted to works cited in the text, as well as a few others of significant interest. Likewise, no effort was made to attempt a detailed list of Rogers' own writings; almost all of his miscellaneous early writing is collected in *PI* (1953).

American Institute of Graphic Arts. *The Work of Bruce Rogers, Jack of All Trades: Master of One. A Catalogue of an Exhibition Arranged by the American Institute of Graphic Arts and the Grolier Club of New York, with an Introduction by D. B. Updike, a Letter from John T. McCutcheon, and an Address by Mr. Rogers.* New York: Oxford University Press, 1939. liv, 127 p. Illustrations.

Barnacles from Many Bottoms, scraped and gathered for B. R. New York: The Typophiles, 1935. 185 p. Portrait. 100 copies printed.

Bennett, Paul A., ed. *Bouquet for B.R. A Birthday Garland Gathered by the Typophiles.* New York: The Typophiles, 1950. 70 p. Illustrations.
   Typophile Chap Book 24.

Bennett, Paul A. *Bruce Rogers of Indiana. An Interview by Paul A. Bennett.* Providence: The Domesday Press, 1936. 30 p., portrait.

Blumenthal, Joseph. *The Printed Book in America.* Boston: David R. Godine, Publisher, in association with The Dartmouth College Library, 1977. xvi, 250 p. Illustrations.

B.R. Marks & Remarks. The Marks by Bruce Rogers, et al., the Remarks by His Friends: H. W. Kent, J. M. Bowles, Carl Purington Rollins [and others]. New York: The Typophiles, 1946. 149 p. Illustrations.
   Typophile Chap Book 15.

BIBLIOGRAPHY

B.R. A Panel Discussion at the Bruce Rogers Centenary Held at Purdue University by Harry Duncan, K. K. Merker, and Ward Ritchie. San Francisco: The Book Club of California, 1981. 64 p. Illustrations. 650 copies printed.

Bradley, Will. "A Visit with B.R." *Hoja Volante* (Los Angeles: The Zamorano Club), no. xxxiv, February 1953.

Bruce, Claire [Hendrickson]. *Through the Mill with B.R., a Play on BRinting.* New York: The Typophiles, 1950. 37 p. Illustrations.
  Typophile Chap Book 21.

Clarke, Bert, and David Way. "Two Views of the Mountain." New York: Privately printed at the Thistle Press, 1955. 23 p.

Crutchley, Brooke. *To Be a Printer.* Cambridge, England: Cambridge University Press, 1980. 192 p.

Dreyfus, John. *Bruce Rogers and American Typography. A Paper Read to the Double Crown Club by John Dreyfus. . . .* New York: Cambridge University Press, 1959. 23 p. Illustrations. 300 copies printed.

Dreyfus, John, ed. *Typographical Partnership: Ten Letters Between Bruce Rogers and Emery Walker, 1907–31. Together with an Unpublished Fragment of Bruce Rogers' Bye-ways of Bookmaking.* With an introduction by John Dreyfus. Cambridge, England: Printed for The Carl H. Pforzheimer Library at the University Printing House, 1971. xvi, 44 p. 350 copies.

Duschnes, Philip C. *Bruce Rogers, a Gentle Man from Indiana.* Address at the 25th annual meeting of the Friends of the Brown University Libraries, 25 March 1963. Lunenburg, Vt.: Printed at the Stinehour Press, c. 1965. 25 p., illustrations.

Fryer, Benjamin N., and James Johnson. *Bruce Rogers and the Figurehead of the Joseph Conrad.* San Francisco: The Windsor Press, 1938. 12 p. Illustrations. 300 copies.

Glick, William J. *William Edwin Rudge.* New York: The Typophiles, 1984. 91 p. Illustrations.
  Typophile Chap Book 57.

Haas, Irvin. *Bruce Rogers: A Bibliography. Hitherto Unrecorded Work 1889–1925, Complete Works 1925–1936.* With a Letter of Introduction by Beatrice Warde. Mt. Vernon, N.Y.: Peter Pauper Press, 1936. vii, 72 p. 425 copies.

Hendrickson, James. "Bruce Rogers." In *Heritage of the Graphic Arts,* Chandler B. Grannis, ed. New York: Bowker, 1972. xii, 291 p., portraits.

BIBLIOGRAPHY

Hepburn, William Murray. *Notes on Bruce Rogers of Indiana*. N.p., 1945. 11 p., colored portrait.

From the *Indiana Quarterly for Bookmen*, July 1945.

Jones, E. Willis. *A Visit to October House. Being notes on a typographic trip to New Fairfield and New York by R. Hunter Middleton and E. Willis Jones in December MCMXLVII, as recorded by the latter*. New York: S. R. Shapiro, 1952. 13 p., illustrations. 75 copies printed.

Lawrence, Thomas Edward. *Letters from T. E. Shaw to Bruce Rogers*. New York: Privately printed by Bruce Rogers at The Press of W. E. Rudge, 1933. 84 p. 200 copies printed.

Lawrence, Thomas Edward. *More Letters from T. E. Shaw to Bruce Rogers*. New York: Privately printed by Bruce Rogers at The Press of W. E. Rudge, 1936. 32 p. 300 copies printed.

Lerner, Abe, ed. *B.R. Today. A Selection of His Books, with Comments*. New York: Grolier Club, 1982. xiv, 41 p. 425 copies designed by Bert Clarke and printed at The Press of A. Colish.

McKitterick, David. "Bruce Rogers at Cambridge, 1917–19." *The Book Collector*, vol. 29, no. 2. Illustrations.

McNitt, V. V. "Bruce Rogers of Indiana." *McNaught's Monthly*, vol. v, no. 3, March 1926.

Meynell, Francis. *My Lives*. New York: Random House, 1971. 332 p.

Moores, Charles Washington. *The Camp Steele Alphabet*. New York: Printed for the Portfolio Club by Bruce Rogers, 1952. 11 p. 250 copies printed at Marchbanks Press.

"Most of the stanzas were written by Charles Moores and myself [B.R.]."

Morison, Stanley. Review of Monotype Centaur in "Type Reviews." *The Fleuron*, no. VII, 1930.

New York Public Library. *Books Designed by Bruce Rogers, Exhibited in Honor of His Eighty-fifth Birthday*. Compiled by Lewis M. Stark. New York, 1955. 16 p., portrait.

PM. An Intimate Journal for Production Managers, Art Directors, and Their Associates. Vol. II, no. 5, January 1936. 44 p.

Contains a number of articles about Rogers.

BIBLIOGRAPHY

Pollard, Alfred William. *Modern Fine Printing in England and Mr. Bruce Rogers.* . . . Newark, N.J.: The Carteret Book Club, 1916. 36 p. 275 copies printed by C. P. Rollins.

Pollard, Alfred William. "Reminiscences of an amateur book builder," *The Colophon*, part 4, no. 1, 1930.

Pollard, Alfred W. "The Work of Bruce Rogers, Printer." *Bibliographical Society Transactions*, vol. 14, 1919.

Rogers, Bruce. *An Account of the Making of the Oxford Lectern Bible.* Philadelphia: Lanston Monotype Machine Company, n.d. 15 p., facsimiles.

Rogers, Bruce. *Books, What They Represent to Some of Those Who Have Written, Read and Loved Them.* Privately printed for Bruce Rogers and his friends, 1945. 19 p.

Rogers, Bruce. *BR to FWG.* Berkeley and Los Angeles: University of California Press, 1940. 21 p.

Rogers, Bruce. *The Centaur Types.* Chicago: October House, 1949. 69 p., 16 p. of specimens. 1,000 copies printed.

Rogers, Bruce. *Champ Rosé, Wherein May Be Discovered the Roman Letters That Were Made by Geofroy Tory and Printed by Him at Paris in His Book Called "Champ Fleury."* New Rochelle, New York: Peter Pauper Press, 1933. 8 p., 24 illustrations.

Rogers, Bruce. *Fine Book Pages. A Portfolio of Specimen Pages from the Distinguished Books Designed by Mr. Bruce Rogers for Composition on the Linotype.* . . . Brooklyn: Printed by W. E. Rudge for Mergenthaler Linotype Company, c. 1925. 8 precis in portfolio.

Rogers, Bruce. *Paragraphs on Printing, Elicited from Bruce Rogers in Talks with James Hendrickson on the Functions of the Book Designer, with Occasional Notes and Illustrations.* New York: William E. Rudge's Sons, 1943. ix, 187 p. Illustrations.

Rogers, Bruce. *PI. A Hodge-Podge of Letters, Papers, Addresses, Written During a Period of 60 Years by Bruce Rogers.* Cleveland and New York: The World Publishing Company, 1953. 185 p. Illustrations.

Rogers, Bruce. *Report on the Typography of the Cambridge University Press, prepared in 1917 at the request of the Syndics . . . and now printed in honor of his eightieth birthday.* Cambridge, England: The University Printer, 1950. 33 p. Illustrations. 500 copies printed.

Rogers, Bruce. *Three Letters from B.R. [and] E. W.* Portland, Me.: The Southworth-Anthoensen Press, 1941. 17 p.

BIBLIOGRAPHY

Two from B.R., one from Emery Walker. Introduction by Edward F. Stevens, recipient of the letters. 350 copies.

Rollins, Carl Purington. *B.R., America's Typographic Playboy.* New York: Printed by R. W. Ellis, 1927. 13 p., facsimiles.
500 copies printed at the Georgian Press.

Rollins, Carl P. "Printing as an Art." *Printing and Graphic Arts*, vol. III, no. 1, February 1955.

Rudge, William Edwin. *A Complete List of Books Printed and Published by William Edwin Rudge.* New York, 1926. 15 p.
Describes many books with typography by B.R.; designed by B.R.

Ruzicka, Rudolph. *On the Aesthetic Values That Are to Be Found in the Printed Work of Bruce Rogers.* New York: The American Institute of Graphic Arts, 1939. 7 p., frontispiece.
Read at the opening of an exhibition of the work of Bruce Rogers at the Grolier Club, November 16, 1938, and originally printed anonymously in the News-letter of the American Institute of Graphic Arts, January 1939.

Ruzicka, Rudolph. *Speaking Reminiscently. Informal Recollections Recorded & Edited by Edward Connery Lathem.* New York: The Grolier Club, 1986. 150 p.; portrait, 16 p. of illustrations.

Targ, William. "The Making of the Bruce Rogers World Bible." Cleveland and New York: The World Publishing Company, 1949. 19 p., illustrations.

Tinker, Chauncey Brewster. *Presentation of the Gold Medal of the American Academy of Arts and Letters to Bruce Rogers. Address by Chauncey Brewster Tinker and Acceptance by Mr. Rogers, 21 May 1948.* Portland, Me.: Anthoensen Press, 1948. 12 p. Typophile Monograph 23. Reprinted from *The New Colophon*, vol. 1, part 3.

Walsdorf, John J., ed. *Men of Printing: Anglo-American Profiles.* Easthampton, Mass.: Pennyroyal, 1976. 85 p., portraits.
Prints B.R.'s obituaries.

Warde, Frederic. *Bruce Rogers, Designer of Books . . . with a List of the Books Printed under Mr. Rogers' Supervision.* Cambridge, Mass.: Harvard University Press, 1925. 77 p. 15 numbered illustrations.

Wells, James M., ed. "Letters from Bruce Rogers to Henry Watson Kent." *Printing and Graphic Arts*, vols. III and IV, 1955, 1956.

Index

An Account of Descriptive Catalogues of Strawberry Hill . . . , 34
An Account of the Making of the Oxford Lectern Bible, 152n, 154–156, 158–159
Address at the Unveiling of the Roll of Honour of the Cambridge Tipperary Club (brochure), 73
Adler, Elmer, 84
A. E. (George Russell), 5
Aesop's Fables, 126, 128, 138, 140, 161, plates 45/46
Aiken, Conrad, 93
Aldus Manutius, 12, 134
Aldus Printers, 169, 170
allusive typography, 29–30
American Academy of Arts and Letters, 177, 178
American Book—Stratford Press, 169
American Institute of Graphic Arts, 30, 83, 172, 173–174. *See also* Kent, Henry Watson
American Type Founders Company, 14, 25, 32, 92, 99, 169. *See also* Bullen, Henry Lewis
Amycus et Célestin, 32
Ancient Books and Modern Discoveries (Kenyon), 92, 96–97, plates 29/30
Angelo, Valenti, 187

Aquatone process, 105
Arents, George, 178
The Arms of Yale University and Its Colleges at New Haven, 179
"Art of the Printed Book: 1455–1955" (exhibition), 134
Arts and Crafts Exhibition Society, 38, 44, 50, 52
Ashendene Press, 29, 39, 65. *See also* Hornby, C. H. St. John
"The Atlantic Charter" (broadside), 174, plate 55
Augustus St. Gaudens, 16

Babington, Percy L., 73
Bailey, Cyril (translator), 169
Bailey, Ted, 163, 164
Ballantyne Press, 6
The Banquet of Plato, 16, 19, plate 12
Barcham Green. *See* J. Barcham Green Mill; papers
Barnacles from Many Bottoms, 173
Bartholomew, A. T., 64, 73, 112, 113
Bartlett-Orr Press, 28
Baskerville, John, 90
Batey, Charles, xviii
Beatty, Chester (collection of), 68
Beerbohm, Max, 185

INDEX

Before Life Began (Hunter), 174
Beilenson, Edna, 137, 188. *See also* Beilenson, Peter; Peter Pauper Press; Walpole Printing Office
Beilenson, Peter, 88, 137, 169. *See also* Beilenson, Edna; Peter Pauper Press; Walpole Printing Office
Benjamin Franklin's Proposals for the Education of Youth in Pennsylvania, 90, plate 21
Bennett, Paul A., 177
Beowulf, 187
Bernier, Julian, 187
Best, Harvey D., 104. *See also* Lanston Monotype Machine Company
Between the Lines, 178
The Bibliographical Decameron . . . (Dibdin), 102–103, plate 32
Bibliographical Society, 37
Binny & Ronaldson, 29
Blake, William, 171
Blashfield, Edwin H., 21
Blazing of Arms (Bernier), 187
Bliss, Gorham, 165, 165n, 166
Blow, Sydney, 111
Blumenthal, Joseph, 88–89, 177. *See also* Spiral Press
Boccaccio, Giovanni, 19
Bodoni, Giambattista, 36, 119
Bombed But Unbeaten (Warde, Beatrice), 174
Book Club of California, 83
Booth, Franklin, 183
Boswell, James. *See The Private Papers of James Boswell* . . .
Botticelli, Sandro, 185, 186
Bowen Merrill, 9

Bowles, Joseph M., 2, 4–6, 7, 9, 177
Bradley, Will, 29, 83, 184
B. R. Associates, 187
Breton, Nicholas, 182
British Museum, 149. *See also* Pollard, Alfred W.
B. R. Marks & Remarks, 177–178
Brooks, Tucker, 165
Brown, Charles Brockden, 4
Brown, Hubert R., 92
Brown, M. Lamont (engraver), 13
Bruce, Claire (Hendrickson), 175
Bryant, William Cullen, 2
Bullen, Henry Lewis, 25–26. *See also* American Type Founders Company
Burch, W. I., 121, 124, 125, 153. *See also* Monotype Corporation
Burlington Fine Arts Club, 39
Burne-Jones, Edward Coley, 141, 142
Burroughs, Bruce (grandson), 106, 109, 114, 118, 126
Burroughs, Bryson, 32

Cambridge University Press, 27, 34, 82, 84, 90, 157, 173; *Fra Luca de Pacioli*, 149; *The Odyssey of Homer*, 131; Rogers at, 53, 62, 64–66, 69–73, 78–80. *See also* Peace, J. B.
Canby, Henry Seidel, 140, 141, 165
The Canterbury Tales (Chaucer), 187
Carl H. Pforzheimer Library, 174, 178
Carnegie Institute of Technology, 181
Carteret Book Club, 31, 42–43
Carter, George, 165
Cather, Willa, 173
Caxton Club, 83, 96, 179
The Centaur, 33, 34, 44, 49, plate 17

INDEX

Centaur type, 32–33, 34–37, 39, 65, 112, 174; adaptation of, 180; books set in, 73, 99, 132, 149, 150, 153–155, 173, 183, 185, 186; Monotype Corporation, 109, 111, 114–116, 121; shipping to England, 51, 54
Century Club, 172
Cerf, Bennett A., 176–177
Champ Fleury, 34, 39, 43, 52, 92, 148, plates 33/34; making of, 97–99, 141. *See also* Tory, Geofroy
Champ Rosé, 136, 137–138
Chapman, R. W., 113
Charles Scribner's Sons, 168
Chaucer, Geoffrey, 23, 187. *See also The Parlement of Foules*
Chiswick Book Shop, 185
Chiswick Press, 57
Churchill, Winston, 174
civilité, 17
Clarke, Bert, 181. *See also* Thistle Press
Clay, John, 64
Cleland, Thomas Maitland, 83, 94
Club of Odd Volumes, 6, 8, 28, 83
Cobden-Sanderson, T. J., 22, 38, 47, 56. *See also* Doves Press
Cockerell, Douglas, 42
Cockerell, Sydney, 64, 68, 110, 112
Coleridge, Samuel Taylor. *See The Rime of the Ancient Mariner*
Cole, Timothy, 32
Colish, Abraham, 175, 186. *See also* Press of A. Colish
A Collection of Books about Cats, 73
The Colophon, 84, 164, 173
Columbia University, 25
The Comedies, Histories and Tragedies of William Shakespeare. *See The Plays of William Shakespeare*
Commercial Controls Company, 180
The Compleat Angler (Walton), 19, plate 14
The Complete Poems of Robert Frost, 170–171, plate 53
The Compromise of the King of the Golden Isle, 94
Conrad, Joseph, 99, 174
The Constitution of the United States of America, 16
The Construction of Roman Letters (Dürer), 95, plate 26
Copeland and Day, 8
Coykendall, Frederick, 136, 148. *See also* Grolier Club
Craig, Edward Gordon, 49, 49n, 177
Cranach Press, 39n, 49n, 58. *See also* Kessler, Count Harry
Crutchley, Brooke, 79, 150
Cuckoo Mill, 107–108
The Culprit Fay, 94
Cumming, John (punch cutter), 14
Curwen Press, 84

Dana, John Cotton, 30–31, 65. *See also* Newark Public Library
Dante Alighieri, 185. *See also The Divine Comedy*
Davis, Esther (housekeeper), 126
Deberny Foundry, 94, 95
The Declaration of Independence (broadside), 16
De Divina Proportione (Pacioli), 148
De Evangelica Praeparatione, 32. *See also* Eusebius

INDEX

de Guérin, Maurice, 33. *See also The Centaur*
Dent, J. M., 44, 44n
de Roos, S. H., 24
de Tournes, Jean, 12, 97
Dibdin, Rev. Thomas Frognall, 102
Dickman, O. Alfred, 88
Didots, 119
Diehl, Edith, 42
The Divine Comedy (Dante), 25, 185–186, plate 56
Double Crown Club, 113, 120
Dove, J. Maury, 100. *See also* Lanston Monotype Machine Company
Doves Press, 20, 29, 44, 54; Bible, 152; type, 36, 39, 56, 65. *See also* Cobden-Sanderson, T. J.
Dowson, Ernest, 93
Drake, Joseph Rodman, 94
Duenewald, Ralph, 88
Dunsany, Lord, 94
Dunster House Bookshop, 93, 95
Dürer, Albrecht, 43, 51, 96. *See also The Construction of Roman Letters; Of the Just Shaping of Letters*
Duschnes, Philip C., 174, 175, 179
Dwiggins, William Addison, 83
Dyke Mill, 33–34. *See also* Rollins, Carl Purington

Early Venetian Printing (Ongania), 14
Ecclesiastes, 19
electrotype, 11, 12–13, 16
Elements of Drawing (Ruskin), 2
Elements of Geometry, Book I (Euclid), 176–177
Emancipation Proclamation (broadside), 16

Emerson, Ralph Waldo, 181
Emery Walker Ltd., 149. *See also* Walker, Emery
Enschedé, 97
Eragny Press, 65
Esarey, Logan, 183
The Essays of Francis Bacon, 169
The Essays of Montaigne, 13, 15, plate 5
Estienne, Robert, 12
Euclid, 176
Euclid in Greek (Heath), 74
Eusebius, 13, 36. *See also De Evangelica Praeparatione*; Jenson, Nicolas
The Extant Works of Epicurus, 169–170

Fabriano (paper mill), 186
Farjeon, Herbert, 162, 164, 168
Fass, John, 88
The Federalist (Hamilton, Madison, Jay), 169
A Few Words About Pipes, Smoking & Tobacco, 178
First Edition Club, 113
Firuski, Maurice, 93. *See also* Dunster House Bookshop
Fitzwilliam Museum. *See* Cockerell, Sydney
The Fleuron, 84
Fonderie Bertrand, 90
Ford, Ford Madox, 99
A Forest Hymn (Bryant), 2
Forrester, Alfred, 179
Foss, Hubert, 113, 153, 153n
Fra Luca de Pacioli, 35, 110, 128, 136, 138, 140–141, 147–151, 165, plates 42/43/44
Franklin and His Press at Passy (Living-

ston), 28, 46, 61, plate 16
Frick Catalogue, 181–182
Frick, Helen Clay, 181
Frick, Henry Clay, 181
Frost, Robert, 170

Gaige, Crosby (producer), 99
Garamond, Claude, 100–102, 117
A Garland for John Donne, 126
Garnett, Porter, 181, 182
Geofroy Tory, 16, plates 6/7
Geometry (Dürer), 43, 51. See also *Unterweysung der Messung*
Gilliss, Walter, 43n, 94
Glick, Milton, 88
Glick, William J., 97
Goudy, Bertha, 137
Goudy, Frederic W., 76, 83, 113, 180; *Fra Luca de Pacioli*, 149; friendship of, 136; Garamont, 100–102; Italian Old Style, 102–103; *Letters from T. E. Shaw to Bruce Rogers*, 137; *Three Essays by Augustine Birrell*, 94
Grahame, Kenneth, 168
Granjon, Robert, 117
Granniss, Ruth Shepard, 59, 113, 114, 138, 140–141. See also Grolier Club
Green, Jack, 133
Grolier Club, 83, 172, 179; *Champ Fleury*, 52, 97–99; commissions, 28, 34, 45–46, 74; exhibition, 173–174; *Fra Luca de Pacioli*, 126, 136, 141, 147–148; Kent as president, 30; *Of the Just Shaping of Letters*, 43, 51, 63; *The Pierrot of the Minute*, 93–95; B.R.'s speech at exhibition, 5, 18, 29–30, 73. See also Kent, Henry Watson
Gulliver's Travels (Swift), 170

Haas, Irvin, 173
Hamilton, Alexander, 169
The Happy Hypocrite . . . (Beerbohm), 185
Harvard University Press, 85, 86, 87, 89–91, 124, 126, 185
Heath, Sir Thomas L., 74
Heintzemann, Carl, 8
Hendrickson, James, 18, 88, 94, 99, 107–108, 159, 175–176, 177
Hesperides Series, 135–136
Hess, Sol, 163, 164
Hewlett, Maurice, 94
The History of Oliver and Arthur, 17
Hofer, Philip, 149
Hoja Volante, 184–185
Homer. See *The Odyssey of Homer*
Homeward Songs by the Way (A. E.), 5, plate 2
Hornby, C. H. St. John, 44, 44n, 46, 47, 51, 58, 113, 117–118. See also Ashendene Press
Houghton, Henry O., 9, 10, 12. See also Houghton, Mifflin and Company; Riverside Press; Riverside Press Editions
Houghton, Mifflin and Company (later Houghton Mifflin Company), 8, 9–11, 13, 24, 119, 173, 185. See also Houghton, Henry O.; Mifflin, George H.; Riverside Press; Riverside Press Editions
Hunter College, 181
Hunter, Dard, 83, 174

INDEX

Il Penseroso. See *L'Allegro* and *Il Penseroso*
The Indiana Home (Esarey), 183
Indiana Illustrating Company, 4
Indianapolis *News*, 4
Indiana University Press, 183
Inland Printer, 19. See also Stevens, Thomas Wood
Isham, Colonel Ralph Haywood, 105, 128, 129, 130
Italian Old Style (brochure), 102–103, plate 32
Ives, George B. (translator), 33, 98. See also *The Centaur*
Ivins, Florence Wyman, 92
Ivins, William M., Jr., 83, 83n, 101

Jackson, Holbrook, 101, 113
Jaffé, Arthur, 183
Jannon, Jean, 101
Janson, Anton, 163
Jay, John, 169
J. Barcham Green Mill, 133, 157, 161
Jenson, Nicolas, 13–15, 32; Doves Press type, 36, 39. See also Doves Press
John Barnard and His Associates, 90
John McCutcheon's Book, 179
Johnson, Henry Lewis, 8
Johnson, John, 116, 120, 124, 135, 140; Oxford Lectern Bible, 153, 154, 156, 158; *The Plays of William Shakespeare*, 162, 165
Jones, E. Willis, 183
Jones, George W., 112, 120, 124
Joseph Conrad (ship), 151–152
The Journal of Madam Knight, 92, plate 23
The Journal Up the Straits (Melville), 173
Jowett, Benjamin, 169
June House Press, 107–108. See also Hendrickson, James
Justowriter Rogers type, 180

Kahoe, Walter, 88
Kelmscott Press, 4–5, 6, 20, 29, 38, 44, 54, 56, 65, 83. See also Morris, William
Kent, Henry Watson, 30–32, 33, 45, 174; correspondence with, 54, 60–63, 66–69, 77–79, 110–114, 118–121, 143; friendship of, 42, 44, 123, 127, 136, 139, 140. See also American Institute of Graphic Arts; Grolier Club; Metropolitan Museum of Art
Kenyon, Sir Frederic J., 96
Kessler, Count Harry, 39, 39n, 49. See also Cranach Press
Keynes, Geoffrey, 113
Kipling, Rudyard, 96
Kis, Nikolas, 163
Klopfer, Donald S., 176
The Knight Errant (magazine), 8
Knopf, Alfred A., 84, 178
Kredel, Fritz, 169

Lakeside Press, 179
L'Allegro and *Il Penseroso* (Milton), 160, 171, 185
Lanston Monotype Machine Company (American), 35, 85, 91, 100–104, 114, 122, 154, 163. See also Dove, J. Maury; *Monotype*; Monotype Corporation; Monotype machine; Monotype type

INDEX

Lanston, Tolbert, 104
Lawrence of Arabia, 109, 128. *See also* Shaw, T. E.
Lawrence, T. E. *See* Shaw, T. E.
Lerner, Abe, 179. *See also* World Publishing Company
Les Points de France, 28
Letters from T. E. Shaw to Bruce Rogers, 136
lettre bâtarde, 17, 99
Lewis, Walter, 113, 124, 149–150
Library of Congress, xvii, 157
Life of Dante (Boccaccio), 16, 19, plate 10
The Life of St. George, 187
Limited Editions Club, 140, 160–171, 177. *See also* Macy, George
Linotype machine, 104
Linotype type, 125
Lippmann, Friedrich, 186, 186n
Livingston, Luther S., 28
A Lodging for the Night (Stevenson), 94
Lohmann, Carl, 165
London *Times*, 27
Loos, Melvin, 88
Ludlow Typograph Company, 155, 170
Luther S. Livingston, 1864–1914 (Winship), 34

Mackail, J. W., 142
Mackenzie & Harris, 171
Macy, George, 126, 151, 160–161, 162, 168, 170. *See also* Limited Editions Club
Madison, James, 169
"The Making of the Bruce Rogers World Bible," 179
Mall Press, 53, 54, 56–58, 63, 65, 173
Malory, Sir Thomas, 187

Marchbanks Press, 171, 183
Mardersteig, Giovanni, 148
Marion Press, 79
Marx, Olga (translator), 178
Mather, William Gwinn, 91. *See also The Portraits of Increase Mather*
McCutcheon, John T., 3, 174. *See also John McCutcheon's Book*
Melville, Herman, 173
Mergenthaler, Ottmar, 104
Merritt, Percival, 34
Merrymount Press, 8, 83. *See also* Updike, Daniel Berkeley
Merton, Wilfred, 51, 62, 120; *Aesop's Fables*, 161; *The Odyssey of Homer*, 129–130
Metropolitan Museum of Art, 28, 30, 31, 65, 83. *See also* Kent, Henry Watson; Museum Press
Metropolitan Museum Press. *See* Museum Press
Meynell, Francis, 74, 124, 134, 165. *See also* Nonesuch Press
Middleton, R. Hunter, 183
Mifflin, George H., 9, 10, 13–14, 17, 21, 123. *See also* Houghton, Mifflin and Company; Riverside Press; Riverside Press Editions
Milford, Humphrey, 113, 135, 153. *See also* Oxford University Press
Milne, A. A., 168
Milton, John, 171
Modern Art, 4, 5, 6, 7, 9
"Modern Fine Printing in England and Mr. Bruce Rogers," 31
Monotype (magazine), 100–102, 104
Monotype Corporation, 33, 35, 79, 121,

INDEX

122, 154, 173. *See also* Centaur type; Lanston Monotype Machine Company; Monotype machine

Monotype machine, 33, 72, 103–104, 115, 180. *See also* Lanston Monotype Machine Company; Monotype Corporation; Monotype type

Monotype type, 100, 102–103, 125

Montague Press, 28, 33, 34, 39, 42, 78, 79, 173. *See also* Rollins, Carl Purington

More, Sir Thomas, 161

Morgan, Ernest, 88

Morgan, J. P. *See* Pierpont Morgan Library

Morison, Stanley, 12, 84, 113, 117, 149; *The Fleuron*, 36; friendship with, 120, 124, 149; writings of, 140, 141, 148

Morley, Christopher, 169, 177

Morris, William, 4–5, 22, 38, 47, 64, 111, 119. *See also* Kelmscott Press

Morte d'Arthur (Malory), 187

Morwitz, Ernest, 178

Mosher, Thomas B., 5–6

Mr. Ryan's Collection, 28

Munder Press, 28

Murdock, Harold. *See* Harvard University Press

Murdock, Kenneth B., 91

Murray, Gilbert, 140

Museum Press, 28, 31, 50. *See also* Metropolitan Museum of Art; Kent, Henry Watson

Nash, John Henry, 83, 94

Nash, Ray, 185

Nason, Thomas W. (illustrator), 170

Nelson, Robert W., 25

Newark Public Library, 31, 43, 45. *See also* Dana, John Cotton

"New Cambridge Shakespeare," 74

New York Public Library, 178, 187

Nichol, R. T. (translator), 43, 63

Night and Moonlight (Thoreau), 92, plate 25

Nobbs, F. G., 150, 150n

Nonesuch Press, 74, 82, 176. *See also* Meynell, Francis

Norton, Charles Eliot, 24, 185

Notes: Critical & Biographical, by R. B. Gruelle, Collection of W. T. Walters, 6, plate 3

The Novels and Stories of Willa Cather, 173

"The Oath of a Freeman" (broadside), 174

October House, 106–107, 125, 126, 136, 172, 184, 187. *See also A Visit to October House*

October House Classics, 187

The Odyssey of Homer, 35, 109, 110, 112, 117, 125, 128–136, 141, 142, plates 38/39/40/41

Officina Bodoni, 148

Of the Just Shaping of Letters (Dürer), 34, 53, 58, 59–63, 65, 98, 148, plates 18/19. *See also* Dürer, Albrecht; Grolier Club

Old Bedford Days, 185

On Dry-Cow Fishing as a Fine Art (Kipling), 96

On Friendship (brochure), 73

Ongania, F. L., 14

INDEX

Oxford Lectern Bible, 35, 110, 116, 120, 128, 138, 140, 152–159, 179, plates 48 and 49
Oxford University Press, 82, 113, 116, 173, 174, 185; *Aesop's Fables*, 126, 151, 161; Hesperides Series, 135; *The Odyssey of Homer*, 134, 135; Oxford Lectern Bible, 152n, 153, 157, 158–159; *The Plays of William Shakespeare*, 162

Pacioli, Fra Luca de, 148, 149. *See also* Fra Luca de Pacioli
Palatino, G. B., 149
pantograph, 32
papers: Æsop, 165–166; Barcham Green, 133, 157, 161; Batchelor, 49, 52, 141, 149, 157; B. R. Wove Antique, 99; Glaslan, 99; Kelmscott, 58; Maidstone, 106; Ronneby, 106; Wolvercote, 157
Papillon, J. B. (engraver), 92
Paragraphs on Printing, 18, 175–176
The Parlement of Foules (Chaucer), 17, 19, plate 13
The Passports Printed by Benjamin Franklin at His Passy Press, 90
Peace, J. B., 64, 65, 67, 69, 79, 80, 124. *See also* Cambridge University Press
Peignot, Charles (typefounder), 90
Pelican Press. *See* Meynell, Francis
The Periodical, xviii
Peter Pauper Press, 137, 173. *See also* Beilenson, Peter
Pforzheimer Library. *See* Carl H. Pforzheimer Library

Phinney, J. W., 14
Photogravure and Color Company, 171
PI (Rogers), 183
Pickering, William, 3, 30
Pierpont Morgan Library, xvii, 31, 40, 42, 44, 134, 171
The Pierrot of the Minute (Dowson), 93, plates 27/28
Pierson, Mrs. (housekeeper), 106, 109, 118, 126, 172
Plantin, Christopher, 117
Plato: The Republic, 169
The Plays of William Shakespeare, 162–167, plates 51/52
Plimpton Press, 134
Poems of Alcman, Sappho, Ibycus, 178
The Poems of Maria Lowell, 19, plate 11
The Poems of Robert Herrick, 136
Poems by the Way, 4–5
The Poems of William Shakespeare, 167
A Political Romance (Sterne), 28
Pollard, Alfred W., 22–24, 31, 37, 41, 42, 44, 45–46, 113, 149; friendship of, 49, 114, 124; writings of, 112
The Portraits of Increase Mather (Murdock), 91
Pottinger, David T., 90, 91, 177
Pottle, Frederick A., 104, 105
Pound, Ezra, 30
Practical Hints on Decorative Printing (Savage), 133
Prang, Louis, 7, 9
Prang Press, 7
Press of A. Colish, 163, 167, 174, 175, 177, 178, 179, 186
Priapus and the Pool (Aiken), 93, plate 24
Price, Julian, 140

printer's marks, xvii, 91, 137, 161, 177, plate 57
Printing Art, 8
Printing as an Art (Nash), 185
Printing and Graphic Arts, 185
Printing House of William Edwin Rudge, 85–89, 91, 92–100, 102, 104–106, 109, 137, 161, 173. *See also* Rudge, William Edwin; William E. Rudge's Sons
Priory Text, 17
The Private Papers of James Boswell from Malahide Castle, 104–106, 109, plates 35/36
"Progress of Modern Printing in the United States" (Rogers), 27–28
Publishers' Weekly, 187
Purdue University, 3–4, 136, plate 1
Pyle, Howard, 21
Pynson Printers, 84

Quattrocentisteria, 94
Quiller-Couch, Arthur, 74, 117. *See also The Tempest*

Rackham, Arthur, 168
Random House, 176–177
"Recollections of Eloise Payne Luquer," 185
Remington, Preston, 140
A Report of the Last Sea-Fight of the Revenge, 14, 15, 21
"Report on the Typography of the Cambridge University Press" (Rogers), 69–73
Ricketts, Charles, 6
The Rime of the Ancient Mariner (Coleridge), 116–117, plate 37
Riverside Press, 7, 9–26, 27, 28, 38, 41, 46, 173, 182, 185
Riverside Press Editions, 11–24, 31, 37, 41
Roberts, S. C., 113, 124
Robin Hood Ballads, 187
Robynson, Ralph, 161
Rogers, Anne (mother), 1
Rogers, Anne (wife), xvii, 34, 79, 106; health of, 65, 106, 114, 118, 126; move to England, 44, 48, 50, 55
Rogers, Bruce: birth of, 1; death of, 188; exhibitions, 31, 37, 43, 44–45, 187; honorary degrees, 109, 136, 174; philosophy of, 15, 19–21; principle of work, 29–30; sailing adventures, 127–128, 143–147; study of binding, 41; style of, 10, 12, 91
Rogers, Elizabeth (daughter), xvii, xviii, 42, 48, 50, 55, 65, 79, 106
Rogers, George (father), 1, 48
Rollins, Carl Purington, 8, 42, 83, 118, 119; *B.R. Marks & Remarks*, 177; correspondence with, 14, 106, 107, 108, 115, 117, 156, 184; friendship of, 33–34, 125, 136; *A Lodging for the Night*, 94; book review, 185. *See also* Dyke Mill; Montague Press; Yale University Press
Ronaldson, James, 28
Ronsard, Pierre de, 19
Roosevelt, Theodore, 17–18
Rosenbach, A. S. W., 169
Rowfant Club, 83, 96, 174, 183
R. & R. Clark, 113
Rubáiyát of Omar Khayyám, 12

INDEX

Rudge, William Edwin, 83, 85–86, 109, 124. *See also* Printing House of William Edwin Rudge; William E. Rudge's Sons
Ruskin, John, 2, 5, 111
Russell, George (A. E.), 5
Ruzicka, Rudolph, 83, 108, 183
Ruzicka, Veronica, 174

Sassetta, Stefano di Giovanni, 183, 183n
Scholderer, Victor, 112, 161
Scott, Geoffrey, 104
Scribner's, 168
Selections from the Life and Writings of St. Francis of Assisi, 183
"Shakespeare: A Review and a Preview" (brochure), 162
Shakespeare, William, 74, 162–167
Shand, James, 113
Shaw, George Bernard, 112, 141–142
Shaw, T. E., 10, 112–113, 117, 128–132, 135, 136–137, 141, 142
Siegfried, Laurence, 29
Simon, Herbert, 88, 113
Simon, Oliver, 84, 113
The Sisters (Conrad), 99–100, plate 31
Small, Maynard & Company (publishers), 92
Society of Printers of Boston, 185
Society of Typographic Arts of Chicago, 183
The Song of Roland, 17–18, 19, plate 8
Songs and Sonnets (Ronsard), 19, plate 9
LXXV Sonnets (Wordsworth), 19, plate 15
Sonnets and Madrigals of Michelangelo, 11, 12, plate 4
Spare Your Good (brochure), 34, 73
Spiral Press, 170, 177. *See also* Blumenthal, Joseph
Stark, Louis M., 187
Starrett, Vincent, 179
Sterne, Laurence, 28
Stevenson, Robert Louis, 94
Stevens, Thomas Wood, 19–22
Stinehour Press, 185
Stone & Kimball, 8, 9
Stratford Press, 169
Suetonius, 13. *See also* Jenson, Nicolas
Summa de Arithmetica (Pacioli), 149. *See also* Fra Luca de Pacioli
The Sun Engraving Company, 168
Sussex House, 56–57. *See also* Mall Press; Walker, Emery
Swift, Jonathan, 170
Syndics, 64, 65, 66, 70, 73. *See also* Cambridge University Press

Tagliente, Giovantonio, 149
Tavern Club, 8
The Tempest, 74, plate 20
Thistle Press, 171, 181, 182, 183, 185, 187
Thompson, Edmund B., 88
Thoreau, Henry D., 92
Tinker, Chauncey Brewster, 90, 104, 171, 178
Tory, Geofroy, 12, 13, 16, 23, 33, 137; *Champ Fleury*, 34, 98. *See also Champ Fleury*
Trafton, Howard, 169, 182
"The Trained Printer and the Amateur..." (Pollard), 35, 114

INDEX

The Tremolino (Conrad), 174, plate 54
Trent, W. P., 171
The Twelve Moneths and Christmas Day (Breton), 182–183
Twelve Prints by Contemporary American Artists (Zigrosser), 86
"Two Views of the Mountain" (Clarke), 181–182
T. Y. Crowell, 9
typefaces: Ancien Romain, 95; Arrighi, 35, 115, 154, 173; Baskerville, 90–91, 105, 168; Bell italic, 137; Bembo, 153; Bernhard Script, 96; Brimmer (Bell), 12, 17, 28; Bulmer, 171, 174, 175; Caslon, 11, 17, 34, 73, 91, 92, 97; Centaur (*see*); Cochin italic, 179; Deepdene italic, 137, 177, 180; Didot, 17; Emerson, 177; Eve, 169; Fell, 116–117, 161, 162; Forum, 76, 180; Fournier, 91, 94, 95; Fry, 28; Garamond, 86, 92, 99, 101, 163, 169, 170; Garamont, 100–102, 170; Georgian Old Style, 73; Goudy Newstyle, 153, 180; Goudy Oldstyle, 99, 180; Goudy Open, 93; Goudy Thirty, 187; Granjon, 135, 169; Hadriano, 174; Italian Old Style, 102–103; Janson, 134, 161, 163, 169, 183; Lutetia, 97, 181; Montaigne, 13–16, 17, 32; Old Style Antique, 6; Old Style, 74; Original Old Style, 17, 93, 169; Oxford, 17, 28–29, 90, 96; Plantin, 154; Riverside Caslon, 16–17, 23, 34, 182; Scotch Roman, 17, 99, 100, 171, 185; Subiaco, 39; Times Roman, 178; Van Dijck, 171, 183

Typophiles, 108, 172, 173; chap books, 97, 174, 177

University Press (Boston), 8
University of Texas Press, 178
Untermeyer, Louis, 168, 170
Unterweysung der Messung, 96. See also *Geometry*
Updike, Daniel Berkeley, 8–9, 11, 13, 19, 43n, 65, 93, 108, 174; *The Plays of William Shakespeare*, 163; Prayer Book, 120–121; use of Oxford type, 29. See also Merrymount Press
Utopia (More), 161, 165, plate 50

Vale Press, 6, 20
Valéry, Paul, 177
Van Doren, Carl, 169
van Krimpen, Jan, 97, 181
Viking (ship), 142, 147
Villiers, Alan, 147, 147n, 151–152
A Visit to October House (Jones, E. Willis), 183

Walker, Emery, 22, 64, 110–111, 112, 126; *Ancient Books and Modern Discoveries*, 96; correspondence with, 125; friendship of, 68, 120, 123, 124, 127, 142; Mall Press, 38–62; *The Odyssey of Homer*, 129–131. See also Emery Walker Ltd.; Merton, Wilfred
Walpole Printing Office, 135, 137. See also Beilenson, Peter
Walters, William T., 6
Walton, Izaak, 19

INDEX

Warde, Beatrice, 101, 173, 174
Warde, Frederic, 35, 87, 88, 99, 115, 161, 173, 174, 177
Watch Hill Press, 99
Way, David J., 181, 182. *See also* Thistle Press
Way & Williams, 9
Weber, Carl, 5
The Wedgwood Medallion of Samuel Johnson . . . (Tinker), 90, plate 22
Wells, Edgar, 88
Wells, H. G., 161
"We Shall Go On To The End" (Churchill broadside), 174
Weyhe, E. (publisher), 86
Whittinghams, 30, 119
Widtman, Earl, 88
Wiebking, Robert, 32
William E. Rudge's Sons, 169, 174, 175, 185
William L. Clements Library, 90
Wilson, Edward A., 175
Wilson, John, 8
Wilson, John Dover (editor), 74

The Wind in the Willows (Grahame), 168–169
Winship, George Parker, 34, 92
Wise, Thomas J., 178
Wood, Roland, 88
Wordsworth, William, 19
The Work of Bruce Rogers, 174
World Bible, 179–180
World Publishing Company, 183
Worthy Paper Company, 165, 165n, 166

Yale University. *See* Tinker, Chauncey Brewster
Yale University Press, 34, 163, 179. *See also* Rollins, Carl Purington
Yates-Thompson, Henry (collection of), 68

Zamorano Club, 184
Zevin, B. D., 179. *See also* World Publishing Company
Zigrosser, Carl, 86

Two thousand copies of this book have been printed on Mohawk Superfine paper in Monotype Centaur composed at Mackenzie-Harris. The text was designed and produced at the press of W. Thomas Taylor; the plates were produced at The Press of A. Colish. There are also 125 copies specially bound and signed by the author.